PENGUIN BOOKS

AMERICAN INDIAN TRICKSTER TALES

Richard Erdoes is an illustrator, photographer, and author of more than twenty books on the American West, including the classics *Lame Deer: Seeker of Wisdom* and *Lakota Woman*. Born in Frankfurt, Germany, and educated in Vienna, Berlin, and Paris, he now lives in Santa Fe, New Mexico. His photographs have been published in *National Geographic, Life,* and many other magazines, and he created the illustrations that appear in this book.

Alfonso Ortiz was born at San Juan, a Tewa pueblo in New Mexico, and was Distinguished Professor of Anthropology at the University of New Mexico. He was a MacArthur Fellow, the author of *The Tewa World,* and the contributing editor of the two Southwest volumes of the Smithsonian's *Handbook of the North American Indian.* He died in 1997.

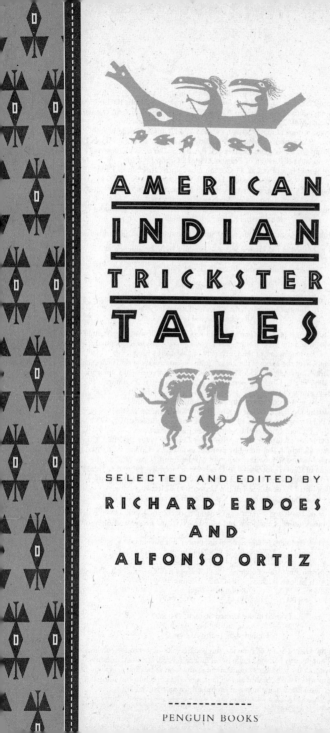

AMERICAN INDIAN TRICKSTER TALES

SELECTED AND EDITED BY

RICHARD ERDOES

AND

ALFONSO ORTIZ

PENGUIN BOOKS

PENGUIN BOOKS
Published by the Penguin Group
Penguin Group (USA) Inc., 375 Hudson Street, New York, New York 10014, U.S.A.
Penguin Group (Canada), 90 Eglinton Avenue East, Suite 700, Toronto, Ontario,
Canada M4P 2Y3 (a division of Pearson Penguin Canada Inc.)
Penguin Books Ltd, 80 Strand, London WC2R 0RL, England
Penguin Ireland, 25 St Stephen's Green, Dublin 2, Ireland (a division of Penguin Books Ltd)
Penguin Group (Australia), 250 Camberwell Road, Camberwell, Victoria 3124,
Australia (a division of Pearson Australia Group Pty Ltd)
Penguin Books India Pvt Ltd, 11 Community Centre, Panchsheel Park,
New Delhi – 110 017, India
Penguin Group (NZ), 67 Apollo Drive, Rosedale, North Shore 0632, New Zealand
(a division of Pearson New Zealand Ltd)
Penguin Books (South Africa) (Pty) Ltd, 24 Sturdee Avenue, Rosebank,
Johannesburg 2196, South Africa

Penguin Books Ltd, Registered Offices: 80 Strand, London WC2R 0RL, England

First published in the United States of America by Viking Penguin.
a member of Penguin Putnam Inc., 1998
Published in Penguin Books 1999

13 15 17 19 20 18 16 14 12

Grateful acknowledgment is made for permission to reprint the following copyrighted works:
"Origin of the Moon and the Sun" from *Indian Legends of the Northern Rockies* by Ella Clark.
By permission of the University of Oklahoma Press.
"Coyote and Eagle Visit the Land of the Dead" from *Indian Legends of the Pacific Northwest*
by Ella Clark. Copyright © 1953 The Regents of the University of California;
© renewed 1981 Ella E. Clark. By permission of the University of California Press.
"The Adventures of a Meatball" from *Comanche Texts* by Elliott Canonge.
By permission of the Summer Institute of Linguistics.
"Where Do Babies Come From?" from "Karuk Indian Myths"
by John P. Harrington, Bureau of American Ethnology Bulletin 107, 1932.
By permission of the Smithsonian Institution Press.
"Napi Races Coyote for a Meal" from *The Sun Came Down* by Percy Bullchild. Copyright
© 1985 by Percy Bullchild. Reprinted by permission of HarperCollins Publishers, Inc.
"How Maasaw Slept with a Beautiful Maiden" and "How Maasaw
and the People of Orayvi Got Scared to Death Once" (retitled "Scared to Death")
from *Stories of Maasaw, A Hopi God* by Ekkehart Malotki and Michael Lomatuway'ma.
Reprinted by permission of the University of Nebraska Press.
Copyright © 1987 by the University of Nebraska Press.

THE LIBRARY OF CONGRESS HAS CATALOGUED THE HARDCOVER AS FOLLOWS:
American Indian trickster tales / selected and edited by Richard Erdoes and Alfonso Ortiz.
p.   cm.
Includes bibliographical references and index.
ISBN 0-670-87829-4 (hc.)
ISBN 978-0-14-027771-5 (pbk.)
1. Indians of North America—Folklore.   2. Tales—North America.   3. Trickster.
I. Erdoes, Richard.   II. Ortiz, Alfonso, 1939–1997.
E98.F6A48   1998
398.2'08997—dc21   97–37763

Printed in the United States of America
Set in Bembo
Designed by Judith Abbate

CONTENTS

PART SIX

PART SEVEN

PART EIGHT

PART NINE
MAGICAL MASTER RABBIT

PART TEN
NANABOZHO AND WHISKEY JACK

PART ELEVEN
OLD MAN NAPI CHOOSES A WIFE

PART TWELVE
GLOOSKAP THE GREAT

INTRODUCTION

Of all the characters in myths and legends told around the world through the centuries—courageous heroes, scary monsters, rapturous virgins—it's the Trickster who provides the *real* spark in the action—always hungry for another meal swiped from someone else's kitchen, always ready to lure someone else's wife into bed, always trying to get something for nothing, shifting shapes (and even sex), getting caught in the act, ever scheming, never remorseful. Tales in which the lowly and apparently weak play pranks and outwit the high and mighty have delighted young and old all over the world for centuries. Each culture usually focuses on one or two characters who turn up in a myriad of disguises and situations. In Germany, it is Till Eulenspiegel; in France they are Reynard the Fox and Gargantua and Pantagruel; in Greece, Karagöz; and in Turkey it's Nasr-eddin, the *hodja* (clown-priest), whose antics are passed on from generation to generation. Loki is the mischief-making sky traveler in Norse mythology, and the famous Punch and Judy puppet shows performed in French parks and country fairs were really Trickster tales played out in a domestic situation.

While in Old World legends and fairy tales the Trickster stories play only a minor part, in Native American folklore Trickster takes center stage. Unlike his European counterparts, who are almost always human males, the New World Trickster is usually the personification of an animal—though he's known to assume human shape if it suits his purposes. The traditions of various tribes feature many different animal characters—Iktomi, the Sioux Spider-Man; Raven; Mink; Rabbit; or Blue Jay—but Coyote is the most popular prankster of all. Tales of Coyote's wild and wicked adventures are told from the Arctic down to Mexico, and across the continent from ocean to ocean. There are probably more tales about Coyote than there are about all the other Native American Tricksters put together, and probably all the other characters, too.

Indian folklore also broadens the role of the Trickster character enormously. In European tales, the Trickster is a jokester and mischief maker, and usually little else. By contrast, Iktomi, the Sioux Spider-Man, and Rabbit Boy are complicated culture heroes. We certainly see them, in classic Trickster style, being clever and foolish at the same time, smart-asses who outsmart themselves. But they are much more than that. Iktomi is a supernatural character with broad powers; Rabbit Boy stars in important creation myths, as the creator. Iktomi is powerful as well as powerless; he is a prophet, a liar who sometimes tricks by using the truth. He is a spider but transforms himself into a man, bigger than life and smaller than a pea. He is a clown, often with a serious message. Like Coyote and Veeho, he has a strong amorous streak and at times seems completely driven by sex.

Coyote, part human and part animal, taking whichever shape he pleases, combines in his nature the sacredness and sinfulness, grand gestures and pettiness, strength and weakness, joy and misery, heroism and cowardice that together form the human character. The tales in this book star Coyote the godlike creator, the bringer of light, the monster-killer, the thief, the miserable little cheat, and, of course, the lecher. As a culture hero, Old Man Coyote makes the earth, animals, and humans. He is the Indian Prometheus, bringing fire and daylight to the people. He positions the sun, moon, and stars in their proper places. He teaches humans how to live. As Trickster, he is greedy, gluttonous, and thieving. During his numberless exploits he often teams up with other animal characters such as Fox, Badger, or Rabbit, usually competing with them for food or women, sometimes winning and sometimes losing.

When it comes to Coyote's amorous adventures, keep in mind that he is no different from the gods of Greek and Roman mythology, who in many classic tales are depicted as philanderers, adulterers, rapists, and child abusers. Mighty Zeus has innumerable extramarital affairs, often with mortal women. Like Native American Tricksters, Zeus and others in the Pantheon are shape-shifters, taking on the form of animals to seduce maidens. With Europa, Zeus disguises himself as a gentle white bull. In the shape of a swan he makes love to Leda. He impregnates Danae in the form of a shower of gold. Assuming the shape of an eagle, he kidnaps Ganymede, a handsome little boy. Hera, wife of mighty Zeus, is often depicted—like Coyote's wife—as a jealous shrew who has her husband tailed (without much success). Coyote also displays, at different times, Pandora's curiosity, Prometheus's daring, and even faces death as well as Orpheus—but all with his own style.

Just as in real life Coyote survives and thrives in spite of traps, poison, and a rancher's bullets, so the Coyote of legend survives the onslaught of white American culture. As Henry Crow Dog, Rosebud Sioux wise man and traditionalist, put it, "Coyote stories will never die."

Iktomi the Spider, Ikto for short, also known as Unktomi, or Wauncha, the mocker, is the principal Trickster of the Lakota and Dakota (Sioux) tribes. Sometimes a wise god, sometimes a fool, Iktomi, according to Lakota tradition, is responsible for the creation of time and space. He invented language and gave the animals their names. As a prophet he foretold the coming of the white man.

According to author James Walker, Iktomi has his roots in Ksa, the god of wisdom: "Because Ksa had used his wisdom to cause a goddess to hide her face in shame and a god to bow his head in grief, Skan, the god of motion, condemned him that he should sit at the feasts of the gods no more, and should sit on the world without a friend, and his wisdom should be only cunning that would entrap him in his own schemes. He named him Iktomi. So Iktomi is the imp of mischief whose delight is to make others ridiculous."

According to various friends from Pine Ridge and Rosebud Sioux tribes:

> Spiders were made from the blood of ancient people who died in a great flood. Ikto can be powerless, a nobody, lower than a worm. But he can also be a creator, more cunning than humans. When he is in the power, Iktomi can do anything. He can uproot mountains. He can transform himself. He is a mischief maker. He is good and bad at the same time—quick thinking, taking advantage of every opportunity. He is puny, a little fellow with tight brown hairy leggings and a red stripe running down the outside of his thighs, the result of being thrown in a fire once. He is the grandfather of lies. He speaks no truth. He brought arrowheads to the people and taught men to wear black face paint when going on the warpath.

Sometimes people are afraid of Ikto and shake their gourd rattles to keep him away from ceremonies. At other times, a medicine man could make an earth altar in the shape of a spider for an Iktomi ceremony.

Despite his bawdy, earthy nature, Iktomi is *wakan*—sacred. Some say you should never squash a spider. If you do, Iktomi will throw sand in your eyes and make them sore. On the other hand, if you make a tobacco offering to Ikto before you go hunting, he will lead you to the game.

Like Coyote, Iktomi is always thinking about sex. He fancies himself to be a great lover. He can transform himself into a handsome young man to court a pretty girl, and he sleeps with both human and animal women. He transgresses the most formidable tribal taboo by making love to his own daughters. He has a love medicine that makes him irresistible to women. He plays the flute beautifully, which makes young maidens come to him. A sexual athlete, he carries his huge penis in a box, and can make it a mile long, or sling it over a river to impregnate a girl on the far shore. He is married, but that certainly does not prevent him from fooling around!

The Cheyenne Trickster Veeho is in many ways the equivalent of Iktomi. He can be a creative genius with vast powers, or (more often) he can be an idiot. In one tale, he spies in the water's reflection a figure curiously like his own, with a piece of meat in its mouth. Never satisfied with what he already has, Veeho tries to snatch the meat from the "stranger's" mouth—and ends up with nothing but a mouth full of water. As it so happens, the name "Veeho" is synonymous with "white man."

Nixant, the Trickster of the Gros Ventre and related tribes, and Sitconski, of the Assiniboine, are strongly related to Iktomi and Veeho. Most of the stories about Nixant are erotic, or invoke his wild sexual adventures and misadventures.

To white people, the idea of a rabbit being a powerful supernatural might seem strange. Not so to the Native American storyteller. Master Rabbit, or Rabbit Boy, stars in the legends of many different tribes. In one Lakota creation tale, Rabbit Boy finds a tiny blood clot and kicks it around until it becomes We Ota Wichasha—First Man. Cherokee legends depict Rabbit as sun-snarer or monster-killer. In Cree stories and in some of the stories in this volume, he is a lying and conniving prankster, an excellent companion to Coyote and Iktomi.

Glooskap, or Kuloskap, is the great supernatural being of the Abnaki, the coastal tribes of New England and eastern Canada, which include the Passamaquoddy, Penobscot, Micmac, and Maliseet (Malecite). Glooskap tales, as you might expect from tribes living near the ocean, often take place on the water or reflect a close relationship with it. Howard Norman, in his collection *Northern Tales*, cites a description of Glooskap as a great giant who could swim with immense strokes. Norman's description of the Northern Trickster can apply across the continent:

> Like a magical hermit, he must live outside civilization, even though his life-lessons, his mesmerizing tricks, nurture the human imagination, make people laugh, and animate life itself. Trickster can never fully marry into human life, just as he can never truly become physically human. Likewise, he cannot inherit our human past, nor does he long for any future. He is the perfect embodiment of the present tense.

Although there is a good deal of Trickster in his nature, Glooskap is more properly a godlike figure. Glooskap represents the good in man; his twin brother, Malsumsis, is evil.

Nanabozho, also known as Winabojo, Manabush, and Manabozho, is the great culture hero of the Algonquian tribes of the northern Midwest and the Great Lakes areas. Sometimes referred to as the Great Hare, he appears in the tales of such tribes as the Menomini, Ojibway (Anishinabe), Winnebago, and Potawatomi. Nanabozho is a full-fledged Trickster—not just the fool or lecher like Veeho or Iktomi, but a much more serious and formidable figure. The Utes tell a story about Ta-wats, the Great Hare, who fights the Sun and shatters him with his arrows; the red-hot splinters set the world on fire. Like Glooskap of the Abnaki, Nanabozho is "the incarnation of vital energy: creator or restorer of the earth, the author of life, giver of animal food, lord of bird and beast," according to author Louis Herbert Gray.

Wesakaychak is the Trickster figure of the Cree and Métis tribes of Canada. *Métis* is the French name for a group of people who are of part French Canadian and part Native American ancestry. Wesakaychak appears often under the Anglicized name of Whiskey Jack, and many of the tales in which he appears have a distinctly European flavor.

Old Man Napi is the featured Trickster of the Blackfoot, Piegan, and related tribes. *Napi* is the term for old man, but its real meaning, according to James Willard Schulz, who lived with a Blackfoot tribe at the beginning of this century, is the dawn, "or the first faint, white light that gives birth to the day," and thus they worshipped the light personified. However, George Bird Grinnell, who lived with the Blackfoot in the nineteenth century, felt that two characters had been accidentally fused into one. "The Sun, the creator of the universe, giver of light, heat, and life, and revered by everyone, is often called Old Man, but there is another personality who bears the same name, but who is different in his character. This last Na'pi is a mixture of wisdom and foolishness; he is malicious, selfish, childish, and weak." *Napi,* like *Veeho,* is also the term for "white man."

The Hopi god Masau'u, the Skeleton Man, is a creator, a germinator, the protector of travelers, the god of life and of death, the peacemaker, and the granter of fertility. But he's also a lecher, a thief, a liar, and sometimes a cross-dresser. Masau'u, also known as Masaaw or Masauwu, is probably the strangest and most multifarious of all Native American Trickster gods. He can assume any shape—human or animal—to lure a maiden to share his blanket. Ruler of the underworld, he is often shown as a skeleton but can also be depicted as a normal, handsome young man bedecked in turquoise. He is said to live in poverty, but he is lord of the land. As Hamilton Tyler recounts in *Pueblo Gods and Myths,* he is said to have brought to the Hopi "a stone tablet which contains the instructions and on which was written all the life plan of the Hopi people. . . . He said, 'The whole earth is mine. As long as you keep this, it all belongs to you.' " This dual character, god and trickster, is a common complication in the tales in this book.

Masau'u is also the boundary maker and the god of planting and agriculture. During Hopi planting ceremonies, a Masau'u impersonator is the center of the action. Ekkehart Malotki and Michael Lomatuway'ma, in their book of Masau'u stories, describe a scene out of a clown act in the circus, as Masau'u takes on any number of "challengers" dressed like cowboys, rival tribespeople, or other characters. He chases the opponent and subdues him with a sack, then robs him of his clothes and puts them on himself, but in a style that's clearly all wrong—moccasins on the wrong feet, sash tied on the wrong side, and so on.

Yehl, the Raven, is the supreme Trickster and hero of the Pacific Northwest coast tribes. He plays a prominent part in the legends of the Haida, Tlingit, Kwakiutl, Tsimshian, and Quileute tribes. He appeared out of the chaos, after the deluge. In the words of writer Marius Barbeau,

> It was then that Yehl, the supernatural Raven of Siberian and Northwestern mythology, began to fly over the desolate wastes. He became a transformer rather than a creator, for in his primeval wanderings through chaos and darkness he chanced upon pre-existing things—animals and a few ghost-like people. His powers were not coupled with absolute wisdom and integrity. He at times lapsed into the role of a jester and a cheat, covering himself with shame and ridicule.

Among the Raven stories are found some of the most abstract and bizarrely plotted of all Native American legends. They seem to unfold in a realm of fantasy, totally divorced from the so-called real world.

The fact that almost all of these Tricksters are animal characters underscores the Native Americans' close identification with nature. Howard Norman perfectly describes this reorientation in the relation between humans and the natural world: "these tales enlighten an audience about the sacredness of life. In the naturalness of their form, they turn away from forced conclusions, they animate and enact, they shape and reshape the world."

All Lakota ceremonies end with the words "*Mitakuye Oyasin,*" meaning "All my relatives," which includes every human being on this earth, every animal down to the tiniest insect, and every living plant. During a television panel show a Christian priest once posed this challenge to Lame Deer, a Lakota holy man from the Rosebud Sioux reservation: "Chief, your religion and mine are the same. The Cross and the Sacred Pipe mean the same thing; so do the suffering of Christ and the suffering your people undergo at the Sun Dance. It is all the same—just the language, the words are different."

"Father," Lame Deer replied, after a long pause, "in your religion, do animals have a soul?"

"You got me there," answered the priest.

Christianity teaches that only humans have souls. Indians believe that even a stone, a tree, or a lake has a soul, a spirit, and there are strict systems of beliefs about the effects of telling certain stories in certain ways or at specific times. Even Trickster stories told principally for entertainment must still be told strictly according to tradition. It used to be that in some tribes, stories were told only in winter. Bad things would happen to the person who told them in summer; he or she might be bitten by a rattlesnake or become sick. In some places, stories could not be told in the daytime because that would make the teller go bald. In some tribes the narrator is forbidden to change or omit a single word in a legend, while others permit free embellishment and modification. Some stories are "owned" by a certain family or even a particular person, and cannot be retold by outsiders. Others wander from tribe to tribe. For instance, the story "Iktomi and the Wild Ducks," in which the Trickster induces his victims to dance with their eyes closed so that he can kill them one by one, occurs in at least a dozen versions among as many tribes. Narrators who could act out a story and mimic the voices of different animals have always been in great demand.

Time and place are evoked "Indian Way." What happens in them is not measured in miles or hours in any conventional European way. A place can be "a hundred sleeps away," or "a thousand paces afar." A story does not begin with "Once upon a time," but with "Sunday is coming along," or "Coyote is walking about." The events in the story have just happened, or are even still going on. In this way the world of Indian legend is more "real" than that of white men's fairy tales.

Tales told in broad, even slapstick comic style sometimes ripen into dramas, too. Sioux Heyoka, sacred clowns sometimes called Thunderdreamers, must act out their dreams publicly, no matter how embarrassing that might be for them. Sacred clowns often take the guise of familiar tribal Tricksters during their dances.

Indian Tricksters are undeniably amorous. Some of the tales are explicit and erotic, but never what white Americans would call pornographic. An earthy innocence surrounds these kinds of stories. Women and children enjoy them as well as men. As Lame Deer used to say, "We are not Christian missionaries. We think differently."

In the book *Stories of Maasaw, a Hopi God*, coauthor Ekkehart Malotki comments,

The Hopi does not give a second thought when referring to sex and related subjects, and will openly talk of these things in the presence of his children. He will also do many things that may be considered repulsive in the eyes of a cultural outsider, but these are not so to him. Thus, characters in a story will urinate and defecate and engage in sexual activities. . . . If a narrator is somewhat of a comic he will embellish his tales along these lines to amuse his audience. In the Plaza [the center of the pueblo], too, the clowns do things of the above-mentioned nature without embarrassment, and people will laugh at them.

The authors of this book can bear witness to this fact. We have often seen the sacred clowns—Kosa, Koshare, Koyemshi, Chiffonetti—doing things that upset the occasional missionary or make an elderly lady tourist blush. These antics are all part of old traditions. In many tribes, during certain dances, modest old grandmothers will say things they would never dare to utter on any other day. It should be noted, too, that there are no "dirty" words in Indian languages. A penis is a penis, not a "dick" or "peter," and a vulva is just that, never a "twat" or "snatch."

Says Howard Norman of the Trickster, "His presence demands, cries out for, compassion and generosity toward existence itself. Trickster is a celebrator of life, a celebration of life, because by rallying against him a community discovers its own resilience and protective skills."

John Fire Lame Deer, traditional Sioux holy man, used to say, "Coyote, Iktomi, and all their kind are sacred. A people that have so much to weep about as we Indians also need their laughter to survive." So take these tales—heroic, tragic, humorous, or erotic—in the spirit of a Lakota, a Hopi, or a Haida: Enjoy!

PART ONE

COYOTE CREATES THE WORLD — AND A FEW OTHER THINGS

THE BEGINNING OF THE WORLD

{Yokuts}

Everything was water except a small piece of ground. On this were Eagle and Coyote. Then the turtle swam to them. They sent it to dive for the earth at the bottom of the water. The turtle barely succeeded in reaching the bottom and touching it with its foot. When it came up again, all the earth seemed washed out. Coyote looked closely at its nails. At last he found a grain of earth. Then he and the eagle took this and laid it down. From it they made the earth as large as it is. From the earth they also made six men and six women. They sent these out in pairs in different directions and the people separated. After a time the eagle sent Coyote to see what the people were doing. Coyote came back and said: "They are doing something bad. They are eating the earth. One side is already gone." The eagle said: "That is bad. Let us make something for them to eat. Let us send the dove to find something." The dove went out. It found a single grain of meal. The eagle and Coyote put this down on the ground. Then the earth became covered with seeds and fruit. Now they told the people to eat these. When the seeds were dry and ripe the people gathered them. Then the people increased and spread all over. But the water is still under the world.

SUN AND MOON IN A BOX

{Zuni}

Here Coyote plays a kind of Pandora role.

Coyote and Eagle were hunting. Eagle caught rabbits. Coyote caught nothing but grasshoppers. Coyote said: "Friend Eagle, my chief, we make a great hunting pair."

"Good, let us stay together," said Eagle.

They went toward the west. They came to a deep canyon. "Let us fly over it," said Eagle.

"My chief, I cannot fly," said Coyote. "You must carry me across."

"Yes, I see that I have to," said Eagle. He took Coyote on his back and flew across the canyon. They came to a river. "Well," said Eagle, "you cannot fly, but you certainly can swim. This time I do not have to carry you."

Eagle flew over the stream, and Coyote swam across. He was a bad swimmer. He almost drowned. He coughed up a lot of water. "My chief," he said, "when we come to another river, you must carry me." Eagle regretted to have Coyote for a companion.

They came to Kachina Pueblo. The Kachinas were dancing. Now, at

this time, the earth was still soft and new. There was as yet no sun and no moon. Eagle and Coyote sat down and watched the dance. They saw that the Kachinas had a square box. In it they kept the sun and the moon. Whenever they wanted light they opened the lid and let the sun peek out. Then it was day. When they wanted less light, they opened the box just a little for the moon to look out.

"This is something wonderful," Coyote whispered to Eagle.

"This must be the sun and the moon they are keeping in that box," said Eagle. "I have heard about these two wonderful beings."

"Let us steal the box," said Coyote.

"No, that would be wrong," said Eagle. "Let us just borrow it."

When the Kachinas were not looking, Eagle grabbed the box and flew off. Coyote ran after him on the ground. After a while Coyote called Eagle: "My chief, let me have the box. I am ashamed to let you do all the carrying."

"No," said Eagle, "you are not reliable. You might be curious and open the box and then we could lose the wonderful things we borrowed."

For some time they went on as before—Eagle flying above with the box, Coyote running below, trying to keep up. Then once again Coyote called Eagle: "My chief, I am ashamed to let you carry the box. I should do this for you. People will talk badly about me, letting you carry this burden."

"No, I don't trust you," Eagle repeated. "You won't be able to refrain from opening the box. Curiosity will get the better of you."

"No," cried Coyote, "do not fear, my chief, I won't even think of opening the box." Still, Eagle would not give it to him, continuing to fly above, holding the box in his talons. But Coyote went on pestering Eagle: "My chief, I am really embarrassed. People will say: 'That lazy, disrespectful Coyote lets his chief do all the carrying.'"

"No, I won't give this box to you," Eagle objected. "It is too precious to entrust to somebody like you."

They continued as before, Eagle flying, Coyote running. Then Coyote begged for the fourth time: "My chief, let me carry the box for a while. My wife will scold me, and my children will no longer respect me, when they find out that I did not help you carry this load."

Then Eagle relented, saying: "Will you promise not to drop the box and under no circumstances to open it?"

"I promise, my chief, I promise," cried Coyote. "You can rely upon me. I shall not betray your trust."

Then Eagle allowed Coyote to carry the box. They went on as before, Eagle flying, Coyote running, carrying the box in his mouth. They came to a wooded area, full of trees and bushes. Coyote pretended to lag behind, hiding himself behind some bushes where Eagle could not see him. He could not curb his curiosity. Quickly he sat down and opened the box. In a flash, Sun came out of the box and flew away, to the very edge of the sky, and at once the world grew cold, the leaves fell from the tree branches, the grass turned brown, and icy winds made all living things shiver.

Then, before Coyote could put the lid back on the box, Moon jumped out and flew away to the outer rim of the sky, and at once snow fell down from heaven and covered the plains and the mountains.

Eagle said: "I should have known better. I should not have let you persuade me. I knew what kind of low, cunning, stupid creature you are. I should have remembered that you never keep a promise. Now we have winter. If you had not opened the box, then we could have kept Sun and Moon always close to us. Then there would be no winter. Then we would have summer all the time."

COYOTE STEALS THE SUN

{Miwok}

There are many different tales of Coyote creating Sun and Moon, or simply stealing them from somebody else.

Coyote is an adventurous fellow. He goes where nobody else dares to go. Coyote lived in the Village of Darkness, on one side of a mountain range. On the other side was the Village of Light. No one had ever gone over the mountains to the other side. They were afraid of what they might find there.

Coyote said to himself: "I want to find out what it is like on the far side. It might be dangerous, but I am curious. Curiosity is always getting the better of me." So Coyote went up one side of the mountains and came down on the other. The land there was bright. It almost blinded him. He was not used to it. There were people there. They were different from the kind of people Coyote knew. They had wondrous things that the people in the Village of Darkness lacked. The people Coyote knew had never heard of such things.

Coyote crept up to the strange people's camp. This was the Village of Light. Coyote crept unseen into the home of a chief. The chief took something out of a basket. It was Sun. At once everything was bright. The chief sent Sun on its path. After a while Sun came back. The chief put Sun back in its basket. Then, at once, everything was dark. The chief took something out of another basket. It was Moon. At once everything was bright again, but not as bright as when Sun was out of its basket. Moon made things much less bright. Moon went on its path and came back. Then Sun came out again. Coyote watched it all with astonishment. He had never believed that such things could be.

Coyote went back to his own Village of Darkness. He told the chief what he had seen. The chief would not believe him. He called Coyote a liar. Coyote said: "They have two wonderful things over there. They call them Sun and Moon. They make things bright."

"You are dreaming," said the chief. "You have lost your senses."

"I will steal Sun and Moon from those strangers on the other side," said Coyote.

The chief mocked Coyote: "We do not need those things. They are of no use to us."

"I will find some use for them," said Coyote.

Coyote again walked over the mountains to the Village of Light. He laid himself across the path that he knew the chief of that village would take whenever he went hunting. Then Coyote transformed himself into a dry branch. The village chief came walking along, just as Coyote had expected. He stumbled over the branch. He looked at what had tripped him. "Ah, this will go on my woodpile," said the chief as he picked up the branch. He took it to his village.

Back at his home, the chief made a fire. He threw the dry branch into it, the branch that was Coyote. At once the branch jumped out of the fire. The chief put it back. The branch formed itself into a hoop going around the fire so that it could not be burned. The chief grabbed the branch a third time and threw it across the fire. The branch quickly stood itself on end at the side of the fire to save itself. "This is a very strange piece of wood," said the chief. "It will not burn. We will see about that."

Coyote used his powerful magic to make the chief drowsy. The chief had just put Sun back into its basket, but had not yet taken Moon out for its nightly journey. The chief fell asleep. He snored. His eyes were shut fast. Coyote quickly assumed his natural form. He seized both baskets and ran away with them. The chief awoke and raised the alarm. Then all his people ran after Coyote to get Sun and Moon back. Coyote is a fast runner. He managed to keep just ahead of his pursuers in spite of his heavy burden. He ran up the mountain slope and over the crest. Then he ran down to his own side.

When his pursuers reached the crest and looked down, they stopped. Before them spread the Land of Darkness. It made them afraid. "This blackness is frightful," they said. "This land is darker than dark. How can one see in such a country? The people there must all be blind. No, we are not used to that kind of thing. We will not go down there." So they gave up.

Coyote came back to his Village of Darkness. He went to the chief's home. All the people followed him. He put the two baskets down in front of the chief. The chief poked them with his feet. He kicked them around a little bit. He said: "I do not trust anything coming from the other side. Everything there is bad."

Coyote opened one bag and let Sun come out. Then everything was bright. The chief said: "I don't like this strange thing. It is bad for the eyes. It could make us blind. We have no use for this." But nobody paid any attention to him. All the people were happy to have light.

Then Coyote took out Moon from its bag. "This will shine in the night," he told the people.

The chief kept grumbling: "This useless thing is also bad, though not quite as bad as the thing called 'Sun.' This will make people go out at night making love instead of sleeping. Then they will be too lazy to hunt or to gather food."

But nobody listened to him. "You have done well," the people told Coyote. Then they made him the chief.

 # ORIGIN OF THE MOON AND THE SUN

{Kalispel}

Here is a moon-stealing story.

Long ago, when the world was very young, the moon was a plaything of a certain tribe of animal people. One day Coyote said to Antelope, "Let our sons go out and learn how to steal the moon."

He and Antelope lived together, and each of them had four sons. Following their fathers' instructions, the eight young men went up into the mountains, each in a place by himself, to fast and to obtain the help of his spirit. Again and again they were sent out. At last Coyote said, "Our boys should be wise enough now to steal the moon."

When the eight young men reached the open space on which the animal people were rolling the great shining ball, they hid themselves at one end of the play field. Now the owners of the moon knew that the boys were coming to steal it. They rolled it toward the boys, sure that it was too heavy for anyone to take away. But the Coyote brothers, one at a time, rolled it toward their home. The owners of the moon caught up with the Coyote brothers and killed them, one at a time. The Antelope brothers took the moon from the youngest Coyote, and they ran so swiftly that no one could catch them.

When they reached home and told Coyote that his four sons had been killed, Coyote began to cry loudly. "Put out the fire and give me that moon," he said to the Antelope brothers. They obeyed him. He took the moon back to its owners, and they gave him his sons, restored to life.

One day Sapsucker said to his grandmother, "Let me go and steal the moon." So he set out. When the moon people saw him coming, they knew his purpose and began to laugh.

"Roll the moon toward little Sapsucker," said one of them. "Let's see what he can do with such a big thing."

When it reached him, he lifted it with difficulty and staggered off with it. Again the people laughed. "Let him go as far as that ridge. But if he passes over it, we will kill him."

They did not know that Sapsucker was very clever. When they reached the top of the ridge, they saw him and the moon at the top of the next hill. He had rolled the moon down the first slope, and its momentum had carried it almost to the top of the second slope. Sapsucker flew over the valley and pushed the ball the rest of the way. The people ran after him until they were tired out, and Sapsucker rolled the moon to his home.

Sadly the people started home without the moon. "Let us make a new moon," they said. "And let us place it in the sky."

"Who will be the new moon?" someone asked.

The people discussed and discussed the matter. Finally they decided that Yellow Fox should be the new moon, and Yellow Fox agreed. They put him in the sky, where he was to shine by day as well as by night. But he made the days so hot that they took him down.

Then they asked Coyote, "Do you think that you would be a good moon?"

"Yes, of course," he replied. "I would like to be the moon, for then I can see everything."

So they placed Coyote in the sky. He did not make the days too hot, but he did see everything. And whenever he saw anything wrong being done, he called out loudly the name of the person and the wrong thing he was doing. The people who wished to do things in secret demanded that Coyote be taken from the sky.

Two young men from the tribe—nicely dressed young men—were desired by four Frogs. The Frogs wanted the two young fellows as their husbands but did not know how to get them. One Frog made a plan. She made everything in the forest wet, so that the young men could only find one dry place in which to sit. That was inside the cedar-bark lodge of Frogs. Instantly one Frog jumped on the face of one of the men and stuck there so fast that he could not remove her. The other Frogs blinded the other young man in one eye.

When the people tried to help the young men, they could do nothing. The blinded one said, "I think I should be the sun. I am ashamed to go about as a man with only one eye."

"I will be the moon," the other man said. "I do not want to go among people with this Frog on my face."

So the people placed the two up in the sky, to be the sun and the moon. The spots we see on the moon are the Frog still sticking to the young man's face. The sun, as we all know, has only one eye.

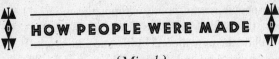

HOW PEOPLE WERE MADE

{*Miwok*}

At one time, quite a while ago, the animals were like people. Falcon said to Coyote: "You have great magic powers. Why don't you make some human beings?"

"It is too much work," said Coyote.

"No matter," said Falcon. "You must do it, because you can do it."

"Well, all right," said Coyote.

Coyote laid down and played dead. Then many crows and buzzards came. They pecked at Coyote's backside. They made a big hole in Coyote's left buttock. They worked their way inside. Then Coyote quickly closed the hole, trapping the scavengers. He went back to his home. He opened the hole in the buttock. He told Falcon to pick the crows and buzzards out. Then he told Falcon to pluck them.

"Now," said Coyote, "we will stick their feathers into various places in all the four directions."

Coyote and Falcon went to work. On every hill they planted one crow and one buzzard feather. The crow feathers became just people. The buzzard feathers became chiefs. As Coyote planted the feathers he gave every site a name, and the next day there were human beings living in all those places.

Coyote said to Falcon: "These new human beings look exactly like us. So now we must assume a different shape. We must become animals. It is your fault. You forced me into making those humans. So now you shall have wings and a beak, and I shall have a tail and fur all over. I shall be Coyote and creep around hunting. You will fly about. You can be the chief if you want."

At once all the original people were transformed into animals and birds. Coyote named them all. "Now I'm tired," he said. "I will rest."

COYOTE STEALS THE SUMMER

{Crow}

At the beginning of time Old Man Coyote was cold. He was almost frozen to death. This was because in those days of old there was no summer. Old Man Coyote was shivering. His tail was frozen stiff, with icicles hanging from it. Then he heard Raven cackling on a branch above him: "Old Man Coyote, I know how you can get warm. I will lead you to the huge tipi of an Old Woman who has many children. This woman is very powerful. She has something that is called 'Summer.' It could make you warm. It could make the whole country around here warm."

"How can I get it?" Old Man Coyote asked.

"You must take five animals with you," said Raven. "A He-Wolf, a Bull Moose, an Elk, a Stag, and a Buck Antelope. When we get to the tipi in which this powerful Old Woman lives, and her many children live, the He-Wolf must bark. Then all of the Old Woman's children will come out of the tipi to see what is going on. Wolf must show himself. Then Old Woman's children will try to catch him, skin him, cook him, and eat him. So Wolf must run away and entice them to follow him. This is the moment for you to act, because you are very smart."

"What must I do?" asked Old Man Coyote.

"While Old Woman's children are pursuing Wolf, you must creep into Old Woman's tipi."

"What do I do when I am inside?"

"I have a powerful herb to give you," said Raven. "This you must smear on Old Woman's lips. You will see two bags in the back of the tipi. One is white and the other is black. You must steal the black one; it contains summer. Under no circumstances take the white one. It contains winter. You do not want it. Grab the bag and run!"

Old Man Coyote did as he was told. He crept into the tipi. Old Woman was sitting there, making moccasins. Old Man Coyote quickly smeared some of the powerful medicine across Old Woman's mouth. It made her voiceless, so that she could not call her children. Old Man

Coyote saw the two bags. He grabbed the black one. Old Woman's children saw him, running as fast as he could. They stopped pursuing Wolf and tore after Old Man Coyote. When Old Man Coyote got tired he passed the bag on to Bull Moose, who was waiting for him at some distance. Bull Moose was lumbering along with his precious burden, Old Woman's children hard on his heels, trying to get the stolen bag. They almost caught Bull Moose, but he was able, just in time, to pass on the bag to Elk, who was waiting for him along the way. So Old Woman's children went after Elk. Just when Elk was on the point of exhaustion, there was Stag, waiting to carry the bag farther. Stag was very fast and Old Woman's children were panting, trying to keep up. When Stag, finally, was about done in, he managed to pass the bag on to Buck Antelope, who was the fastest of them all. Old Woman's children were left far behind. They gave up. Buck Antelope arrived at Old Man Coyote's village. Raven was already there. They waited for their friends to come, for He-Wolf, Bull Moose, Elk, Stag, and Buck Antelope. Old Man Coyote was the last to arrive. He was given the honor to open the bag. As he opened it, summer jumped out.

At once there was warmth. Flowers bloomed, green grass was shooting up. Leaves appeared upon the naked tree branches. The earth rejoiced.

Then Old Woman's children appeared before Old Man Coyote's

tipi. "You evil thief," they said. "You have stolen our mother's bag, you and your evil friends. You have robbed us. You have stolen Summer. Give it back!"

"I will not," said Old Man Coyote. "I like it too much!"

"Then we will make war upon you," said Old Woman's children. "We shall fight to the death!"

Old Man Coyote did not want to have a war on his hands. He was a peaceful fellow. He thought that fighting to the death was a very bad idea. He said: "Oh, Old Woman's children, there is nothing to be gained by killing each other. Let us agree on this: You shall have summer for half a year, and then we will have winter for the other half."

"That is fair," said Old Woman's children, and they all agreed to do it this way.

COYOTE AND EAGLE VISIT THE LAND OF THE DEAD

{Yakima}

In the days of the animal people, Coyote was sad because people died and went away to the lands of the spirits. All around him was the sound of mourning. He wondered and wondered how he could bring the dead back to the land of the living.

Coyote's sister had died. Some of his friends had died. Eagle's wife had died and Eagle was mourning for her. To comfort him, Coyote said, "The dead shall not remain in the land of the dead forever. They are like the leaves that fall, brown and dead in the autumn. They shall come back again. When the grass grows and the birds sing, when the leaf buds open and the flowers bloom, the dead come back again."

But Eagle did not want to wait until spring. He thought that the dead should be brought back without delay. So Coyote and Eagle started out together to the land of the dead, Eagle flying along over

Coyote's head. After several days they came to a big body of water, on the other shore of which were a great many houses.

"Bring a boat and take us across the water!" shouted Coyote. But there was no answer—no sound and no movement.

"There is no one there," said Eagle. "We have come all the way for nothing."

"They are asleep," explained Coyote. "They sleep during the day and come out at night. We will wait here until dark."

After sunset, Coyote began to sing. In a short time four spirit men came out of the houses, got into a boat, and started toward Coyote and Eagle. Coyote kept on singing and soon the spirits joined him, keeping time with their paddles. But the boat moved without them. It skimmed over the water by itself.

When the spirits reached the shore, Eagle and Coyote stepped into the boat and started back with them. As they drew near the island of the dead, the sound of drums and of dancing met them across the water.

"Do not go into the house," warned the spirits as they were landing. "Do not look at the things around you. Keep your eyes closed, for this is a sacred place."

"But we are hungry and cold. Do let us go in," begged Eagle and Coyote.

So they were allowed to go into a large lodge made of tule mats, where the spirits were dancing and singing to the beating of the drums. An old woman brought to them some seal oil in a basket bottle. Dipping a feather into it, she fed them from the oil until their hunger was gone.

Then Eagle and Coyote looked around. Inside the lodge everything was beautiful, and there were many spirits. They were dressed in ceremonial robes, beautifully decorated with shells and with elk teeth. Their faces were painted, and they wore feathers in their hair. The moon, hanging from above, filled the big lodge with light. Near the moon stood Frog, who has watched over it since he jumped into it long ago. He saw to it that the moon shone brightly on the crowd of dancers and singers.

Eagle and Coyote knew some of the spirits as their former friends, but no one paid any attention to the two strangers. No one saw the basket that Coyote had brought with him. In the basket he planned to carry the spirits back to the land of the living.

Early in the morning, the spirits left the lodge for their day of sleep. Then Coyote killed Frog, took his clothes, and put them on himself. At

twilight the spirits returned and began again a night of singing and dancing. They did not know that Coyote, in Frog's clothing, stood beside the moon.

When the dancing and singing were at their gayest, Coyote swallowed the moon. In the darkness, Eagle caught the spirit people, put them into Coyote's basket, and closed the lid tight. Then the two started back to the land of the living, Coyote carrying the basket.

After traveling a great distance, they heard noises in the basket and stopped to listen.

"The people are coming to life," said Coyote.

After they had gone a little farther, they heard voices talking in the basket. The spirits were complaining. "We are being banged around," groaned some. "My leg is being hurt," groaned one spirit. "My legs and arms are cramped," groaned another. "Open the lid and let us out!" called several spirits together.

Coyote was tired, for the basket was getting heavier and heavier. The spirits were turning back into people.

"Let's let them out," said Coyote.

"No, no," answered Eagle quickly.

A little later Coyote set the basket down. It was too heavy for him.

"Let's let them out," repeated Coyote. "We are so far from the spirit land now that they won't return."

So he opened the basket. The people took their spirit forms and, moving like the wind, went back to the island of the dead.

Eagle scolded at first, but soon he remembered Coyote's earlier thought. "It's now autumn. The leaves are falling, just as people die. Let us wait until spring. When the buds open and the flowers bloom, let us return to the land of the dead and try again."

"No," replied Coyote, "I am tired. Let the dead stay in the land of the dead forever."

So Coyote made the law that after people have died they shall never come to life again. If he had not opened the basket and let the spirits out, the dead would have come to life every spring as the grass and flowers and trees do.

COYOTE STEALS FIRE

{Klamath}

There was a time when people had no fire. In winter they could not warm themselves. They had to eat their food raw. Fire was kept inside a huge white rock that belonged to Thunder, who was its caretaker. Thunder was a fearful being. Everybody was afraid of him. Even Bear and Mountain Lion trembled when they heard Thunder's rumbling voice.

Coyote was not afraid of Thunder. He was afraid of nothing. One day, Thunder was in an angry mood and roared and rumbled his loudest, so that the earth trembled and all animals went into hiding. Coyote decided that this was the time to get the fire away from Thunder. Coyote climbed the highest mountain on which Thunder lived. Thunder was at home. "Uncle," said Coyote, "let us play a game of dice. If you win, you can kill me. If I win, you have to give me fire."

"Let us play," said Thunder.

They played with dice made from the gnawing teeth of beavers and woodchucks. The beaver teeth were male dice. The woodchuck teeth were female dice. A design was carved on one side of these teeth. The teeth were thrown on a flat rock. If the male teeth came up with the carved sides, they counted two points. If the female teeth came up with the carved sides, they counted one. If the dice came up uneven, they did not count. There was a bundle of sticks for counting, for keeping track of the points scored.

Now, Coyote is the trickiest fellow alive. He is the master at cheating at all kinds of games. He continuously distracted Thunder so that he could not watch what Coyote was up to. Thunder was no match for Coyote when it came to gambling. Whenever Thunder took his eyes off Coyote's hands, even for just the tiniest part of a moment, Coyote turned his dice up so that they showed the carved sides. He turned Thunder's dice up so that they showed the blank sides. He distracted Thunder and made him blink. Then, quick as a flash, he took a counting stick away from Thunder's pile and added it to his own. In the end, Thunder was completely confused. Coyote had all the counting sticks, Thunder had none. "Uncle, I won," said Coyote. "Hand over the fire." Thunder knew that Coyote had cheated but could not prove it.

Coyote called upon all the animals to come up to the mountaintop to help him carry the big rock that contained the fire. That rock was huge and looked solid, but it was very fragile, as fragile as a seashell. So all the animals prepared to carry the rock away. "Not so fast," growled Thunder. "Coyote won the game and so I give him the fire. But he cheated, and for that I shall take his life. Where is he so that I can kill him?"

Now, Coyote had read Thunder's mind. He had anticipated what Thunder was up to. Coyote could pull the outer part of his body off, as if it were a blanket, so he put his skin, his pelt, his tail, his ears—all of his outside—close by Thunder, and with the inside of his body, his vitals, moved a distance away. Then he changed his voice so that it sounded as if it were coming not from a distance, but like from just a few feet away. "Here I am, Uncle," he cried. "Kill me if you can." Thunder picked up the huge rock containing fire and hurled it at what he thought was Coyote. But he hit only the skin and fur. The rock splintered into numberless pieces. Every animal took a little piece of the fire and put it under its armpit or under its wing, and they hurried all over the world, bringing fire to every tribe on earth. Coyote calmly put on his outer skin and fur again. "Good-bye, Uncle," he said to Thunder. "Don't gamble. It is not what you do best." Then he ran off.

{Salish}

■

Coyote was wandering about, enjoying himself, singing a merry tune. On the branch of a tree sat Tomtit. As Coyote walked beneath it, the little bird chirped: "Grandfather, I am hungry. Do you have something for me to eat?"

Always, when wandering about, Coyote carried with him a bag of pemmican—dried meat pounded together with kidney fat and berries. A handful of this could keep him going for a whole day. He took the pemmican and broke off a few small pieces, which he fed to the little bird. Tomtit said: "Thank you, grandfather. You have been kind to me. In return I will do something for you. I will give you good advice. Toward the north, where you are going, lives Terrible Monster. He swallows up whoever goes there."

"How does Terrible Monster look?" asked Coyote. "How do I recognize him?"

"Grandfather," Tomtit answered, "Terrible Monster is so big, eyes cannot encompass him. His body is so large, it stretches from horizon to horizon. You might imagine you are entering a valley and find out that

the valley is Terrible Monster's mouth. He eats up everybody who enters this valley."

"I guess I can distinguish a valley from Terrible Monster's mouth," said Coyote.

"Don't be so sure," said the little bird.

Coyote wandered on. He came to a pine tree. It was the tallest one in the world. Coyote had an idea. He uprooted the tree and laid it across his shoulders. He carried it that way. "Now Terrible Monster cannot swallow me. This tree trunk is too long. It would stick out of Terrible Monster's mouth on both sides. So he could never gulp me down."

Coyote came to a broad, mile-wide canyon. Immensely tall reddish cliffs rose on either side. "This is neither a valley nor a monster's mouth," Coyote said to himself. "This is safe to enter."

Coyote wandered on. Then he noticed that the canyon floor was entirely covered with dry bones. They made a crackling noise under Coyote's feet. "This is most peculiar," Coyote said to himself. "I am walking through a desert of bones." He saw a man sitting on a heap of human skulls. The man was as thin as a reed. He was horribly emaciated—almost a skeleton himself.

"Friend, have you something to eat?" said the man in a very weak voice. "I am dying of hunger." Coyote gave him a few handfuls of pemmican from his possible bag. "Thank you," said the living skeleton. "You have saved my life—for a little while, at least. But tell me, why are you carrying this enormous pine tree across your shoulders? It must be heavy."

"I carry it," said Coyote, "so that Terrible Monster cannot swallow me."

"My poor friend," said the thin man, "it is already too late. You are already inside Terrible Monster. We are in Terrible Monster's belly."

"Then let us hurry back to where we came in."

"It's too late. Look, way back. There is no light at the canyon entrance. The mouth is already closed. Terrible Monster will wait now until we are dead. Then he will open his mouth again for the next batch of victims. There is nothing to eat here, not the tiniest bit. We won't last long, friend. You'll just live a little longer than I, because you were swallowed up later."

"What are these strange things dangling high above us?" Coyote asked.

"These are Terrible Monster's entrails," said the thin man. "They might be nourishing if only we could reach them."

"That is no problem," said Coyote. "How smart of me to bring this pine tree." He leaned the tall pine tree against a wall that was part of the inside of Terrible Monster's belly. Coyote climbed up the trunk until he could reach Terrible Monster's intestines. He took his sharp flint knife and cut off lengths of Terrible Monster's guts. He munched on them, saying: "Ah, this is good, this is tasty." He threw some of the entrails down for the thin man to eat. The thin man wolfed them down.

Coyote climbed higher and higher. He came to a strange, huge dark red lump, as big as a mountain. This thing contracted and expanded, making a noise like rushing water. It pounded rhythmically, sounding like a gigantic drum. It was so loud it almost busted Coyote's eardrums. "This must be Terrible Monster's heart," it occured to Coyote. With his flint knife he cut the heart to bits. Terrible Monster's body shook violently. It was like a strong earthquake. Then all was still. Terrible Monster was dead. At once there was light shining through nine gigantic body openings. Bones formed themselves up into skeletons. Skulls joined up with spines. The bones covered themselves with flesh, then with skin. All the dead people Terrible Monster had swallowed came to life again. They all shouted, "War honors to Coyote! He has saved us." Then they streamed out into the sunlight through Terrible Monster's nine body openings. They left in huge crowds. Coyote recognized Thin Man waving to him. He was no longer thin. He had put on weight. He looked plump and strong. He laughed. Coyote said: "Let's get out of here!" They left through the opening underneath Terrible Monster's tail.

{Nez Percé}

■

*The Seven Devils Gorge, or Hell's Canyon of the Snake
River, forms part of the boundary between Oregon and
Idaho. On the Idaho side of the gorge, which is said to be
the deepest canyon on the North American continent,
seven high peaks stand in a semicircle. They are called the
Seven Devils Mountains. The Blue Mountains are in
eastern Oregon and Washington.*

Long, long ago, when the world was very young, seven giant brothers
lived in the Blue Mountains. These giant monsters were taller than the
tallest pines and stronger than the strongest oaks.

The ancient people feared these brothers greatly because they ate
children. Each year the brothers traveled eastward and devoured all the
little ones they could find. Mothers fled with their children and hid
them, but still many were seized by the giants. The headmen in the villages feared that the tribe would soon be wiped out. But no one was big
enough and strong enough to fight with seven giants at one time.

At last the headmen of the tribe decided to ask Coyote to help them.

"Coyote is our friend," they said. "He has defeated other monsters. He will free us from the seven giants."

But Coyote really did not know what to do. He had fought with giants. He had fought with monsters of the lakes and the rivers. But he knew he could not defeat seven giants at one time. So he asked his good friend Fox for advice.

"We will first dig seven holes," said his good friend Fox. "We will dig them very deep, in a place the giants always pass over when they travel to the east. Then we will fill the holes with boiling liquid."

So Coyote called together all the animals with claws—the beavers, the whistling marmots, the cougars, the bears, and even the rats and mice and moles—to dig seven deep holes. Then Coyote filled each hole with a reddish-yellow liquid. His good friend Fox helped him keep the liquid boiling by dropping hot rocks into it.

Soon the time came for the giants' journey eastward. They marched along, all seven of them, their heads held high in the air. They were sure that no one dared to attack them. Coyote and Fox watched from behind some rocks and shrubs.

Down, down, down the seven giants went into the seven deep holes of boiling liquid. They struggled and struggled to get out, but the holes were very deep. They fumed and roared and splashed. As they struggled, they scattered the reddish liquid around them as far as a man can travel in a day.

Then Coyote came out from his hiding place. The seven giants stood still. They knew Coyote.

"You are being punished for your wickedness," Coyote said to the seven giants. "I will punish you even more by changing you into seven mountains. I will make you very high, so that everyone can see you. You will stand here forever, to remind people that punishment comes from wrongdoing.

"And I will make a deep gash in the earth here, so that no more of your family can get across to trouble my people."

Coyote caused the seven giants to grow taller, and then he changed them into seven mountain peaks. He struck the earth a hard blow and so opened up a deep canyon at the feet of the giant peaks.

Today the mountains are called the Seven Devils. The deep gorge at their feet is known as Hell's Canyon at the Snake River. And the copper scattered by the splashings of the seven giants is still being mined.

PART TWO

UP TO NO GOOD

COYOTE TAUNTS THE GRIZZLY BEAR

{Kutenai}

■

This is a typical rendition of a Kutenai story.

Coyote went along. There was a hill. He went up and saw Grizzly Bear eating there. Coyote thought: "I will play with him." He said to him: "Grizzly Bear, Short Tail!" He hid behind the hill.

Grizzly Bear heard Coyote talking, calling him bad names. Grizzly Bear thought: "You are sure to say that again." Grizzly Bear did not look.

After a while Coyote looked again at Grizzly Bear. He said to him: "Grizzly Bear, Left-Handed One!"

Then Grizzly Bear knew that Coyote was on the hill calling him. He pretended to eat again. He was looking without letting Coyote see it.

It was not long before Coyote looked over the hill at Grizzly Bear. He said to him: "Grizzly Bear, Small Eyes!" Coyote hid again.

Then Grizzly Bear ran. He pursued Coyote. It was not long before he looked over the hill again to say something to Grizzly Bear. Coyote said: "Grizzly Bear—" He stopped quickly in his speech. Coyote saw that Grizzly Bear was already coming right up to him. Then Coyote

began to run away. He was pursued by Grizzly Bear. Coyote said: "Things that want to catch each other do not run fast together." Then Coyote left him behind.

Coyote was going along. He turned in a circle and got up to Grizzly Bear from behind. Grizzly Bear was going along in the tracks of Coyote. Coyote heard him panting. He was getting near him. He thought he would catch up with him on the right side. Then Coyote jumped along his side. Then he jumped around on the left side of Grizzly Bear. Coyote went past. Grizzly Bear was going along, and Coyote did the same again.

Grizzly Bear thought: "Now I'll catch Coyote. I'll bite him." Coyote jumped along on the other side. Then Grizzly Bear turned to the right side quickly to catch him, but again he could not catch him. Grizzly Bear went along a short distance and saw Coyote. He was going along tired. Grizzly Bear overtook him. Then Coyote was looking from one side to the other. His tongue was lolling. There was a big stone.

Coyote thought: "Now Grizzly Bear will bite me." Grizzly Bear chased him around the stone. Then Grizzly Bear was about to catch him, and Coyote was out of breath. Coyote fell down there. He lay there for a time, and thought: "Why doesn't Grizzly Bear bite me?" Then he felt something on his hands. He looked at it, and saw that he had his hands in the horns of a Buffalo Bull. He looked at the Grizzly Bear. He was standing by his feet. Coyote stood up quickly and ran after him. He spoke to him in the way a bull bellows. The bear trembled. Then Coyote knew that Grizzly Bear was afraid of him. He pursued him. The way Grizzly Bear had done, that way Coyote did to him. He also did the same. Grizzly Bear looked from side to side over his shoulders.

There was a river. Grizzly Bear started to swim. Coyote put out one of his hands with the horn where Grizzly Bear was swimming ahead. He hit him with it. He hit his backside, and he put out the other one and with it also he hit the backside. Grizzly Bear swam across there.

Coyote sat down. When Grizzly Bear was across, he looked back. Coyote was sitting down. Coyote said: "Grizzly Bear, you were going to bite me. It should be once that Grizzly Bear bit Coyote." Grizzly Bear did not speak. He was afraid. It is true, Coyote was never bitten by Grizzly Bear, and he was helped by his friend Buffalo Bull. Enough.

{Zuni}

Locust was sitting on the branch of a piñon tree. He was playing his flute. It made a high, chirping sound. Now and then, he stopped piping away to shout as loud as he could (not very loud), in a high, quavering voice: "I am Locust, the best flute player in the world!"

Coyote happened to be in the neighborhood. He heard Locust's flute; he heard Locust's boasting. "Who can that be, making this tiny fluttering piping?" thought Coyote. He was curious. He followed the sound. He came to the piñon tree. He saw Locust sitting on the branch with his flute. Locust was singing a little song in his tiny, shrill voice:

> *Kokopelli is hump-backed,*
> *Kokopelli's feet are backward,*
> *Kokopelli has a flute,*
> *Kokopelli is a fine flute player.*
> *So am I.*

"My friend," said Coyote, "this is a very pretty song. Will you teach it to me?"

"Why not?" said Locust, and taught Coyote the song. They practiced. They sang the song together, Locust with his high, quavering voice, Coyote with his deep, hoarse, grating voice.

"Didn't we do beautifully?" Coyote asked. "Is not our singing together something wonderful?"

Secretly, Locust thought: "We do not harmonize very well. Coyote really has a very unpleasant, croaky voice. It makes one shudder. He

will never make a good singer." Aloud he said: "It went passably well. Our voices surely are very different."

"Of course," said Coyote, "yours is high, and mine is low. It harmonizes delightfully."

"Hmmm," said Locust.

"Friend, I have to go now," said Coyote. "Thank you for having taught me this pretty song."

"Don't mention it," said Locust.

Coyote went on, memorizing the song as he walked. He stumbled over a dead branch lying in his path. He fell hard. He scraped his knees. He was upset. The accident had made him forget the song. "Well, little old Locust is probably still sitting where I left him. He will refresh my memory." Coyote went back to Locust. Already from a distance he heard him piping away.

"Friend," he told Locust, "a bad fall has hurt me. This made me forget your song. Please teach it to me once more."

"Well, all right, but pay attention this time." Locust sang the song again. "Have you got it?" he asked.

"Oh, yes," said Coyote, "now it is firmly implanted in my mind."

Coyote went homeward again, trying to memorize the song. He went about twice as far as before. He did not watch where he was going. He fell into a stream. He almost drowned. This made him forget the song. So a second time he went back to see Locust. "This is really time-consuming," he thought. To Locust he said: "I fell into a stream and almost drowned. This made me forget your song. So now I have to bother you again. I can't help it."

"He is really not very bright," thought Locust. "He can't concentrate. He can't remember things." Aloud he said: "I will sing the song once more for you, but try real hard to memorize it. This is really tiresome." Then Locust sang the song once more in his reedy, piping voice.

"Now I've got it," vowed Coyote. "Now I will never forget this pretty song. Thanks for taking the trouble."

"It's all right," said Locust, "glad to be of help." Coyote left once more. "He won't memorize it this time, either," Locust said to himself, "it is hopeless."

Coyote now went three times as far as before. He walked along a cliff. A loose rock fell from above and knocked him senseless. When Coyote came to, he had, of course, forgotten the song. "Let me think," he said to himself. "What was this song about? Was it about Corn Maiden? Was it about Dragonfly? Was it about the Winged Serpent? I can't remember. This rock really rattled my head. I have to go back to Locust and let him teach me his song once more. He is a friendly little fellow. He won't mind." So back Coyote went, retracing his steps.

Back on his piñon branch Locust thought: "That stupid Coyote will be back here any moment. He will want me to sing that song for him again. I am fed up with this. I shall play a trick on this mindless fellow." It was just about time for Locust to shed his shell, which had become too small for him. He split his hard shell in the middle and crawled out. He saw a shiny pebble. He put it inside his old shell and propped it up on the piñon branch. The shell looked like a real live Locust. "This will fool him," thought Locust. He flew up into a nearbly juniper tree. He settled down to watch while making himself a new, larger shell.

Sure enough, Coyote came back. He went right up to the shiny shell sitting on its branch. He thought it was Locust.

"Friend," said Coyote, "I have to inconvenience you once more. I was hit in the head with a stone. That made me forget the song. I'm sure you understand."

The shell was silent. "Come on, old fellow," Coyote urged, "sing that song for me."

The shell was silent.

"I am getting angry now," said Coyote, "sing that ugly song for me or else."

The shell remained silent. In the juniper tree Locust was watching.

"I see that I have to play rough, you puny thing with your squeaky voice. Either sing that song at once or I'll crush you between my teeth and eat you!"

There was no answer. Coyote snapped at the shell, clamping down hard on it. His teeth met stone. His teeth broke. They fell out of Coyote's mouth. He howled with pain. He did not understand what had happened. He could not figure it out. Up in his juniper tree Locust said to himself: "Never try teaching a good song to a half-wit." So it was.

COYOTE-GIVING

{Paiute}

Every man should have his own song, and no one else should be allowed to sing it, unless the owner permits it. At the high points in a man's life, when he kills his first deer, when he first makes love to a woman, out of this kind of happening he makes up his own song. He sings his song on great occasions. He might leave it to his son.

There was a man called No-Song. They called him that because this poor man owned no song. At a corn dance or a rain dance he would sit apart from the others. Often he tried to hide or lose himself in a crowd, because people would point him out to each other, saying: "Over there is that pitiful man who has no song." And because of his sad condition, he was too shy to court the young maidens.

So one day this man No-Song had harvested a big load of corn. He also had a big pot bubbling full of delicious venison stew. Coyote smelled it from afar. Coyote came running. "Oh, my," he thought, "I must get this corn, I must get this wonderful stew!" He was slavering. He said: "Hey, No-Song, what will you swap for your corn and for that sweet-smelling stew?"

"You are Coyote, the Song-Maker. You can have all this for a song."

"What kind of song?" asked Coyote.

"A song that will make the heart of young women flutter," said No-Song. "I wish for a song to make glad the people so that they will admire me. Also I don't want a Coyote song, because Coyotes are the kind of fellows who want to take their gifts back."

"I would never do something so bad," said Coyote, whose mouth kept on watering.

"Give me your word that this will not be what they call a 'Coyote giving.' "

"I promise, I promise, as long as the song is wisely used for its purpose—to court a maiden and, on a special occasion, to gladden the hearts of the people."

"How can you think that I would not use the song in the right way?" said No-Song, somewhat insulted. Then Coyote gave him a song and he gave to Coyote all the corn and the big pot of venison stew. Both were very happy with the bargain they had made.

Soon there was held a great feast and dance, a fine occasion for No-Song to sing. All the people were astonished and delighted at this song. "How come," they asked, "suddenly No-Song can sing so sweetly?" All the people clapped their hands and expressed their delight. At once a beautiful maiden suggested to No-Song that they should go behind some bushes, to a hidden place, and there do something that the teller of this story will not elaborate upon. And No-Song went from feast to feast, and from dance to dance, singing his song, and all who heard it were enchanted. And No-Song changed his name to "Singing Wonderfully."

Now, this singing of his song had gone on for months, and he had sung his song wherever he found people to listen, and their praise went to his head. And the one who called himself Singing Wonderfully sang his song for many purposes for which it was not designed, and he sang it so often that people grew bored with it and fell asleep while he was singing. And so, one night when this man calling himself Singing Won-derfully was asleep, Coyote crept up to him and took the song back. Coyote felt justified in doing this, because Singing Wonderfully had misused the song. And when the singer awoke, the song was gone. He could not remember a single word of it and neither could anyone else. And the people called him No-Song again. So now he is sitting there every day with a huge bag of corn before him and a huge bubbling pot of venison stew, but, so far, Coyote has not come back.

PUTTING A SADDLE ON COYOTE'S BACK

{Northern Pueblo}

■

This tale pits two Tricksters, Coyote and Rabbit Boy,
against each other.

Rabbit Boy was resting inside his snug burrow when, suddenly, Coyote's head was appearing in the entrance hole.

"Good morning, little friend," said Coyote. "You look good enough to eat."

"That's a bad joke, uncle," said Rabbit Boy. He was frantically trying to think of a way to save himself.

"Yes," Coyote went on, "you look very appetizing."

"I was just leaving for a party—my aunt is giving a big feast tonight for all her relatives."

"A big feast," thought Coyote. "There will be many rabbits. And many rabbits are better than just one measly rabbit!" It was exactly what Rabbit Boy wanted him to think. "You can come along, uncle," he told Coyote, "and share in the feast, provided you let me ride on your back. My aunt's home is quite a way off, my legs are short, and I tire easily. Also, by myself, I could not get there in time."

"Why, sure, hop on my back, little brother," said Coyote, smiling to himself at the thought of a large pot of succulent rabbit stew.

"Uncle, I am a very poor rider," said Rabbit Boy. "I cannot do without a saddle."

"Why, sure, of course not, little brother," said Coyote. "I live nearby. I'll get a saddle for you, and not only a saddle, I will also get a bridle to make things easier for you."

"That will be fine, uncle. Make it a strong bridle."

Coyote ran off as fast as he could to get these things. During the short time when Coyote was away on this errand, Rabbit Boy plucked two long, sharp thorns from a thornbush, hiding them in his fur. Soon Coyote was back, crying: "Here I come, little brother, saddled and bridled."

"You will make a fine horse for me, uncle," Rabbit Boy told him. "Please face the other way, so that I can mount you from behind." Coyote turned around and, quick as lightning, Rabbit Boy fastened the two large thorns to his heels, intending to use them as spurs. Then he hopped onto Coyote's back.

"Off you go, uncle," he cried. "Get a move on! Run!" And he jabbed his spurs into Coyote's flanks. "Faster, faster!"

Coyote howled with pain: "Ow, ow, ow,! Little brother, have pity on me!" Coyote arched his back, bucked, twisted, and tried to shake off his rider, but Rabbit Boy stuck to him like a burr. Thus they arrived at the home of Rabbit Boy's aunt. In a flash, Rabbit Boy jumped off Coyote's back and, at the same time, tied the bridle to a piñon tree. He did this in the twinkling of an eye, in one blurred motion.

All of Rabbit Boy's relatives were there. Already they were feasting.

Tied to the tree, Coyote had to watch the rabbits stuffing themselves with good food, having a good time, eating, drinking, and telling stories. The feast lasted a long time. When it was over at last, Rabbit Boy went over to Coyote, accompanied by a cousin, another rabbit, of course.

"As soon as I'm on this ugly fellow's back," Rabbit Boy told his cousin, "untie him and throw the bridle to me!" His cousin did as he was told. At the moment Coyote was untied, Rabbit Boy dug in his spurs. Again and again he struck at Coyote's sides.

"Off with you, back to my home, faster, faster, you lousy Coyote!"

Again Coyote howled with pain: "Ow, ow, ow!" he was helpless. He was thinking: "I won't stop at this evil rabbit's place. I'll rush right by it, back to my den. There my wife will help me get this pest off my back. Then he won't be able to escape us. My wife and I will catch that no-good rabbit. I'll skin him alive. I'll put him in my pot. I'll make soup of him!"

It did not work out this way. As soon as they were passing his home, Rabbit Boy jumped off Coyote's back and, quick as lightning, dashed into his hole, shutting the door behind him. In vain Coyote tried to get in. In vain he pounded at the door, scratched, and dug. He could not get in. He heard Rabbit Boy laughing at him from behind his door, calling him names. At last Coyote gave up.

When Coyote got home, his wife asked him: "What's the matter with you, husband? You are in a cold sweat. You are foaming at the mouth. Your sides have blood all over."

"Old woman, mind your own business," said Coyote.

A SATISFYING MEAL

{Hopi}

Coyote and Fox are not very fond of each other, because they are always competing for the same kind of food. So whenever he has a chance to play a trick on Fox, Coyote will do it.

One day Fox managed to catch a prairie dog. He killed it. He said: "This is a fine, fat prairie dog. It will make a tasty meal."

Fox got some wood and made a fire. When the wood had been reduced to glowing embers, Fox pushed the prairie dog under the hot ashes to roast it. "It will take a while until the meat is done," Fox said to himself. "I think I'll have a little nap in the meantime." So he went to sleep.

Not far away, Coyote came walking along, scrounging for something to eat, sniffing around. The wind brought to him a scent of roasted meat. Coyote's nose quivered with delight. "Ah," he said, "I am smelling something good."

Following his nose, Coyote came to the spot where Fox was sleeping. He dug out the prairie dog from under the still-glowing embers. He ate it up in no time at all. He said: "This meat is very tender, cooked just the way I like it." He left only the bare bones. He took a little of the fat and smeared it around Fox's mouth. Then Coyote went off laughing.

Fox woke up. He noticed that his mouth was greasy. He said: "I must have eaten the prairie dog. Funny, I don't remember it." He dug underneath the ashes and pulled out what was left—the prairie dog's bones. "I was right," he said, "I did eat the meat, even though I don't remember it."

Fox sat down on a rock. He was thinking. He said to himself: "If I had eaten that prairie dog, I should feel sated. Instead I am hungry, very hungry. Therefore I did not eat that meat." He jumped up: "Now I know what happened. That evil trickster, that no good Coyote, has stolen my meat. I will find him and kill him!"

Fox followed Coyote's tracks. Coyote saw him coming. Coyote said to himself: "Fox is faster than I am. I cannot get rid of him by running away." So Coyote stood up and leaned against an overhanging cliff. Fox came running. "Watch out, Coyote, you miserable trickster," he cried. "I've come to kill you!"

"Fool," Coyote cried. "Halfwit! Don't you see that I'm holding up this overhanging cliff, which is about to crush us both to death? Here, you lean against the cliff and hold it up while I go for a tree trunk to wedge against this rock wall, so that we both can get out from under it without being crushed. Lean against it real hard or it will flatten you. I'll be right back!" Fox leaned against the cliff real hard. He waited and waited, but Coyote did not come back. "This evil Coyote has tricked me again," said Fox, as he jumped away from the rock wall, still looking up to see whether it would fall down on him. "Yes, Coyote has made a fool out of me."

Once more, Fox followed Coyote's tracks. He found him sitting on a tree stump near a stream. Again Coyote did not try to flee. Fox came running, foaming at the mouth: "Watch out, Coyote, this time I'll make an end of you, once and for all. I'll tear your throat out!"

It was sunset. The red setting sun was reflected in the stream's water. "Nitwit!" Coyote shouted, pointing at the sun's reflection. "Idiot, look at this hunk of fine red meat in the water. Instead of bothering me, you should try to get it before the current sweeps it away. Here, I'll hold on to your tail to pull you up after you've grabbed the meat!"

Fox fell for it. As he jumped into the water, Coyote quickly tied a heavy rock to Fox's tail. Fox drowned. "Finally I'm rid of this pest," said Coyote. But of course he was wrong. No matter how often Coyote and Fox kill each other, they always come to life again.

A STRONG HEART

{Arikara}

The Coyote was going along when he saw an old Buffalo bull sitting down on the side of a hill. The Coyote went up to him and said, "Well, my grandfather, are you sitting here sunning yourself?"

The Buffalo said, "Yes."

The Coyote said that he was hungry, that he would like the Buffalo to give him something to eat.

The Buffalo said, "Why are you not like myself, a big Buffalo eating grass?"

The Coyote said, "Well, my grandfather, I wish that you would make a Buffalo out of me."

So the Buffalo said, "All right. You will then have to break up your bow and arrows, for you will need them no more." So the Buffalo

placed the Coyote, and said, "Now you must keep a strong heart; do not get scared." The Buffalo rushed at the Coyote, and just as he was about to hook the Coyote, the Coyote jumped sideways. Then the Buffalo said, "Why did you get scared? Now stay right at this place, and I will come and make a Buffalo out of you." But every time the Buffalo ran toward him, the Coyote would jump away.

The last time the Coyote stayed, and as the Buffalo went up against him there were two Buffalo bulls. They locked horns. Then the Buffalo told the Coyote-Buffalo to eat grass. The Coyote-Buffalo obeyed and ate until he was filled. Then the Buffalo said, "We must go to the Buffalo herd, for there is one bull there who has control of all the female Buffalo, and we will fight him, and when we have killed him we can have all the female Buffalo." So they went to the Buffalo herd. The Buffalo bull was going around among the Buffalo. They were waiting to fight him when it should come time. They fought, and they killed the Buffalo bull.

Now each bull took many cows to look after. When they all came together they lay down in a hollow for the night. The next night the Buffalo all jumped and traveled toward the western country. When the Coyote-Buffalo got up he saw that he had been left behind, all alone.

He arose, but did not follow the other people. The Coyote-Buffalo came across a Coyote and said, "Why are you not as I am? I was a Coyote once, but now I am a Buffalo." The Coyote-Buffalo told the Coyote to throw his bow and arrows away, for he was going to make him into a Buffalo. He sat the Coyote in a certain place and made a rush at him. The Coyote jumped sideways. Three times did the Coyote-Buffalo try to run into the Coyote, but every time the Coyote jumped sideways. The last time, the Coyote-Buffalo said, "Now you must close your eyes and let me run over you." The Coyote obeyed and the Coyote-Buffalo ran into him, and there were two Coyotes instead of the Buffalo-Coyote and the Coyote. So the Coyote-Buffalo turned back into a Coyote.

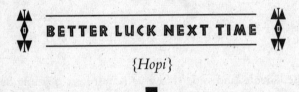

BETTER LUCK NEXT TIME

{Hopi}

Water Turtle was walking one day, nibbling at moist leaves and succulent plants. He was so wrapped up in eating that he didn't notice how far he had strayed from the water. He got farther and farther away. The sun rose in the sky. It grew hotter and hotter. At noon it was unbearable. Water Turtle could not stand the heat. A cool stream was his home. The heat was about to kill him. He crawled toward the water, but his crawling was very slow and the stream was too far. Water Turtle crawled into a hole and started to cry: "Ow, ow, ow."

Coyote was coming along. He heard Water Turtle crying. He said, "Somebody is singing." He followed the sound. He found Water Turtle in his hole. Coyote said, "Your song is very pleasing."

"I am not singing," said Water Turtle, "I am crying."

"It doesn't matter," said Coyote. "You will teach me some turtle songs and then I will make a fire and cook and eat you."

"You are very ignorant," said Water Turtle. "Otherwise you would know that turtles are fireproof. Flames cannot hurt us. We cannot be cooked."

"Then I will put you on your back in the sun and when you get tired and relax, and your shell opens, I will dig out your meat and eat it."

"You are really stupid," Water Turtle told him, "or you would know that we never get tired and our shells open only when we want."

"Then I will climb to the top of a cliff," said Coyote, "and drop you on the hard stones below. Then your shell will crack into pieces and I'll make a dinner of you."

"You are the greatest fool I ever came across," said Water Turtle. "Don't you know that our shells are harder than flint, harder than anything else in the world? Our shells never crack."

"Then I'll drop you into the nearest stream and the water will dissolve your shell and you'll drown and then I'll eat you!"

"Ow, ow, ow, please, please, please don't do that!" cried Water Turtle. "It would kill me. I'd drown. My shell would melt. Water would be the death of me. Please, dear, dear Coyote, don't put me in the stream."

"Who is stupid now?" Coyote laughed. "You dumb Water Turtle, you've given yourself away!"

Coyote grabbed Water Turtle between his jaws and ran as fast as he could to the nearest stream. He dropped Water Turtle into the stream. Water Turtle stuck his head out above the surface. He was grinning. He shouted: "Thank you, thank you, dear Coyote, you've brought me home. You've saved my life!"

Coyote went off, shaking his head, growling: "Water Turtle had more brains than I thought. He has outsmarted me. Better luck next time."

 ## LONG EARS OUTSMARTS COYOTE

{Pueblo}

Coyote was walking along, looking for what he could get. On the road he overtook a donkey on the way to market with a big load of fine round cheeses. Right away his mouth began to water. "Good morning, Long Ears, may I walk along with you?"

"With pleasure," said the donkey. "I always love to have company." They went along. They came to a river. They had to cross it, but there was no bridge.

"Señor Long Ears, I hear that you are a wonderful swimmer," said Coyote. "I'm told you can outswim everybody. Would you take me across?"

"Gladly," said the donkey. "Hop on my back, but be careful that none of the cheeses falls off."

"I'll be very careful," said Coyote. While donkey was swimming across, Coyote ate up all the cheeses. When they reached the other shore, Coyote told the donkey: "Señor Long Ears, here our ways part. Thank you so much for ferrying me across. I hope you get a good price for your cheeses."

"*Adiós,* Señor Coyote," said the donkey. He was unaware that Coyote had eaten up all his cheeses. He arrived at the market and found a buyer for his wares. They agreed on a price, but when the buyer looked inside the bags the donkey was carrying, there were no cheeses there. "What are you trying to pull on me?" said the buyer, and went off cursing. The donkey was very disappointed. "How could Coyote repay my kindness by stealing my goods?" he exclaimed. "How could he be so evil?"

The donkey returned to his master, who cried, "You stupid beast, you've ruined me!" The master got a big, heavy stick and beat the donkey unmercifully. "Go, catch this thieving Coyote and bring him to me. If you don't, I'll beat you some more. I'll break every bone in your body!"

The donkey ran off in a panic. He had no idea where to find Coyote. He searched far and wide without any luck. Then he heard someone laughing, guffawing. The laughter was very loud, the side-splitting kind. The donkey followed the sound. It led him to Coyote's cave. Inside, Coyote was bragging to his wife and his little ones: "That foolish Señor Long Ears. Hah, hah, he must have been very surprised when he got to market with an empty load. I just love to play tricks on such fools. No wonder they call a stupid person a dumb ass!"

The donkey heard it. He lay down in front of the cave's entrance. Then he waited. After a while Coyote's wife came out to get water. The donkey played dead. Coyote's wife ran back to the cave. "Quick, quick," she called, "there's a dead donkey lying at the door. The body is still warm, the meat fresh. We'll have a big feast."

They all ran out—Coyote, his wife, and the little coyotes. One of them cried: "Dear father, I want the heart, bring me the heart."

Coyote said: "All right!" It was his favorite child who had asked for it. Coyote opened the donkey's jaws wide and stuck his head way down its throat to tear the donkey's heart out. The donkey promptly clamped his teeth down hard upon Coyote's neck. Coyote was caught.

In the meantime, Coyote's wife and children had gone back inside the cave to make a fire and get pots and pans ready for a big feast. They had not seen that Coyote's head was stuck fast between the donkey's jaws. While they were inside, the donkey dragged Coyote off. When Coyote's wife came out again with her great big butcher knife, she could find no trace of her husband or the donkey. She didn't know what to make of it. "What could have happened?" she said to the little coyotes. "It must be witchcraft."

The donkey dragged Coyote all the way back to his master. "You no-good thieving trickster!" cried the master. "Now you must pay for my cheeses!" Then he tore Coyote's pelt and skin from his back, saying: "This will make a nice rug before my bed."

Coyote ran back to his cave, all naked, without his fur. His wife did not recognize him. "Stranger," she said, "you are surely the ugliest creature I've ever met. You have a coyote's shape, but you are pink and hairless like a pig. You are truly ugly."

"Stupid woman," said Coyote, "it is me. Don't you recognize your own husband?"

Coyote was ashamed. He went deep inside to the farthest corner of the cave. He wanted nobody to see him until his fur had grown back.

OLD MAN COYOTE AND THE BUFFALO

{Crow}

*Driving buffalo over the edge of a high cliff was a
hunting technique practiced by Plains Indians
for hundreds of years.*

Once, when Old Man Coyote saw some buffalo, he wanted to eat them
and tried to think of a scheme to do this.

He approached the buffalo and said to them: "You buffalo are the
most awkward of all animals—your heads are heavy, your hairy legs are
chopped off short, and your bellies stick our like a big pot."

The buffalo said to him: "We were made this way."

Old Man Coyote said to them: "I'll tell you what let's do—we
will run a race." And all went to a level place with a steep cut bank at
the end.

Old Man Coyote said to himself: "I will go and put my robe over the edge of the bank," and turning to the buffalo, he said: "Just as we get to the place where my robe is, we will all shut our eyes and see how far we can go with our eyes closed."

The race was started, and just before getting to the robe, all of the buffalo shut their eyes and jumped over the steep cut bank and were killed; and Old Man Coyote feasted off the dead buffalo.

COYOTE AND BOBCAT HAVE THEIR FACES DONE

{Ute}

At the beginning of time, Bobcat had a long nose and tail. One day he was sleeping in front of his den when Coyote happened to be passing by. "Ah, Bobcat is sound asleep," Coyote said to himself. "Here is my chance to play a trick on him." Coyote pushed Bobcat's face in and cut off most of his tail.

When Bobcat woke up, he felt different. He felt behind him for his long, bushy tail and there was nothing, just a little stump. Bobcat felt his face, and where his long nose used to be, there was nothing. "How could this have happened?" Bobcat lamented. He had been so proud of his long, bushy tail and he did not at all like his new, stubby nose. "It must have been that evil prankster, Coyote, who has done this to me," he thought. "But I'll get even with him."

Now, in those long-gone days, Coyote had a short nose and just a little stump of a tail. One day he was sleeping in front of his lodge. He was dead to the world. A thunderclap could not have awakened him. Bobcat happened to be passing by. He saw Coyote sleeping, smiling in his dreams. "Here is my chance," said Bobcat. He pulled hard at Coyote's nose and tail. He made them long.

When Coyote woke up, he noticed that something was not right. He said: "What is there dragging behind me?" he felt around and discovered that his tail had grown long. He said: "What is this strange thing sticking out in front of my face?" He felt it and found that it was his nose. He did not like it. "Could it be that flat-faced fellow, Bobcat?" he wondered. He went home, his long tail dragging behind him. When his wife saw Coyote's long nose, she had a good laugh.

THE ADVENTURES OF A MEATBALL

{*Comanche*}

Long ago, it is said, there somewhere, a big pounded meatball went loping. As it went loping along the road, one (Coyote) was lying there beside the road. That loping one said: "That's Coyote. Are you lying there?" That Coyote said: "Yes, I am lying here. I am about to die from hunger." That big meatball said to him: "You must take one big bite of me." That one Coyote took a big bite of it. Then Coyote said: "I am going." Coyote ran along the road, again stopped and lay down over there in front of the meatball.

That big meatball was rolling here along the road. Coyote again was lying here in front of it. The big meatball said to him: "Are you lying there?"

"Yes," said Coyote, "I am about to die of hunger."

Meatball said to him: "Take a big bite from me, once."

Coyote, along there, took a big bite of it. Coyote said: "I am going."

Meatball said: "Along here it is this way, one after another." Big meatball was rolling off again at this place. Coyote stopped and lay down here in front of it again. Big meatball said to him: "Are you lying there?"

Coyote said: "Yes, I am lying here. I am about to die of hunger."

Big meatball said: "You must take a big bite from me."

Coyote, along here, took a big bite of it. Coyote ran.

Meatball said: "Along this road, it is this way, one after another."

Here again Coyote stopped and lay down in front of it. As he lay down here, big meatball came, rolling toward him. Meatball said to him: "Are you lying here?"

"Yes," said Coyote, "I am about to die of hunger." He was about to take a big bite of it. When he opened his mouth wide, big meatball saw it, Coyote had meat between his teeth.

Big meatball said to him: "Oh, you are the same one, moving along, cheating me." At this place, when meatball recognized him, Coyote ran.

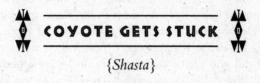

COYOTE GETS STUCK

{Shasta}

Stories of Trickster stuck in tar or pitch occur among many tribes. Indian legends were possibly the source of Uncle Remus's "Tar Baby" stories.

Coyote was roaming. He encountered Pitch. Coyote greeted him: "How are you, uncle?" Pitch did not answer. Coyote said: "Did you not hear me?" Pitch remained silent. Coyote was annoyed: "Hey, I am speaking to you. Why don't you answer?" Pitch said nothing.

Now Coyote was really angry: "You rude, impolite fellow, don't you hear me? Are you deaf?" There was still no answer. Coyote was furious. "I'll teach you a lesson!" he cried. Coyote struck Pitch with his right fist. It got stuck.

Coyote growled: "Let me go or I'll kick you." Pitch did not move.

Coyote kicked him with his right foot, which got stuck. Coyote tried to balance himself on one leg.

He shook his left fist into Pitch's face and threatened: "You evil, no-good fellow, I'll knock you senseless!" He gave Pitch a good whack, but now his left hand was stuck.

Coyote got more and more frustrated. "I'll knock you with my other foot," he shouted. He got no reaction. He kicked with all his might and his left foot was stuck.

Coyote shouted: "You nasty lump! I shall whip you with my tail!" He struck Pitch with his tail, but it, too, got stuck.

Finally Coyote threatened Pitch: "My teeth are sharp. I will bite you to death!" Pitch still did not react. Coyote sank his teeth deep into Pitch and, of course, his mouth got stuck. He was helpless, glued to Pitch, unable to move. He could hardly breathe. He croaked: "Oh, my aunt! Help me!"

Coyote's aunt was powerful. She came running to his aid. "Set fire to him! Set fire to him!" Coyote cried. Aunt took a burning stick and plunged it into Pitch's side. As soon as the flame touched Pitch, he grew soft. He began to melt. Then Coyote could extricate himself. Coyote told his defeated opponent: "You will be nothing but pitch. People will call you pitch. Now you are no longer a person, you are just a gooey, sticky, unpleasant lump." Then Coyote and his aunt went off to attend to some matter.

 # ANYTHING BUT PIÑON PITCH!

{Navajo}

One day Coyote was out walking. He was walking in the forest. He saw Rabbit. He started to chase Rabbit. Rabbit ran in a hole. Coyote said: "I'll get you out of that hole. Let me think." Coyote sat down to think. "Now I know. I'll get you out. I'll get weeds. I'll put them in the hole. I'll set fire to them. Then you will come out," said Coyote.

Rabbit laughed. "No, I will not come out, my cousin. I like weeds. I'll eat the weeds."

"Do you eat milkweeds?" asked Coyote. "I'll get milkweeds."

"Yes, I like milkweeds. I'll eat milkweeds," said Rabbit.

"Do you eat foxtail grass?" asked Coyote. "I'll get foxtail grass."

"Yes. I like foxtail grass. I'll eat foxtail grass."

"Do you eat rabbit brush?" asked Coyote. "I'll get rabbit brush."

"Rabbit brush? I like rabbit brush best of all. I'll eat rabbit brush, too," said Rabbit.

"I know," said Coyote. "Piñon pitch."

Rabbit looked sad. "You will kill me. I do not eat piñon pitch," said Rabbit.

Coyote was happy. He ran from piñon tree to piñon tree. He gathered piñon pitch. He put the piñon pitch in the hole. He set the piñon pitch on fire. He bent low. He blew on the fire.

"Come closer," said Rabbit, "blow harder." Coyote came closer. He blew harder. "I'm nearly dead," said Rabbit, "come closer. Blow a little harder."

Rabbit turned. He kicked hard. The fire flew in Coyote's face. Rabbit ran away. He was laughing very hard.

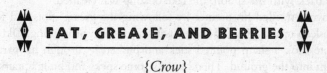

FAT, GREASE, AND BERRIES

{*Crow*}

Coyote was walking along and met four men and every part of their bodies was made of fat, grease, and all kinds of berries, fruits, etc. Before the four men saw him, he transformed his body into that of a poor dog, and he got in front of them, when they came nearer, so they would have pity on him, and they patted his head while he licked them to get the grease of which they were made. They passed and went on their way and Old Man Coyote went over the hill and got in front of them again. This time he had transformed himself into a larger dog than the previous one, and he licked them again and occasionally bit small pieces off them. Again they passed on and he met them again, a still larger dog, and bit larger pieces. The fourth time, he met them and bit still larger pieces, and then they discovered it to be Old Man Coyote; so they began to run. Old Man Coyote took a young sapling and knocked them down in an old lake bed, and they all melted into a soup.

As Old Man Coyote started to drink up the soup, he called to his partner to come, and when his partner came, he said, "Now you go after my spoon" (which was the tail of the lynx). His partner started for the spoon and shortly returned, claiming that his moccasins were worn out on the bottom. So Old Man Coyote fitted him out in rawhide moccasins, but his partner, after going but a short distance, took a sharp piece of rock and made holes in the soles, returned again, and again complained of his moccasins. Again he was fitted out, this time with stone-sole moccasins. These he smashed on the rocks and again returned and complained. Old Man Coyote said: "You stay here—you know nothing—and when I reach the top of the hill, you dip your hand in the soup and lick it for me." When Old Man Coyote went over the first hill for his spoon, his partner drank a lot of the soup, and when the last hill was reached by Old Man Coyote, the partner had drunk the last of the soup and then ran away. When Old Man Coyote came back with the spoon, the lake of soup was cleaned.

Coyote tracked his partner by following the grease spots and found him asleep under a big shade tree with his rectum protruding. Old Man Coyote took a sharp pointed stick and pushed it through his partner's rectum into the ground. Then he took some sticks and built a prairie fire to the windward of his sleeping partner. Old Man Coyote shouted that the prairie was on fire and the sleeping partner was quickly aroused, and dashed away to avoid being destroyed by the fire. As he ran, his intestines became unraveled and stretched out across the country. Old Man Coyote took the end of the rectum which was pinned to the ground and began to suck out the soup. He kept on sucking until all the soup had been taken, but he insisted that there must be more of it, and continued sucking, which caused Old Man Coyote to vomit all the soup.

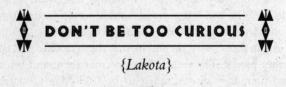

DON'T BE TOO CURIOUS

{Lakota}

Shunka Manitou, Coyote, came walking along, scrounging, as usual. He met Mastincala, Rabbit, who was carrying a leather pouch on his back. *"Hau, kola,"* Coyote said, *"toniktuka hwo?* How are you?"

"Middling well," said Mastincala.

Coyote wanted to know what was in the pouch. He guessed: "Oh, you have *chanshasha* [tobacco] in that pouch on your back. I sure would like something to smoke. Give me some. You've got more than you need for your size. You are small, I am big."

Rabbit did not answer. "Come on, you greedy, no good *Hlete,* don't be stingy." Rabbit walked on.

"Hey, you long-eared fellow, let me see what you got there on your back!"

"Nothing you would want," Rabbit finally answered.

"Well, let me see that nothing."

"No, you would be sorry. You would be angry with me."

Coyote was dying with curiosity. "If it's not tobacco, what, then?" he insisted.

"I said already that you would not want what is in this pouch," said Rabbit.

Then, in a big rage, Coyote tore the pouch from Rabbit's back and opened it. The pouch was full of fleas, so many nobody could count them. They all went on Coyote. He ran off in a frenzy, scratching himself, howling.

Rabbit yelled after him: "I told you so!" Ever since that time you can hear Coyotes howling all over the place. They howl because the fleas are biting and make them itch. That's why they howl.

PART THREE

COYOTE'S
AMOROUS
ADVENTURES

COYOTE'S AMOROUS ADVENTURES

{Shasta}

Once Coyote perceived two girls walking along the road; and he said to himself, "I should like to have these girls. I wonder how I can get them." A small creek ran parallel to the road.

"I will go into the creek and turn into a salmon," said Coyote. He did so, and pretty soon the girls came to the creek. Upon seeing the salmon darting to and fro, one girl exclaimed, "Oh, here is a salmon! Let us catch it!" So the girls sat down on opposite banks of the river, and the salmon swam back and forth, entering their bodies.

The elder girl said to her sister, "Do you feel anything queer?"

And her sister answered: "Yes, I feel fine."

Thereupon Coyote came out of the creek in his true form, and laughed at the girls, saying, "You thought it was a salmon, but I fooled you."

The girls were angry, and cursed him.

He kept on going downstream, and after a while he saw two girls digging camas on the other side of the river. He began to wonder how to get possession of them. He made his penis grow into a stalk going under the river and coming up on the other side like a plant. While the girls were bending over digging camas, the stalk entered between their legs. One of the girls then found a strange object on the ground and wanted to find out what the object was. So she looked around and saw a little stalk, which she tapped with her camas-digger.

Thereupon Coyote began to yell from across the creek, because the stalk was part of his own body, and it hurt him when it was struck. He pulled it back.

The girls, perceiving the deception, become angry and said, "It was that old Coyote who played this trick on us."

TWO RASCALS AND THEIR WIVES

{Pueblo}

There was a hill. Old Man Coyote lived on one side of it, Old Man Beaver and his wife lived on the other. So they were neighbors. They were friends, but Old Man Coyote loved to play tricks even upon friends. One day he went over to Old Man Beaver's place. Beaver said: "Come in friend, sit down by the fireplace. Have a smoke."

"Thank you, brother," said Old Man Coyote. "I've had an idea—let's you and I go out hunting rabbits. You go hunting over to the west, I will go toward the east. The rabbits I'll catch I'll bring to your wife. The rabbits you catch, you'll bring to my wife."

"All right," Old Man Beaver agreed, "but why should I bring my rabbits to *your* wife, and why should you bring your rabbits to *my* wife?"

"Brother, I hate to say this, but you're slow-witted. Don't you get it? This way we will swap wives. Wife-swapping is fun. You'll bring lots of rabbits to my wife. She will be so overjoyed that she will love to copulate with you. And your wife will be so glad with the rabbits I shall be bringing her, that, right away, she will want to sleep with me. This will be fun!"

"I never thought of this," said Old Man Beaver. "Well, all right, I'll get my rabbit stick."

Old Man Coyote was always in the mood to copulate. He knew that Old Man Beaver was not as eager to do it. He did it only once in a while. Also Old Man Coyote knew that Beaver was not a very good hunter. How could he be, always swimming around in a pond and eating nothing but twigs and saplings? So Old Man Coyote was very sure of himself.

Old Man Coyote and Old Man Beaver went off to hunt early in the morning. Beaver Woman was full of anticipation. She was singing a little song:

> *"Old Man Coyote,*
> *come soon*
> *with many rabbits.*
> *Old Man Coyote,*
> *you're such a great lover,*
> *Old Man Coyote,*
> *sleep with me."*

Old Man Coyote came back very late. He had not caught a single rabbit. He went to Old Man Beaver's house. Beaver Woman scolded him: "You braggart, always boasting of what a great hunter you are. You brought me nothing to eat. I won't sleep with a no-good fellow like you. Get out!"

Old Man Coyote was not very happy. He went over to his own place. Old Man Beaver was already there. He had brought a whole sack full of rabbits. He and Coyote Woman had eaten their fill until they could not eat a single mouthful more. Old Man Beaver was already copulating with Coyote Woman. She was crying out loud: "Agh, agh, agh!"

Old Man Coyote was sitting outside, in front of the door, listening. He called out: "Oh, oh, brother Beaver, don't hurt my wife!"

Coyote Woman called back: "Old Man Coyote, you fool! I'm crying because I like it!" Old Man Beaver and Coyote Woman did it several times. They couldn't stop themselves.

Finally they were done. Old Man Beaver came out of the house. He told Old Man Coyote: "Brother, don't complain. This was your idea!"

COYOTE SLEEPS WITH HIS OWN DAUGHTERS

{Southern Ute}

Coyote had two daughters and a son, a little boy. One evening Coyote was lying on his blanket. It was raining and the roof of his shelter was leaking. Water dripped on Coyote and he got wet. He told one of his daughters to climb up and fix it. While she was doing this he caught sight of her exposed vulva. Coyote became excited and amorous. He felt his penis stirring. He said to himself: "Oh, this looks nice and juicy. I want to copulate with her soon." Then he told his other daughter: "Climb up there and fix the leak!" As she did so, Coyote got a glimpse of her vulva. "Oh, how lovely and red," he said to himself. "I must copulate with her too." The thought made his penis stand up. He thought: "How can I do this with these girls, my daughters? It is forbidden to a man to sleep with his own kin." After a while he told himself: "Never mind, I'll find a way."

Coyote told his wife: "I am going hunting for rabbit." He went out of his lodge. He thought: "My wife is getting old and ugly. It is no longer fun to copulate with her. It will be much more fun with my daughters." He picked up a sharp, broken bone. He scratched his chest with it until it bled. He went home. He told his wife: "Woman, an enemy stabbed me. I am dying." He fell down on the floor of the lodge.

His wife and daughters rushed to his side: "Oh, poor man, don't leave us! Don't die!"

Coyote told them: "It cannot be helped, I'm done for. Dear wife, dear daughters, after I am dead, wrap me in my blanket and put me on a woodpile. Burn me up. Then go to the next village and make a new life for yourselves. When you go, let none look back or something bad will happen."

Coyote played dead. He made it look real. The women wrapped him in his blanket, put him on a woodpile, and set fire to it. "Let no one look back," said his wife. Then they went away weeping.

The little boy looked back. He cried: "Father slipped out of his blanket. It's only the blanket that's burning."

"How can you say such a wicked thing?" his mother scolded him. "Your poor father is dead."

"I saw him roll off the woodpile," said the boy.

"It was his ghost you saw," said his mother. "Your father is dead. He is burned up."

They all went to another village and put up a lodge there.

Not long after, a good-looking young man arrived at that village. The stranger was dressed in rich otter fur. He wore a hat made of otter skin. He had an otter-skin quiver slung over his shoulder. He was riding a fine gray horse. It was Coyote, who had the power to change himself into anyone or anything he wished. His wife, daughters, and little boy were sitting before their lodge. Coyote dismounted in front of them. Coyote said to his wife, who did not recognize him: "You look like a good cook. I have a lot of good-tasting buffalo-hump meat in my possible bag. Let's cook it and have a feast!"

They all went into the lodge, cooked and ate the meat. Coyote's daughters looked at the handsome stranger and thought that they would like to have him for a husband. Their mother thought that he would make a good son-in-law. Coyote told his wife: "You have two beautiful daughters. I wish to marry them."

His wife told him: "I would be proud to have you as a son-in-law."

Both daughters said: "I want him for my husband."

The little boy said: "This man looks a lot like our father."

"How can you say such a foolish thing?" his mother scolded him. "Your poor father is dead. Also your father was old and ugly. This one is young and handsome."

"He has the same look in his eyes as Father," the little boy persisted.

"Be quiet," said his mother.

Coyote married his daughters. "Take whomever you want first," said Coyote's wife. "I am going to bed."

"I'll start with your eldest daughter, dear mother-in-law," said Coyote.

That night Coyote copulated with his eldest daughter. "Oh, oh, it hurts!" she cried.

"Only the first time," said her mother. "From then on it feels good."

The next night Coyote slept with his younger daughter. "Oh, oh," she cried, "it hurts!"

Her mother told her: "It was the same with me. It hurts the first time. Later you can't get enough of it."

Coyote said to himself: "This is so much better than with the old woman."

Some time later his wife said: "Son-in-law, I feel like eating rabbit. Could you get some for me?" Coyote left to hunt rabbits. He took his little boy with him. Coyote had the power to make himself big or small to fit any situation. He made himself small and crept into a rabbit hole and killed all the rabbits inside. He ate the biggest and threw the others out of the hole to take home.

"That is exactly how Father used to do it," thought the boy. He told this to his mother.

"Your father is dead," said his mother. "And no man ever marries his daughters. It is forbidden. One cannot even imagine it."

A few days later Coyote again went out with his boy to hunt. They did not catch anything. "Let's sit down and rest awhile," said Coyote. He began telling his son funny Trickster tales. He laughed at his own stories, grinning from ear to ear. Then the little boy saw that Coyote had four teeth missing, one at the upper left and one at the upper right, one at the lower left and one at the lower right. This was something Coyote had not been able to change. The son ran back to his mother, crying: "It is Father! It is Father! You can tell by his teeth! He has done what one cannot even imagine!"

The mother asked her daughters: "What does your husband do when you make love?"

"He sucks our breasts," the daughters told her.

"That's what he does with me!" cried their mother. "It is your father! The boy was right!"

Just then Coyote came home. His wife went after him with her skinning knife, screaming: "You unspeakable man, you have done the unimaginable!"

Coyote was running away from her, crying: "Calm down, old woman, from now on I sleep only with you!"

His daughters were so ashamed they flew up onto the sky and became stars.

OLD MAN COYOTE MEETS COYOTE WOMAN

{Blackfoot}

In the beginning there were only two human beings in this world— Old Man Coyote and Coyote Woman. Old Man Coyote lived on one side of the world, Coyote Woman on the other. By chance they met.

"How strange," said Old Man Coyote. "We are exactly alike."

"I don't know about that," said Coyote Woman. "You're holding a bag. What's in it?"

Old Man Coyote reached into his bag and brought out a penis. "This odd thing."

"It is indeed an odd thing," said Coyote Woman. "It looks funny. What is it for?"

"I don't know," said Old Man Coyote. "I don't know what to use it for. What do you have in your bag?"

Coyote Woman dug deep into her bag and came up with a vagina.

"You see," she said, "we are not alike. We carry different things in our bags. Where should we put them?"

"I think we should put them into our navels," said Old Man Coyote. "The navel seems to be a good place for them."

"No, I think not," said Coyote Woman. "I think we should stick them between our legs. Then they will be out of the way."

"Well, all right," said Old Man Coyote. "Let's put them there." They placed these things between their legs.

"You know," said Coyote Woman, "it seems to me that the strange thing you have there would fit this odd thing of mine."

"Well, you might be right," said Old Man Coyote. "Let's find out." Coyote stuck his penis into Coyote Woman's vagina.

"Um, that feels good," said Coyote Woman.

"You are right," said Old Man Coyote. "It feels very good, indeed. I have never felt this way before."

"Neither have I," said Coyote Woman. "It occurred to me that this might be the way to make other human beings. It would be nice to have company."

"It certainly would," said Old Man Coyote. "Just you and me could become boring."

"Well, in case doing what we just did should result in bringing forth more human beings, what should they be like?" said Coyote Woman.

"Well, I think they should have eyes and mouth going up and down."

"No, no," said Coyote Woman. "Then they would not be able to

see well, and food would dribble out of the lower corner of their mouths. Let's have their eyes and mouths go crosswise."

"I think that the men should order the women about," said Old Man Coyote, "and that the women should obey them."

"We'll see about that," said Coyote Woman. "I think that the men should pretend to be in charge and that the women should pretend to obey, but that in reality it should be the other way around."

"I can't agree to this," said Old Man Coyote.

"Why quarrel?" said Coyote Woman. "Let's just wait and see how it will work out."

"All right, let's wait and see. How should the men live?"

"The men should hunt, kill buffalo and bears, and bring the meat to the women. They should protect the women at all times."

"Well, that could be dangerous for the men," said Old Man Coyote. "A buffalo bull or a bear could kill a man. Is it fair to put the men in such danger? What should the women do in return?"

"Why, let the women do the work," said Coyote Woman. "Let them cook, and fetch water, and scrape and tan hides with buffalo brains. Let them do all these things while the men take a rest from hunting."

"Well, then we agree upon everything," said Old Man Coyote. "Then it's settled."

"Yes," said Coyote Woman. "And why don't you stick that funny thing of yours between my legs again?"

 ## COYOTE AND FOX DRESS UP

{*Nez Percé*}

Coyote and Fox were wandering. They were hungry. Coyote said: "I am too lazy to hunt for myself. Let somebody else provide food for me."

"You mean for *us,*" said Fox.

"Well, all right, for us."

"How do we do this?" Fox asked.

"You take after your father," said Coyote. "He was slow-witted, and so are you. I take after my father, who was wise; therefore I am very clever. Let us marry some men who are good hunters and will provide for us."

"How can we marry men when we ourselves are men?"

"We will disguise ourselves by putting on women's clothes. They won't know that we are men."

"They will find out when they want to cohabit with us. They will want to right away."

"Don't worry," Coyote assured him. "Leave it all to me."

Coyote and Fox put on women's clothes. They went to a place where two Wolf Brothers lived. Coyote had heard that these Wolves were mighty hunters. They arrived at the Wolves' lodge. They went inside. The Wolf Brothers were there, eating.

"We are two maidens come to marry you," said Coyote. "Your parents and our parents, who live in that camp beyond those mountains, arranged it for us."

"Well, yes," said the Wolf Brothers, "we always wanted to marry comely maidens like you. Well, we consider ourselves married already."

The one brother pointed to Coyote and said: "I will marry you, and my brother will take this one," pointing at Fox.

"Yes," said the other brother. "I will take my new wife to that corner over there, and you, my brother, will take yours to the far corner over there. We will cohabit right away."

"Not so fast," said Coyote. "Before we marry and sleep with you, we must make sure that you can provide for beautiful maidens such as us. For four days you shall feed us—only the best, mind you. Then, after we have satisfied ourselves that you are skilled hunters, we will marry and cohabit."

"Well, you are certainly very demanding," said the Wolves, "but we will do what you want."

For four days the Wolves went out hunting. Every evening they came back with loads of meat—buffalo, elk, deer, antelope, fowls of every kind. Coyote and Fox gorged themselves. At the end of the fourth day, bloated with food, Fox whispered to Coyote: "There arises now a situation difficult to handle."

"Just watch me," Coyote whispered back.

"Well," said the Wolves, "it is now time to get married and cohabit."

"Yes, certainly," said Coyote. "You have shown us that you are great hunters, but first I have to answer a call of nature." To Fox he whispered: "Brother, pretty soon these wolves will be in a hurry to leave this lodge. Then run for your life!" Coyote went out.

After a short while the Wolves said to Fox: "Your sister takes her time relieving herself." In the meantime, Coyote had run to a nearby lodge belonging to the Wolf Brothers' mother. Coyote crept into the lodge. The Wolf Mother was sleeping. Coyote quickly lifted her skirt and entered her. Wolf Mother woke up and realized what was done to her. She howled with anger and anguish. Her howl reverberated through the forest. The Wolf Brothers heard it. They tore out of the lodge to run to their mother's aid. Then Fox ran for his life. Coyote was already doing the same. They got clear away. They joined up some time later.

"Brother, you are very smart, indeed," said Fox.

"Let's get out of these women's clothes," said Coyote.

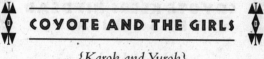

COYOTE AND THE GIRLS

{Karok and Yurok}

Coyote went to visit a village where the Indians were having a feast. There was much deer, fish, and acorns to eat and they were planning to have a big dance. There were, however, two girls who were very beautiful but who had never joined the other Indians at a dance, and who lived alone on a nearby hill. Everyone had tried to get the girls to come to the dance, but had failed. Coyote was told about the girls, and he said that he would get them to come down.

Coyote caught a cricket and put it behind one ear. He caught a bird and put it behind the other ear. As the dance began, Coyote danced and swayed with the others and soon the cricket and the bird began to sing. Coyote mouthed the songs, causing people to think that he himself was doing the singing. The two girls heard the songs and thought that they were the loveliest that they had ever heard. Finally they could resist the singing no longer and came down to see who was at the dance and who was singing such songs. They saw Coyote and danced with him, one on each side. The people marveled at the sight. Finally, as the other people became tired, they left, and Coyote and the two girls were alone.

When they tired, they lay down to sleep, with Coyote in the center and a girl on each side. When Coyote fell asleep he snored and swayed and this started the bird and cricket to sing again. The girls looked behind Coyote's ears and found the cricket and the bird, and knew that they had been tricked. The girls looked about and found two logs and put them alongside Coyote. They were put so close to Coyote that he was unable to move. Coyote finally awoke and saw the logs pinning him down. The girls had gone back to their home on the hill and Coyote knew that he had been tricked himself and repaid for what he had done.

 ## COYOTE KEEPS HIS DEAD WIFE'S GENITALS

{Lipan Apache}

Coyote's wife died. Before he disposed of her body, he cut her genitals off, and after that he dried them and pounded them to a powder, which he put in a pouch. Every time he got lonely for his wife, he took this package out and sprinkled some of the powder on his penis. It caused an orgasm every time.

Coyote had several sons. They saw their father go away by himself with his pouch several times. They snooped around and finally saw what he was doing.

One time when he was away they stole his pouch. They stood around and sprinkled the powder on their penises. It caused erections and orgasms, and they were ejaculating in all directions.

Just then Coyote came in and found them at it. He was very angry. He scolded them and beat them. "It was just for myself," he said. "You had no business taking it. Which of you did it work on?"

"It didn't work on me," the smallest son said. "No white stuff came out, though my penis grew big. I had only a pouch."

THE TOOTHED VAGINA

{Yurok}

Coyote was a young man. He came out and saw two girls picking hazelnuts. They had a sweetheart, Cotton Tail Rabbit. Coyote came along and asked, "Where are you going?"

They said, "We are going to camp out."

Then Coyote said, "Can I go with you?"

"Sure," they said, so he went with them.

They said to him, "We're going to camp right here on this sandbar," so they laid down and slept. Coyote slept in the middle between the girls, while Rabbit slept crossways at the foot.

The blanket was narrow. Every time they pulled it, they tore it in the middle, and Coyote pushed with his elbows and said, "Don't get so close to me, your breasts are too big. Don't get so close to me, I am going hunting tomorrow." Then he went to sleep and snored.

The girls did not like him. They felt sorry for Rabbit sleeping at the foot and they said, "Let's run away from Coyote."

Rabbit said, "All right," and they put logs on both sides of Coyote so he would think they were still there, and went across the river and stayed.

About noon they saw Coyote come out across the river. He said to Rabbit, "Take me across." Rabbit would not do this, so Coyote got angry. He picked up rocks; he was going to fight that Rabbit. He swam across, carrying the rocks. Rabbit got frightened. He made medicine to cause the river to be rough, so that Coyote would not be able to land. Soon Coyote drowned, and Rabbit thought he had two wives now and would never see Coyote again, because he was drowned.

Coyote landed way down the river, nothing but bones. Some thought they saw some nice wood in the river. They thought they would go and chop it. When they hit him, Coyote got up and said, "I was just sleeping right there," and went along up the river. He came across a camp where he saw many children. He thought, "I bet those are Rabbit's children." So he frightened all those children and made them go to sleep. Then he set fire to the camp and all the children were burned and he ran away up the river.

He had heard that there was a woman up the river who had killed many men. Every man who slept with her she killed. There was nothing but bones outside, and nobody ever passed that way anymore.

He knew how she killed them: When a man had intercourse with her, she killed him. There were teeth inside her. Coyote decided to go up and see her. So he made sticks. He took those sticks and went up there and thought he was going to kill her.

He stood around near her house. Soon she came out. "Ah, come on," she said. She wanted him to sleep with her right away. Coyote thought everything was all right, so when the woman wanted him to have intercourse with her, he took one of the sticks and did what she wanted. Soon he felt the stick was wearing out, and he put another in its place. He had ten sticks. The woman kept talking about it. She said, "I'm glad, my husband." He changed sticks five times. After that she quieted down. At about the eighth time she was saying something only once in a while. The tenth time he killed her. Coyote blew his breath and said, "These Indians are going to have a good time with women from now on. They aren't going to be killed."

 # SOMETHING FISHY GOING ON

{*Athapascan*}

Coyote was walking along. He saw too young girls by a lake about to take a bath. He thought: "I sure would like to have these girls. I sure would like to cohabit with them." He hid himself among the reeds and watched. The girls were taking their clothes off. Coyote turned himself into a fish and slipped into the water. He was darting back and forth.

One of the girls said to the other: "Look at that pretty little fish."

"It's just a fish," said the other.

They were naked. They waded into the lake. When it was deep enough, they began to swim. One girl said to the other: "I feel something tickling me between the legs, something slippery." Coyote entered that girl. Her body almost swallowed him up. "I feel something strange down there," said the girl. After a while Coyote slipped out of her.

Then the other girl said: "Something is tickling me, too, between

my legs." Coyote entered her. The girl said: "I also feel something strange wiggling down there, but it feels rather good." Coyote did what he wanted and slipped out of her. The girls finished bathing, dressed, and went home.

After some time, one of these girls said to the other: "My belly has swelled up. It must be all the good fatty meat and kidneys we are eating."

"That must be it," said the other girl. "We are lucky that our father is such a good hunter."

After some more time one of these two girls said to the other: "My belly is really big now. What can be the matter?"

"My belly is swollen up, too," said the other girl. "I think we are pregnant."

"How can this be?" asked the first girl.

"Remember when we were swimming in the lake? It must have been that little fish that got between our legs."

"But how can a fish get us pregnant?"

"It was Coyote, that evil fellow, who played this trick on us."

"I hope we'll be giving birth to humans," said the other, "and not little coyotes."

Well, Coyote was on his way to make mischief again. He came to a stream. On the far shore he saw two girls digging camas. "These girls are pretty, even from this far away," Coyote said to himself. "I will enter them." He sent his penis across the water. It came out on the other riverbank. With his Trickster power, he make it look like a stalk.

"I have been sitting on some plant stem," one of the girls said to the other. "It got into me by accident." The penis was enjoying himself. Coyote, on the far bank, was enjoying it. He took his penis out of this girl and slipped it into the other.

"I, too, sat on some kind of root," said the other girl. "It also got into me." Coyote was having a good time.

"There is something strange about these roots," said the first girl. "Let's look and see what it is."

They looked. "It's just some kind of plant," said the first girl. She gave the stalk a whack with her camas-digger. At once there was a loud cry of pain from the other side of the river: "Oh, oh, it hurts, it hurts!" The girls looked to where the cry was coming from. They saw Coyote there, howling. They examined the strange stalk again and discovered that it was a part of Coyote's body. The girls got very angry and shook their fists at Coyote, crying: "It's that evil, scabrous lecher who has tricked us."

"Someday," one of the girls shouted, "I'll get him with my skinning knife!"

"This is not the day," Coyote shouted back, pulling his member across the stream. He rolled his penis up and flung it over his shoulder. He laughed, waved at the girls, and ran off.

{*Karuk*}

It was Coyote who first made a baby. Then Coyote said: "Human will make a baby the same way."

Coyote and Lizard were talking in the sweathouse about what human is going to do. And one said: "They ought to cut a woman open; they ought to take the baby out of her belly."

Then Coyote said: "No. There won't be many people. How quick will he lose his wife, though he paid so much for her."

Then they all said: "How will the baby travel through?"

Then some said: "Let him out of her mouth."

Then Coyote said: "No, that won't do. Let the baby come out behind."

Then Lizard said: "Yes, that's good."

Then Coyote said: "One will be a female, and the next will be born a male. That's the way we will do. The female will be mixed with them."

Then Lizard said: "That's good. I am going to make the boy's hands, and his feet, and his penis, too, I am going to make. His hands and his

feet will grow first of all, when he is water yet. When he is earliest embryo."

They measured what size a baby was to be. "If it grows over this the woman will die," they said. "If it is growing beyond this the mother will die." There will be some herb medicine. The Ikxareyavs, the Immortals, will leave some herb medicine. There will be lots of herb medicine. Human will have herb medicine."

They instructed the boys that way: "Ye must not kill Lizard." And they told the little girls: "Lizard is your husband."

And it (the baby) is small yet, they (the Lizards) tell when it is asleep, when the baby is dreaming about something sometimes it laughs when asleep, and then people say: "It is dreaming about Lizard; lizards are telling it: 'Laugh, laugh!' And sometimes Lizards tell it: 'Cry,'" and people say: "Lizards are telling it: 'Cry, cry, cry,'" when the little baby is asleep.

When it is asleep, when it cries, they tell it: "The Lizards are pinching the baby."

Lizard said it: "I will be bothering Human's little baby."

They were talking in the sweathouse, that Human is going to come, they were talking about it. And today Lizard likes it on top of the sweathouse. He hugs his chest toward it repeatedly (with raising and lowering motion toward the sweathouse roof board). That's why he likes it there, because it is warm. It is too bad for the lizards, that there

are no more sweathouses. We never see lizards anymore in the Indian *rancherias;* they only live in rocky places now. They do not stay around the *rancherias* anymore.

WINYAN-SHAN UPSIDE DOWN

{Sioux}

There was this chief's daughter. She was beautiful. Coyote was thinking: "This one is for me." He was hanging around her tipi, he was courting her, but she would have nothing to do with him. What was to be done?

Now, at that long-ago time, the White Man had already come, but he was still only in a narrow strip along the eastern sea. Except for a few tribes living there, Indians had not yet seen their first White Men, and they knew nothing of the many new strange things they had brought. Now, Coyote knows everything that is going on long before anybody else. He senses what is going on far away. He can travel there in no time. So Coyote went there fast, in a magic way, to see what those White Men had brought. He went there and came back in a flash with four things no Indian had ever seen.

Back in the village, Coyote put up his tipi right next to the one in which the chief's daughter lived. All night he made a great noise, drumming, rattling, pounding sticks together, howling.

The chief's daughter heard it. She could not sleep. She told her sister-in-law: "Sister, go over there where they make this noise and make them stop."

The sister-in-law went to Coyote's tipi. She told him: "Stop that racket. Don't you know people are sleeping here?"

"I can't help it," said Coyote. "I am making some wonderful new strange things, the kind no one has ever seen. Beautiful and useful things."

"Why don't you make these wonderful things during the day, when people are up and awake?"

"These things can be made only during the night."

The sister-in-law went and told this to the chief's daughter.

The next morning the chief's daughter was thinking about this. She was curious. She said: "Sister-in-law, why don't you go over there and bring this man and the wonderful thing he has made? I want to see what it is."

The sister-in-law went there. She came back with Coyote. The chief's daughter asked: "Well, where is the thing you made? I hope it is something worthwhile, worth the great noise you made."

Then Coyote showed it to her. It was a bead choker made of the White Man's wonderful colorful glass beads. The chief's daughter had never seen anything so beautiful. Naturally she wanted to have it. "What do you want for this?" she asked.

"Nothing much, just a kiss, *imaputake,* kiss me," said Coyote.

"Really, just one kiss?"

"Yes, just one."

"Sister-in-law," the chief's daughter whispered, "do you think there is any harm in that?"

"No," the sister-in-law answered. "What harm can there be in just one little kiss? I can't imagine giving away such a valuable thing just for this."

So the chief's daughter gave Coyote a kiss, and he thanked her many times and went off. The chief's daughter was very happy with what she had gotten and with what she had paid for it.

Now, the next night, Coyote was making a lot of noise again. In her tipi, the chief's daughter was thinking: "I wonder what this man is making now!" In the morning she said: "Sister-in-law, I can't wait to see what was made this night. Go over and bring Coyote to me, together with whatever he has made."

The sister-in-law brought Coyote. "Let me see it," said the chief's daughter, "the thing I think you have fashioned last night." Then Coyote showed it to her. It was an iron kettle for making soup. No one had ever seen the like of it. The chief's daughter had never seen anything made of iron. It was so much better than cooking in a buffalo's paunch.

"What do you want for this?" the chief's daughter asked.

"Oh, well, nothing much. I just want to fondle one of your breasts. Only once and quickly."

"Sister-in-law, what do you think?" the chief's daughter whispered.

"Why, what harm can there be in it? This man is foolish to give such things away for almost nothing."

"All right," the chief's daughter told Coyote, "you may do this once, but be quick about it!"

So Coyote fondled her breast a little and went off. "I think this was a very good bargain," said the sister-in-law.

"I think so, too," said the chief's daughter.

That night there was a lot of noise in Coyote's tipi again. "Sister-in-law, quick," said the chief's daughter in the morning, "bring this man over here with whatever he has made."

The sister-in-law did this. "Well, what is it this time?" asked the chief's daughter. "I want it already, though I have not yet seen it."

Coyote showed it to her. It was a bright red wool blanket with black, white, and blue stripes. The chief's daughter had never seen anything so beautiful or useful. She felt the blanket and marveled at how warm and soft it was. "Well, all right, fondle my other breast and be quick about it," she told Coyote.

"No," he said, "what I want for this blanket is to feel one of your buttocks."

"Sister-in-law, what do you think?"

"Why, what is the harm in that? He already got a kiss. He already fondled a breast. What does a buttock matter?"

"Well, all right, you can do it. Just once. Do it quickly." Coyote fondled her buttock quickly, thanked her, and went away.

"It wasn't too much to ask for this blanket," said the chief's daughter.

The following night Coyote made a greater noise than in all the previous nights put together.

"Quick, quick," the chief's daughter said in the morning, "get Coyote. I am sure he has made something really wonderful this time."

Coyote came. "Show it to me at once, whatever you have made this time," the chief's daughter said. Coyote showed it to her. It was a *miloglas*, mirror. The chief's daughter beheld her own face for the first time reflected in a White Man's *miloglas*. "This is truly wonderful," she said, turning her head this way and that, admiring herself. "What do you want for this?"

"Oh, not much, really. Just to look between your legs. Only once."

"Sister-in-law," whispered the chief's daughter, "what do you think?"

"Why, what harm can there be in just a look?"

"All right," said the chief's daughter, "you may look, once." The chief's daughter spread her legs. "There, be quick, just a glance."

Coyote looked. He shook his head. "Oh, my, oh, my, too bad, too bad!"

"What is too bad?" asked the chief's daughter.

"Your *winyan-shan* is upside down. It has to be remade. It can't stay like it is. What a pity!"

Coyote thanked the chief's daughter and went off someplace.

The chief's daughter wept. "What is the matter?" the sister-in-law asked.

"This man has said that my *winyan-shan* is upside down. It has to be redone. Who is there who can do this job?"

"Why, the man who made the bead choker, and the kettle, and the blanket, and the wonderful *miloglas,* of course. Who else?"

"Sister-in-law, you are right. Get Coyote, quickly."

PART FOUR

THE TROUBLE
WITH ROSE
HIPS

COYOTE, SKUNK, AND THE BEAVERS

{Wichita}

Coyote was roaming, searching for what he could get. He surprised Skunk, waddling alongside a stream.

"Little Brother," said Coyote, "I am truly sorry, because I have to kill you. You seem to be a nice fellow, but I need your meat. I and my family, we have to eat. Don't take it personally."

"Whoa, wait a moment," said Skunk, "don't kill me. If you abstain from making a meal out of me, I'll show you how you can get many animals much fatter than myself, which are excellent eating."

"How will you do that?" asked Coyote.

"I know a place where the beavers are having a medicine dance. Beavers are fat and delicious. I will bring them to you one by one. Then we can knock them on the head and kill them. There will be more than enough for you and me and our families."

"How will you make them come, one by one?" asked Coyote.

"That's my business," answered Skunk.

"Well, all right, you seem like an honest fellow, I'll take a chance on you."

Skunk went to the place where the beavers were having a medicine dance. They were all medicine men, skilled at doctoring. Skunk went up to the fattest beaver. "Uncle," he said, "you are a famous healer. I have a brother waiting for me a little way off. He is very sick. He is too sick to come here. Please go with me and see what you can do for him. They tell me that you are the greatest medicine man of them all. Also I will give you many fine horses and other gifts."

The fat beaver was flattered. Also he was thinking of the gifts that he wanted badly. So he went along. Skunk led the beaver to where Coyote was lying, pretending to be sick.

"Which is the spot that is hurting?" asked the beaver.

Skunk turned Coyote over and lifted the tail, exposing the hole beneath it. "This is where it hurts," Skunk explained.

"Let me have a closer look," said the beaver. He put his face right up to Coyote's anus. A cloud of suffocating stench came out of it. "Your brother is indeed very sick," said the beaver, coughing and sputtering. "I think the only thing to do is make a brand-new anus for your brother. The one he has now is very sick, as you can tell by the smell. It will take some time and will cost you many horses."

"Is that so?" said Skunk, and knocked the beaver over the head with a heavy war club, killing him instantly.

"The plan is working all right," said Coyote.

"I'm going for some more beavers," Skunk told him. Skunk went back to where the beavers were having their dance. Again he picked out the fattest one. "Uncle," he said, "your relative couldn't heal my sick brother. I gave him many horses and much buffalo-hump meat, but it was no use. I guess that relative of yours is not as good as you when it comes to healing."

"You spoke the truth, little nephew," said the beaver. "Nobody is as good as myself. Lead me to your brother quickly so that I can doctor him." This beaver was already dreaming of horses and hump meat.

"Where does it hurt?" the beaver asked after they got to the place where Coyote was lying. Again Skunk turned Coyote over and lifted his tail. "It's his anus," he said. "It has been ailing for a long time. I'm afraid it can't be cured."

"Nonsense," said the beaver. "There's not one anus in the whole world that I cannot cure, no matter how sick. Let me have a look." He peeked closely under the tail and Coyote let out a stupendous fart, which almost choked that beaver to death. Sputtering and holding his nose, he told Skunk: "This is the sickest anus I've ever come across. You can tell by the awful smell. Also this nether-hole is all worn out from too much farting. I must make a new anus for your brother."

"I'm sure you are the right man to do this," said Skunk, knocking him over the head and killing him.

"We have a very good partnership, little brother," said Coyote. "I'm sure glad I did not make an end of you."

"So am I," said Skunk. "Well, I think I'll go for some more beavers."

In this way the two of them lured and killed one beaver after another. "I am really glad to have met you," Skunk told Coyote.

"Likewise," said Coyote. They divided the meat fairly and went home.

MONSTER SKUNK FARTING EVERYONE TO DEATH

{*Cree*}

Monster skunk was killing people and animals in most unpleasant ways. He would break wind against them, or discharge his juice against them, or shit on them. He killed them all one way or another, and then ate them.

A crier ran through the village, shouting: "Save yourselves! Save yourselves, the Monster Skunk is coming. He will fart you to death!"

The people were in a panic, taking their tents down, wrapping up their children, running here and there, not thinking at all, not thinking because they were too afraid to think. Some of the elders said: "We must have a meeting. We must keep our heads."

They had a meeting. "Who will go and scout?" said one old man. "We need a volunteer to go and tell us from where this monster is coming. Otherwise we might flee to just the spot where he is waiting to kill us."

The mouse squeaked: "I will go, but somebody must go with me. I won't go alone."

So the weasel volunteered to go with the mouse.

"You are small," said the old man, "but you are brave."

The mouse and the weasel went together. They came to something very big, big as a hill. "What is this strange thing?" asked the weasel.

"Be quiet," whispered the mouse. "It is the Monster Skunk's foot."

The monster had not noticed them—they were too small. They ran as fast as they could back to their camp, to tell the people Monster Skunk was coming from the east. He was not far away.

Then Bobcat and Coyote, who were the bravest, offered to try to kill the Monster Skunk. "I shall get him by the throat," said Bobcat.

"I shall get him by the balls and by the buttocks," vowed Coyote. "I shall get him at the part with which he kills people."

They painted themselves for war. They sang their death song and made medicine.

In the meantime, the Monster Skunk came walking. He met a person on his path trembling with fear. "What are you afraid of?" Skunk Monster asked this person.

"I am afraid of Monster Skunk when he farts." Monster Skunk turned around and farted this person high into the sky, and then dropped him to his death.

Monster Skunk walked on and met another man. The man was scared. "What are you scared of?" asked Monster Skunk.

"I am afraid of Monster Skunk when he shits." Monster Skunk turned around and suffocated the man under a mountain of shit.

Monster Skunk walked on. He met a third person, whose teeth were chattering with fright. "What are you afraid of?" asked Monster Skunk.

"I am afraid of Monster Skunk when he sprays his fluid." Monster Skunk turned around and drowned him in his fluid.

Monster Skunk went on. A woman saw him. Monster Skunk ran after her. The woman threw her awl case behind her, crying: "Awl case, stand up! Turn into a mighty forest!" And it did, but Monster Skunk farted it out of the way.

A woman threw her whetstone behind her, crying: "Whetstone, become a big mountain, a mountain as slippery as you are. The whetstone turned itself into a slippery mountain, but Monster Skunk farted it away, too.

A woman threw her basket behind her, crying: "Basket, become a thick hedge." The basket became a thick hedge. Monster Skunk dissolved it with his fluid.

A woman threw her water bag behind her, crying: "Water bag, become a great river." The water bag turned itself into a big river. The Monster Skunk swallowed it up. He caught up with the woman and farted her to pieces. Then he went on.

A grandmother and her granddaughter saw him coming. "Quick," said the grandmother, "lie down and play dead."

The Skunk Monster found them. "I wonder what killed these two?" said the Monster. He turned the old woman over. He saw her vagina. "Ah," he said, "this is the wound that killed her. It must have been made by a big, flat knife. Let's see whether she has been dead for a long time." He stuck two of his fingers into the old woman's vagina. He smelled them. He said: "This one is already rotting." He then stuck two fingers into the granddaughter's vagina and smelled them, saying: "Ah, this one has not been dead for long. This one is still fresh. But it does not matter. Dead is dead, and I don't eat dead things." He walked on. This old woman and her granddaughter were lucky.

The Monster Skunk then came to the place where Bobcat and Coyote had hidden themselves to ambush him. As he went by, they jumped out of their hiding places. Bobcat sprang for Monster's throat and fastened his fangs upon it. Coyote seized Monster Skunk's buttocks and fastened her teeth upon his balls. So they struggled. They bit and clawed but could not harm Monster Skunk. Coyote was clever. She got hold of a large, round rock. She stuffed it up Monster Skunk's anus. She stopped him up. His farts could not come out. Nothing could come out. His belly swelled up to a tremendous size until at last Monster Skunk was blown apart by his own farts. The big stink filled the whole country. After it abated, the people held a big feast. Coyote was given the best parts.

COYOTE SELLS A BURRO
THAT DEFECATES MONEY

{*Lipan Apache*}

Coyote found a burro. He came a little off the side of the road with it. He took some of the money and stuck it under the tail of the burro, in the anus. Every time Coyote hit him on the small of the back with a stick, the burro had to let one of the pieces of money drop.

Some people came along. They asked Coyote what he was doing.

"Oh, I'm here to show you something. This burro defecates nothing but money. Every time I hit him with this stick, nothing but money comes out." He did it for them and they were surprised.

They wanted to buy the burro, so he sold the burro. He made a good trade and got money and goods for it.

These people went one way and Coyote went another. Then those people hit the burro with sticks. At first a few pieces of money fell out, but soon it was all used up and nothing more came out. Then the burro started to defecate. They saw that he did it the same way as any other burro. These people moved off with their burro.

COYOTE THE CREDULOUS

{*Taos*}

Coyote went out to hunt. He went to Road-earth and there was Puakauuna (a ratlike animal) sleeping there. Coyote said to him, "Grandchild, you are fat and pretty!" Puakauuna was afraid of Coyote and did not say anything when Coyote spoke to him. Coyote said, "Why don't you speak?"

And the little Puakauuna said, "Wait! Wait, grandfather, listen to what the people who live way below are saying."

"What, grandchild?" said Coyote.

"Now, grandfather, I will tell you what they are saying below. They are saying, 'All who have been urinating and defecating on the road or on top of the stones anywhere in the world are going to die.' "

Coyote was scared and said, "It's too much! Grandchild, you must not tell; just a little while ago I urinated and defecated in the road. You must not tell." He jumped and ran away. And he never came back there.

Puakauuna said, "Coyote always gets scared at any little thing. And he won't come back and I shall live well."

 # THE TROUBLE WITH ROSE HIPS

{*Lipan Apache*}

Coyote went on. Along the path he saw some rose hips. They looked red and ripe. "Oh, they might be good to eat!" he thought.

The rose hips said among themselves, "We'd better tell him we are not fit to eat."

He stopped there and said, "How sweet you look. I wonder whether you are good to eat."

"No, we are not good to eat at all."

"What will happen if someone eats you?"

"Oh, if anyone eats us, he will have to break wind so hard that it will toss him up into the sky."

"Well, I just want to try one," said Coyote. He picked one and ate it. The berries nudged each other. "Oh, you are sweet," he said. He ate another and another until he was full. He gathered them by the handful. They didn't nudge each other anymore.

He started to sing:

"When I look up I see many berries,
When I look down I see many more;
The ripe ones, the soft ones; they are the ones I eat."

He had had enough. They all nudged each other when he had gone a little distance away.

They began to work on his insides. He ran for a tree and hung on. He went off like a horse. He had to do this again and again.

Far away in the flats he saw a black thing moving. He went out there. He saw what it was. There were two people looking around on the ground. They were two crows. He stopped there. He said, "You two fellows must have killed a good fat buffalo."

"Yes, our children were hungry. So we killed this buffalo. We are butchering it."

"Well, leave your work. We'll play a little game first."

"No, let us alone."

He insisted. Finally they asked, "Well, what is this game?"

"Let us see who can defecate over this buffalo."

"No, that's a dirty thing. We don't do anything like that over the game we kill, over the things we eat."

"Oh, only a little will get on it, perhaps."

He kept begging and they finally gave in. They wanted him to do it first. But he said, "No, you do it first."

The first crow tried. He jumped and defecated. It went only a little way, about halfway across.

But Coyote said, "That's pretty good. I don't think I can do that well." The other crow tried it then and did no better. Now it was Coyote's turn. He whirled around and bent down. It came out red and went straight across.

They had agreed that the one whose excrement went all the way over could have all the meat. Coyote had won all the meat. They had agreed because they thought no one could do it. The crows begged him to leave a little fat in the eye sockets, a little meat between the ribs, and some on the joints.

Coyote went back home with the meat. The two crows were there blaming each other. That has all been carried on to this day. If two are going along somewhere and meet someone going the other way, this fellow will persuade them to change their plans. Then they do something unwise, for they do not think it over. And it has a meaning in a different way. Some are not honest in playing games and trick others. One must watch out for these people, for they start trouble.

Before these two crows parted, they said, "Now our children will go hungry because we were fooled." And that's the way it is today. People spend their money foolishly and their children go around badly clothed and ill fed. Today some Indians do not listen to the advice of an older brother or a parent and gamble and drink and get into trouble.

PART FIVE

IKTOMI THE
SPIDER - MAN

SEVEN TOES

{Assiniboine}

*Though Sitconski is the preeminent Trickster of the
Assiniboine, they also have Iktomi tales.*

All the earth was flooded with water. Iktomi sent animals to dive for
dirt at the bottom of the sea. No animal was able to get any. At last he
sent the Muskrat. It came up dead, but with dirt in his claws. Iktomi
saw the dirt, took it, and made the earth out of it.

Iktomi was wearing a wolfskin robe. He said, "There shall be as
many months as there are hairs on this skin before it shall be summer."

Frog said, "If the winter lasts as long as that, no creature will be able
to live. Seven months of winter will be enough." He kept on repeating
this, until Iktomi got angry and killed him. Still Frog stuck out seven of
his toes. Finally, Iktomi consented and said there should be seven
winter months.

Iktomi then created men and horses out of dirt. Some of the Assiniboine and other northern tribes had no horses. Iktomi told the Assiniboine
that they were always to steal horses from other tribes.

{*Sioux*}

At one time there lived two little boys and their grandmother in the west. She is always telling them stories about Ikto, Iktomi, the smart-ass Spider-Man. They want to know whether Iktomi is a man or a spider. He is both; he is a spirit of the mind. These boys are listening to their grandmother's voice. They say: "Things that we don't know, we want to know."

Some people talk Iktomi language; they are right and they are wrong, they are smart-foolish. Iktomi, Ikto, can do anything, almost. He tricks people and he can be tricked.

One day Iktomi is walking, looking for something to eat. He is hungry. All of a sudden he sees *mastinčala*, a bunch of rabbits. Iktomi likes rabbit stew, but the *mastinčala* is very fast. Too fast for him. The rabbits are having a feast.

"*Hau, kola*, friends, how are you?" says Iktomi as he approaches the rabbits. "I see you are having a powwow. But you don't sing good. You hardly sing at all. You see that bundle I carry on my back? In this bundle I have all the good songs. Just what you need for your feast."

"Open the bundle," say the rabbits. "Let us have some songs to dance by."

"No, no, *hiya,* I can't give you these songs for nothing." "We will give you something good for your songs, like these fine *timpsila,* wild turnips, here, and these fine leaves to nibble on."

Ikto doesn't like *timpsila* or leaves. He likes meat, rabbit meat. "Friends, whatever you'll give me, these songs are too sacred."

"Oh, but we want so much to dance."

"*Ohan,* cousins, since you want it so much, I'll sing you some songs. I'll open the bundle and let out some rabbit songs and the rabbit dance. But this is powerful medicine. You must dance two by two and keep your eyes closed all the time, real tight, or your eyes will turn red. You might go blind."

Ikto sings the rabbit dance song and the *mastinčala* dance until they are tired. Ikto is looking to see which one is the fattest. "Cousins, don't look around. Keep your eyes closed or you'll go blind. These songs are powerful!" Iktomi takes a club out of his bundle—that's the only thing in there, a club—and he knocks the four fattest rabbits on the head.

One smart little rabbit opens one eye. He starts shouting: "Brothers, Iktomi is going to kill us all." So all the other rabbits run away.

Ikto says to himself: "Well, I got more than enough. Those stupid *mastinčala.* I'll have a good feast now. *Lila talo ota*—lots of good meat." He makes a fire and starts to cook those rabbits.

On the other side of the hill are two young coyotes. They smell something. Something good: roasting meat. Their noses are twitching. One coyote comes down the hill, the other circles around and sneaks up behind a clump of trees. There are two trees, an oak and an ash, close together. In the wind the trunks are rubbing together, making a mournful sound.

"*Hau, mishunkala,*" says the coyote who came down from the hill to Iktomi. "Listen to what the spirit in that tree is telling you."

"I can't make it out."

"You can't? And I thought you were smart. He's hungry. He's saying: 'Give me some of that meat and I'll give you a very valuable present in return.'"

The trees go on making that sad noise. "Be quiet," says Iktomi. "I'll give you something to eat."

"Be careful," says the coyote. "You can't trust nobody these days. The valuable gift is where the trees form a cross. In that crotch you will find it. And put the meat in there. Be careful."

"I can take care of myself, *pilamaya,*" says Iktomi, and goes over to the trees.

"First get the present before you put the meat there," the coyote advises him.

Iktomi puts his hand into the crotch, trying to find his present. The second coyote does something to make the trees snap together and Iktomi's hand is caught. It hurts. He can't free himself. He has to watch while the coyotes eat up the good meat. "Cousins, save me a little meat," he begs, but the coyotes just laugh. They eat everything up, even the bones.

So that Trickster is tricked. A big wind comes and knocks the trees apart. Iktomi falls down. All the food is gone except the four heads. Iktomi walks on. All of a sudden he hears a song. He sees a buffalo skull lying there and out of it comes this song. He looks in through an eye socket and he sees all these little yellow bugs, the *tumunga,* dancing and having a powwow. He sees this big yellow bug singing. Steady and slow. "Cousins, what are you going to eat at your feast?"

"There's plenty of *tunkče,* honey."

"Cousins, let me come in and dance with you." He says this, but all he is thinking was how to get the honey.

The bees know what he is up to. Iktomi is going around the skull

trying to find a way to get in. The yellow bugs say to each other, whispering: "Let's trap that wicked spider." Aloud they say: "Stick your head in through the eye hole here and lick up that good *tunkĉe* we are having."

Iktomi does as they tell him and his head gets stuck. He can't go ahead and he can't go back. "Cousins," he cries, "pity me. Let me go." But the *tumunga* fly away. Iktomi stumbles around with his head in the buffalo skull. He tries to shake it loose, but he stays caught.

Just nearby two young boys are playing with bow and arrows, with Indian slingshots. They come across Ikto. With his little body and the big buffalo skull, he is quite some sight. "What's your name?" ask the boys.

When he hears the boys, the Spider-Man cries: "I'm Iktomi. Help me get this thing off. In return I'll help you."

"What can you do?"

"I can do most everything. I'm all-powerful."

"Then why don't you knock that skull off by yourself?"

"This is a very special case." So the boys knock the skull apart with a rock and free Ikto. Iktomi tells them: "I can do everything. Whoever believes in me, I do great things for him. But first you must bring me deer meat. Plenty of it."

"And what will you give us?"

"Before the sun goes down bring me a piece from the rays of the sun, and ten rawhides. Find a mud turtle. Whenever the mud turtle farts, put the farts in this medicine bag here. That's powerful medicine. And bring me the heart of the tiniest ant. This medicine will give you many good songs and stories."

The boys get him the rawhides. But they can't catch the sun rays. They say: "We tried to make the mud turtle fart into this bag, but whether the farts are really in there, we don't know."

"They are, they are, I can smell them. This will make good medicine. Where is the meat?"

Iktomi eats and says: "The turtle farts are already working. I feel a good story coming on. Sit close by me, boys."

He tells the story of three young warriors who go out on the warpath and get themselves all killed. "They told me the story themselves."

The boys are suspicious: "How come they could tell you the story when they are dead?"

"Through my magic," Iktomi explains. "Through this red weed. (He pulls out some red grass and shows it.) This is a messenger. Now get me a fine buffalo robe. I need one. It's already getting cold." He is making an Ikto web, a spider web formed like a circle, because he is akin to a witch doctor. So he makes a *wihmunge*, a magic thing that bewitches. The boys take Iktomi to their camp. He tells the chief: "Iya is coming to eat you up."

"How are we going to stop him?" asks the chief. We'll put up a good *wakan wohanpi*, a sacred feast. I'll perform it."

"What will you use for that ceremony?"

"Get me a joint from a female deer leg. We must have plenty to eat for this *wakan wohanpi*."

They start out with a sweat lodge—Iktomi, the chief, and the two boys. Iktomi sings a song. He says: "*Hau,* the spirit is here." He pretends to speak to the spirit, but he is faking. There is no spirit.

"Ask the spirit," says the chief. Ikto mumbles like he is talking spirit language. He pretends to listen. He tells the chief and the boys: "They'll do what I ask them. The spirits are stopping Iya. I can do everything. Now get me a lot of good meat. And two fine buffalo hides. And a piece of the Morning Star while you are about it."

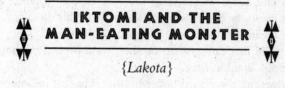

IKTOMI AND THE MAN-EATING MONSTER

{*Lakota*}

Iktomi, the tricky Spider-Man, was walking along. He saw a vine dangling down from a huge rock. Iktomi cannot resist dangling vines. He has to climb them. So also that time, he crawled up this vine. At once he was sorry for having done so, because on top of the rock Man-Eating Monster was lying in wait. He was fearful to behold. Iktomi was very scared.

Iktomi said to the Monster: "Younger brother, I have been looking for you. I am glad I found you."

The Monster looked at Iktomi, saying: "I have not had much to eat."

"Is that so?" said Iktomi. "It is much too early for dinner."

"I have not eaten breakfast," said Monster. "I could do with a bit of food. You look good enough to eat." Man-Eating Monster was smacking his lips.

"Younger brother," said Iktomi, "I could not even fill a cavity in one of your teeth—I am not worthwhile eating."

"Since when am I your younger brother?" said Monster. "To call me younger brother is an insult."

"When were you born?" asked Iktomi.

"I was born when the earth was made," replied Monster.

"Hah, it was I who made the earth," said Iktomi, "and I also made the Sun, the Moon, and the Stars. Come to think of it, I made you. You were then only a little itsy-bitsy dirty thing, and I threw you away."

"Well, all right," said Man-Eating Monster, "I will call you older brother. Then I will eat you, though you are very small."

"Hold on, younger brother," said Iktomi, "I have something better for you than just little me. I know where there is a large camp with many people. I'll eat half of them, and I'll let you eat the other half."

"Well, yes, that is good," said Man-Eating Monster. "Let's go." Monster came down so fast from the rock that he panted. When he caught his breath he almost sucked Iktomi down his throat.

"Please breathe in some other direction."

"Let's go to that camp, older brother," said Monster, whose mouth was watering. "I am hungry."

"Why, yes, let's hurry, younger brother, but first tell me what you are afraid of," Iktomi asked.

"Why do you want to know?" asked Man-Eating Monster.

"So that I can make sure there is no such thing where we are going."

"Well, all right. There are only three things that I am afraid of—a rattle, a whistle, and a woman who is on her moon, a menstruating woman."

They went on. When they got near to the camp Iktomi told Man-Eating Monster: "Younger brother, wait here. I want to make sure that we don't come across the things you are afraid of."

"Well, all right, but hurry!"

Iktomi went ahead to the camp. He called the people together. "Big Man-Eating Monster is coming! He wants to eat you up. If there is a woman among you who, just now, is on her moon, let her come forth. Let her shake a rattle and blow a whistle when Man-Eating Monster arrives. That will scare him off."

Iktomi hurried back to where Man-Eating Monster was waiting. "Everything is in order," he said. "There is no woman on her moon, no whistle, and no rattle."

"Good," said Man-Eating Monster. "But it is unfair that you want half of all the people to eat. You are small. I'll let you have one or two. Don't be greedy."

"Well, all right," said Iktomi. "Just let me have one."

When they came to the camp, the woman on her moon greeted them, blowing a whistle and shaking a rattle. It so frightened Man-Eating Monster that he dropped down dead.

{Lakota}

Iktomi and Flint Boy were old friends. Once they were traveling together, and they were going merrily along when suddenly out of the woods dashed a ferocious grizzly. The bear attacked them. Iktomi ran away and hid himself. Flint Boy stood his ground. With his sharp flint knife he stabbed the grizzly. He stabbed him repeatedly. The bear died.

Iktomi came out of hiding. "*Kola,* friend," he said to Flint Boy, "you did a great deed."

"It was nothing," said Flint Boy. He was skinning the bear with his flint knife. "This will make a fine, warm robe for my bed," he commented. Then he cut off the claws. "This will make a fine bear-claw necklace," he added.

"I am impressed," said Iktomi. "I am so impressed I will call you from now on *mishunkala,* younger brother."

"No, no," said Flint Boy, "you must call me elder brother, because it was I who killed the bear. I will call you little brother."

They argued, they quarreled about it. They came to a lake. "*Kola,*" said Iktomi, "let's make up. Aren't we old friends? What does it matter what we call each other?"

"You are right, friend, let's never quarrel again," said Flint Boy.

"Come over here," said Iktomi, who was standing at the lakeshore, right at the edge. "Look down here, look at this big fish." Flint Boy went to the lake and looked into the water. Iktomi came up behind Flint Boy and toppled him into the lake. The waters were deep. Flint Boy sank immediately way down to the bottom. He could not swim up because he was so heavy. He was made of flint rock. He never came up again. He drowned. You can still see the bubbles at the spot where Iktomi pushed him in.

IKTOMI AND THE BUFFALO CALF

{*Assiniboine*}

Iktomi was going along a buffalo trail. He followed a creek and found a young calf that had been trampled in the mire by the other buffalo. It could not get out of the wallow. Iktomi stripped, washed off the mud, and extricated the calf. Then he said, "Younger brother, let us travel. You are able to walk now."

They traveled for two or three days. One day Iktomi asked, "Do you think you can locate people in the direction we are traveling?"

"Yes, we'll soon meet people by a big lake. Before we get there, I'll make myself grow. I did not think I would get out, but now I am glad. I have strayed from my mother, and she must be seeking me now."

Iktomi took the lead, and the calf followed. The calf rolled over several times, and stood up a little larger than before. They continued on their way, the calf leading. After a while, it again asked Iktomi to go ahead, and repeated the same proceedings. When it rose again, it was as big as a two-year-old.

"You look like a buffalo now," said Iktomi.

"Yes, by the time we arrive, I'll be one of the biggest buffalo."

They went on. After a while, the calf again asked Iktomi to walk ahead. It rolled over, and again stood up bigger than before. "How do I look now?"

"You look like a big buffalo now."

The calf told him that they would soon reach a big camp, and the painted lodge would be the buffalo chief's residence. "Brother," it said, "you had better roll over in the same way as myself."

Iktomi obeyed, rose, and was transformed into a two-year-old buffalo. He was surprised. "We must roll over once more," said the calf. "Then we'll go to the camp." So they rolled again, and the calf stood up a real big buffalo, while Iktomi also got to be of a good size.

They went closer and hid in a coulee until dark. When it was dark, the calf said, "I'll steal a woman from the camp; wait for me here." The calf went, and soon returned with a white cow. "Now, brother, you go, but don't go near the painted lodge. Its owner is powerful; he will know if you get close."

Iktomi went, thinking, "I wonder what would happen if I went there." So he went to the painted lodge and near it found a spotted cow, the chief's wife. She asked him when he had arrived in the camp. "I have just come a little while ago with a band of people. Do you want to see them?"

Her husband was away, so she agreed to go with him. They got to where the calf was standing with his mate. They all decided to run off. The calf led, and they fled for four nights, when they arrived at a woods. There Iktomi said, "Let us rest here. They can't catch up."

The calf said, "They may be near us. Look toward the sunset. If you see dust ascending, it will be from the buffalo." Iktomi looked there and saw the dust approaching like a prairie fire.

The buffalo chief's horns were of iron. He ran up over the hills, followed by his herd. He dispatched a messenger to the fugitives. "Tomorrow you will have to fight those two buffalo whose wives you have stolen."

At noon the calf got ready to fight. The two enemies approached each other slowly and began to butt. Iktomi thought, "I have raised this calf, and I will help him."

The calf said, "Step back, don't help me." But Iktomi hooked the bull and threw him up into the air again and again until all his bones were broken.

Then it was Iktomi's turn to fight the chief. The calf now helped him, and they continued throwing the bull into the air until all his bones were broken. The other buffalo turned around and went home. Iktomi and the calf kept their wives.

The calf said, "Iktomi, stay here. I'll go west to find my parents. Every fall I am going to visit you with the buffalo, and if any people live here, they will have plenty of buffalo."

{*Rosebud Sioux*}

There was a *Woinihan*, a frightful monster. Its name was Siyoko. Everybody was afraid of him. Siyoko could uproot forests and flatten mountains. He could swallow a whole buffalo with one gulp. Even Unktehi, the terrible Water-Monster, took refuge at the bottom of the river when Siyoko was around. And also Anung-Ite, the horrifying two-faced Woman Spirit, kept out of Siyoko's way.

Ehanna, a long time ago, Siyoko was playing a hand game. The gamblers were singing, joking, and making faces, trying to confuse and distract their opponents. But Siyoko always guessed right. He always knew in whose hand the plum pit was hidden. He was winning all the time. He boasted: "I am the great Siyoko! I have the power! Who is there who can resist me? I conquered the Water-Monster. The frightful double-faced witch hides herself if she sees me coming. I could kill any *Woinihan* with the flick of my hand! There is nobody left to challenge me."

Among the gamblers was Iktomi, the tricky Spider-Man. Iktomi told Siyoko: "You don't frighten me. I could whip you with one hand."

"Hah, hah," Siyoko snorted. "Don't make me laugh! You, the puny spider, whip me? You are *witko*—crazy!"

"As a matter of fact," said Ikto, "even my little Takoja, my six-month-old grandson, could defy you. You can't even frighten a little child. All you can do is brag."

Siyoko could not stop laughing, but he also grew angry. "How dare you tell me that a spider baby could best me? Me, the great and terrible Siyoko! Have you lost your mind?"

"No, baby spider is mightier than you. Do you want to bet?"

"*Kanji,* cousin." Siyoko laughed. "I have already won your best horse in this game. Are you brave enough to bet everything you own, even your wife?"

"Yes, I know baby spider can beat you. Are you ready to bet everything you own, even your wife?"

"It's a bet," said Siyoko, still laughing, but inwardly he was just a tiny bit worried. Iktomi was tricky and full of mischief. He had hidden powers. He was a *wicamunge,* a wizard. Could he have something up his sleeve?

But Iktomi's Takoja, his grandson, turned out to be just an ordinary little *hokshila,* a baby like any other. "Is this tiny crawling thing the one I am supposed to lick, defeat, subdue, and frighten?" Siyoko was outraged. He growled: "Can you not pit me against someone worthy—a giant, an ogre, a great wizard?"

"No," said Ikto, "it is this little one you have to beat."

"Well, all right. I hope your wife is pretty. I hope you have many fine ponies and buffalo robes to lose."

Siyoko roared like Igmoo-Tanka, the Mountain Lion. "This will scare him," he thought. "This will make him cry." But the little boy cackled with delight.

Siyoko turned himself into a snarling Igmoo-Gleza, a fierce Bobcat. The baby took him for a pet, stroked him and chucked him under his chin.

Siyoko changed himself into Unktehi, the big, ugly Water-Monster, with flames shooting out of his nostrils. The baby stuck his grandmother's awl into the monster's nose and cackled delightedly. Siyoko's nose was bleeding. It hurt.

Siyoko transformed himself into a Wakinyan, a Thunderbird. Lightning shot out from his eyes and whenever he opened his mouth there was a deafening thunderclap. The baby thought this was great fun and laughed.

Siyoko turned himself into Waonze, the Grizzly. He uttered the fearful sound grizzlies make when they are about to kill: "Grr, grr!" The baby growled right back at him.

Siyoko turned himself into a giant buzzard. He grabbed the baby with his huge talons and flew off with him, flapping his enormous wings and screeching loudly. The baby loved the ride, smiled, and giggled happily.

Siyoko then put on the mask of Anung-Ite, the horrid, double-faced witch, a sight that makes one's blood curdle. "This will really scare him," Siyoko hoped. The little boy liked the mask. He would not leave it alone. He wanted to keep it as a toy.

Siyoko was exhausted. He said: "Let's rest awhile." He sat down and put the baby on his lap. The little boy pissed on him. He dirtied him all over. He covered Siyoko's lap with *chesli*.

At this moment the baby's mother came in. She scolded the little one, saying: "What have you done!" The baby got scared and cried.

"I give up," Siyoko told Iktomi. "You win. This baby is mightier than any *Woinihan* I ever fought."

"Kanji," said Iktomi, "I'll take your horses and buffalo robes. You can keep your wife. She's too ugly for me."

THE CHEATER CHEATED

{*Lakota*}

This happened when the first white traders came to Lakota country. They came with a little peddler's hand cart and soon they had a big trading post and a fancy house. They started with nothing and in no time were rich. They took the fat of the land. There was a French trader who boasted that he could cheat the stingiest man alive out of his last dollar. He boasted that he could make an Indian trade two hundred dollars' worth of furs for two dollars' worth of whiskey. He boasted that he could get five hundred dollars' worth of beaver skins for five dollars' worth of powder and tobacco. He said he could beat a Comanche at horse trading and everybody knows that this is impossible.

Somebody told this trader: "I know a fellow who is better at cheating than you."

"That person doesn't exist."

"Yes, he does. His name is Iktomi."

"Bring him to me. I want to see the fellow who can beat me in a deal."

The man brought Iktomi to the trader: "Here he is—Ikto, the Spider-Man. He is the slickest guy around. He can beat you at cards, he can beat you in a horse race. He can steal money right out of your pocket and you won't notice it."

"I hear you are good at cheating," the trader said to Iktomi. "Let's see how good you are at it. Let's have a cheating contest."

"Well, all right, but I don't have my cheating medicine with me."

"So what are you waiting for? Go get it!"

"That will take a while, but if you lend me your horse I can be back in no time."

"All right, get on, but go easy on him. That's my finest horse." The trader dismounted and handed the reins to Iktomi.

"This horse is frisky. It snorts. It won't let me get on," said Iktomi. "Lend me your coat and hat so that the horse thinks I'm you."

"Well, all right." The trader took off his fine, fringed coat, which was decorated with quillwork, and put it on Iktomi. He took off his costly beaver hat and put it on Iktomi's head.

"The horse is still shy and dancing around. I think you should also let me have your boots; otherwise the horse won't let me ride him."

"Well, all right." The trader took off his boots with silver spurs on them. Iktomi put them on. The spurs made a pleasing tinkling sound. Iktomi got on the horse and trotted off.

The trader suddenly had second thoughts. He called after Iktomi: "Hey, come back! I have the feeling you won't return my goods!"

"That's funny," Iktomi yelled back. "I have the same feeling." Iktomi rose in the saddle, lifted his breechcloth, showing the trader his bare backside. Then he laughed and galloped off.

"*Sacre bleu!*" cried the trader. "*Ce salaud sauvage! Ce voleur rouge! Il m'a trompé. Merde!*"

Thus the cheater was cheated.

THE SPIDER CRIES "WOLF"

{*Rosebud Sioux*}

Iktomi was walking about, looking for what he could find. He came across a herd of Hehaka, elk. It was summer. The grass was high. There was food aplenty. The elk were sleek and fat. With their huge antlers they looked so handsome, stately, and powerful. Iktomi envied the elk's beauty and way of life. He looked at his reflection in the nearby stream. "How shabby I am," he said to himself, "ugly, small, pitiful, insignificant."

Iktomi sought out the tallest among the elk. "This must be the chief," he thought. Humbly he approached, saying: "*Lekshi,* uncle, you are so handsome, so imposing, every inch a great chief, and I am so small, homely, hairy—a nobody. But we have one thing in common. You, mighty Hehaka, are known to have the love magic, the power to make women love you. You have the love charm, the love wink in your eye. Insignificant nobody that I am, I, too, am a great lover."

"Is that so?" said Hehaka.

"*Mi lekshi,* uncle of mine, you have the power, you can do anything. Make me like yourself; let me join your tribe."

"I have heard about you. They are saying bad things about you. You have a very bad reputation."

"It's just mean gossip, uncle, you know how people are. They are always bad-mouthing me because of my luck with women. They are just envious."

"They also say that you are a sniveling coward."

"Uncle, they are lying," Iktomi protested. "I am a mighty warrior. I have taken many scalps in battle. I have earned eagle feathers. I am invincible!"

"Can you spy an enemy from far, far away?" asked Hehaka. "Can you discover buffalo and other game from a great distance?"

"My eyes are sharper then those of the eagle," said Iktomi.

"Can you hear an enemy creeping stealthily up on our camp?"

"My sense of hearing is so keen," said Iktomi, "I can hear a mouse walking from a hundred paces away."

"Can you detect the scent of grizzlies, wolves, or cougars creeping up on our herd?"

"My sense of smell is so acute," said Iktomi, "I could detect their odor from a mile away, even from upwind."

"Well," said Hehaka, "you might make a good member of our tribe."

"*Pilamaya,* thank you, uncle, but I would not like to join the Elk Nation in the puny shape I am in. Uncle, you are so very powerful, you can do anything you want. Please make me as big and tall as you are."

"Well, all right," said Hehaka, and he made Iktomi big and tall.

"And could you give me a handsome shiny coat like yours?"

"Well, all right, I'll do it," said Hehaka, and gave Iktomi a new coat.

"And, uncle, would you be so kind as to also give me a pair of mighty antlers?" Iktomi kept on begging.

"Well, all right," said Hehaka, "but that's enough. Don't be greedy." And so he gave Iktomi a pair of magnificent antlers.

Iktomi was capering and prancing about, showing off his new coat and antlers. "Is there anybody as handsome as I?" he crowed. "Is there anybody stronger and braver?" Already he assumed the pose and manners of a chief. Thus he joined Hehaka Oyate, the Elk Nation.

Some weeks later, as Iktomi was resting among his new relatives, a small twig from a tree fell upon him. He was seized by a panic: "Help! I've been hit by an arrow!" he screamed. "Enemies, hunters, cougars!" Then all the elk stampeded, with Iktomi way in front, leading the flight.

After a while the elk noticed that there were no hunters or predators in sight. "You scare easily," they told Iktomi. "Don't make false alarms."

A day or two later they were all resting again. An acorn fell down upon Iktomi. "Help!" he screamed. "Enemies, hunters! I've been hit by a bullet!" Again the elk stampeded, with Iktomi far in front.

After running at top speed for a while, the elk discovered that they were all alone on the empty prairie. "Didn't we tell you to give us no false warnings?" they scolded Iktomi.

Again, a few days later, as they all were walking slowly, grazing, wandering from one grassy spot to another, Iktomi was caught and scratched by some thorns. "Help, help!" he cried. "I've been cut by a knife! I've been torn apart by the fangs of wild wolves!"

"There are no hunters with knives here, and no wolves," said the Hehaka Itancan, the Elk Chief. "Have we not told you to stop scaring us with your wild imaginings? You lied. You are not a mighty warrior."

Again, a few days later, in the middle of the night, Iktomi awoke, hearing something rustling in the bushes. "Help, help!" Iktomi screeched. "Wake up! Enemies are coming! There must be hundreds of them!" The whole camp was in an uproar. Then, in the silvery light of a full moon, the elk discovered that it was only a little rabbit that had terrorized Iktomi.

The morning after, when Iktomi was out of earshot, the elk were whispering to each other. It had to do with Iktomi. That evening they camped and went to sleep. At sunrise, when Iktomi woke up, he found that he was all alone. The elk had gone, he knew not where. And he was no longer an elk. He was no longer big and tall. His antlers had disappeared. Once again he was the undersized, puny, hairy, pitiful Spider-Man. It was his own fault. He had cried "wolf" once too often.

TIT FOR TAT

{Omaha}

Iktinike is the Omaha name for their Trickster, who is a clone of the Lakota Iktomi.

Iktinike was walking along. On his way he met Coyote. "My younger brother," said Iktinike, "how are you doing?"

"Very well, honored elder brother," replied Coyote. He pointed to a sleeping horse, lying on its side. "I found this dead pony. Friend, let us drag it to my place and have a big feast."

"How can we drag it?" asked Iktinike. "It is too heavy for us."

"Not at all, friend," said Coyote. "I'll tie your hands to its tail, then you pull. At the same time, I'll pull on the hind legs."

"Yes! Let's try!"

Coyote tied Iktinike's hands tightly to the horse's tail. "Now pull!" cried Coyote. "Pull real hard, honored elder brother!"

Iktinike did and the horse jumped up. It wasn't dead, after all. It stampeded. Galloping away at a dead run, the horse dragged Iktinike through thornbushes and shrubs wuth long, sharp spikes. Iktinike was all scratched up. He was bleeding. Still the horse ran on, kicking furiously with its hind legs in order to free itself, kicking Iktinike with his hooves so that he was badly bruised. Finally the length of rope that tied Iktinike's hands to the horse's tail broke, leaving Iktinike lying on the ground, hurt and panting. Coyote laughed, fit to burst, wiping tears of merriment from his eyes. Shaking with laughter, he walked off. He had succeeded in something he had wanted to do for a long time—playing a trick on Iktinike.

Limping away, Iktinike was thinking of revenge. He bided his time. Summer turned into fall, fall into winter. Iktinike was placing himself along a path often taken by Coyote. Iktinike was sitting there with a big fish by his side. Coyote was coming along. He saw Iktinike and took particular notice of the big fish. "Honored elder brother," said Coyote, "where did you get such a fine, big fish?"

"My friend," answered Iktinike, "come with me and I'll show you." Iktinike led Coyote to a nearby lake that was entirely covered with ice. "Here is where I get my fine big fish in the wintertime."

"How, honored elder brother, how do you get them?"

With his tomahawk Iktinike chopped a hole in the ice. "Here, friend," said Iktinike. "Drop your tail through this hole and the fish will come and bite," said Iktinike. Coyote dipped his tail through the hole in the ice that Iktinike had made. "Just sit still and be patient," Iktinike advised Coyote.

After a while, Coyote said: "Honored elder brother, I think a fish is biting."

"It's too early," said Iktinike.

The ice was closing in on the hole. Coyote felt it pinching his tail. "Elder brother," he cried, "I really feel them biting now!"

"Patience, friend," Iktinike told him. "The big one is still to come. You don't want to go home to your wife with a measly, small-sized fish."

"Well, all right, I'll wait a little longer," said Coyote. The hole froze completely over. The ice pinched Coyote's tail badly. It held him in its grip. "Oh! Oh!" cried Coyote. "A big fish is biting my tail. It is biting on it hard. It has sharp teeth."

"Well, friend," said Iktinike, "I think this time you got the big one. Pull him out! Pull hard!"

Coyote pulled and pulled, but he was stuck in the ice. He could not extricate his tail. "Help! Help, elder brother!" Coyote wailed. "The fish clamped its teeth so hard on my tail that I cannot get it out. Help!"

"Here, take hold of my hands," said Iktinike. "We'll both pull." They pulled so hard, they tore Coyote's tail off. It remained stuck in the ice. Only a short, bleeding little stump was left.

"Oh, it hurts!" Cried Coyote, rubbing his sore backside.

"Maybe you should have gone for a smaller fish," said Iktinike.

"Oh, my beautiful tall Elder brother, you have done me wrong. You played an evil trick on me!"

"I've only done to you, friend, as you did to me," said Iktinike, walking off laughing.

IKTOMI TAKES BACK A GIFT

{Rosebud Sioux}

■

*Tunka, Inyan, the Rock, is the oldest
divinity in the Lakota cosmology. Everything
dies; only the Rock is forever.*

Iktomi, the tricky Spider-Man, was starving. There had been no game for a long time. Iktomi was just skin and bones. His empty stomach growled. He was desperate. Then it occurred to him to go for help to Inyan, the Rock, who has great powers, and who might answer his prayers.

Iktomi wrapped himself in his blanket, because it was late in the year and cold. Then he went to a place where a large upright rock was standing. This rock was *lila wakan*, very sacred. Sometimes people came to pray to it.

When Iktomi arrived at that place he lifted up his hands to Inyan: "*Tunkashila, onshimalaye,* grandfather, have pity on me. I am hungry. If you do not help me, I will starve to death. I need meat, grandfather."

Iktomi took his blanket from his shoulder and draped it around Inyan. "Here, grandfather, *tunkashila,* accept this gift. It is the only thing I have to give. It will keep you warm. Please let me find something good to eat."

After praying to Inyan for a long time, Iktomi went off to search for food. He had a feeling Inyan would answer his prayers, and he was right. Iktomi had not gone very far when he came upon a freshly killed deer. It had an arrow piercing its neck, the feathered nock sticking out on one side of the neck and the arrowhead on the other.

"*Ohan,*" said Iktomi, "the deer has been able to run for a distance after being hit and the hunter has lost it. Inyan has arranged it that way. Well, that is only fair. Did I not give him my blanket? Well, anyhow, *pilamaya, tunkashila*—thank you, grandfather!"

Iktomi took his sharp knife out of its beaded knife sheath and began to skin and dress the deer. Then he gathered wood and, with his strike-a-light and tinder, made a fire. There was not much wood and it was wet. It wasn't much of a fire. And it had grown very cold. Iktomi was shivering. His teeth were chattering. He was saying to himself: "What good is my blanket to Inyan? He is just a rock. He does not feel either cold or heat. He does not need it. And, anyway, I don't think Inyan had anything to do with my finding this deer. I am smart. I saw certain tracks. I smelled the deer. So there, I did it all by myself. I did not have to give Inyan anything. I shall take my blanket back!"

Iktomi went back to the sacred rock. He took the blanket off him. "*Tunkashila,*" he said, "this blanket is mine. I am freezing. You don't need this blanket; I do."

Iktomi wrapped the blanket tightly around his body. "Ah, that feels good," he said. "Imagine, giving a blanket to a rock!"

When Iktomi came back to the place where he had left the deer, he discovered that it had disappeared—vanished, gone! Only a heap of dry bones was left. There were no tracks or any signs that somebody had dragged the deer away. It had been transformed into dry bones by a powerful magic.

"How mean of Inyan," said Iktomi, "and how stupid of me. I should have eaten first and then taken the blanket back."

IKTOMI AND THE WILD DUCKS

{Minneconjou Sioux}

One day, Iktomi, the spider fellow, was talking a walk to see what he could see. Tiptoeing through the woods, he saw water sparkling through the leaves. "I am coming to a lake," Iktomi said to himself. "There might be some fat ducks there. I shall creep up to this lake very carefully so that I cannot be seen. Maybe I shall catch something."

Iktomi crept up to the water's edge on all fours, hiding himself behind some bushes. Sure enough, the lake was full of nice, plump ducks. At the sight of them Iktomi's mouth began to water. But how was he to catch the birds? He had neither a net nor his bow and arrows. But he had a stick. He suddenly popped up from behind the bushes, capering and dancing.

"Ho, cousins, come here and learn to dance. I have eight legs and I am the best dancer in the world."

All the ducks swam to the shore and lined up in a row, spellbound by

Iktomi's fancy dancing. After a while Iktomi stopped. "Cousins, come closer still," he cried. "I am the gentle, generous Spider-Man, the friend of all the birds, cousin to all fliers, and I shall teach you the duck song. Now, when I start singing, you must all close your eyes in order to concentrate better. Do not peek while I sing, or you will be turned into ugly mud hens with red eyes. You don't want this to happen, do you? You have, no doubt, noticed my stick. It is a drumstick with which I will beat out the rhythm. Are you ready? then close your eyes."

Iktomi started to sing and the foolish ducks crowded around him, doing as he had told them, flapping their wings delightedly and swaying to and fro. And with his stick Iktomi began to club them dead—one after another.

Among the ducks was one young, smart one. "I better check on what's happening," this duck said to himself. "I don't quite trust that fellow with the eight legs. I'll risk one eye. One red eye isn't so bad." He opened his left eye and in a flash saw what Iktomi was up to. "Take off! Take off!" he cried to the other ducks. "Or we'll all wind up in this man's cooking pot!"

The ducks opened their eyes and flew away, quacking loudly.

Still, Iktomi had a fine breakfast of roast duck. The Spider-Man's power turned the smart young duck into a mud hen.

This is why, to this day, mud hens swim alone, away from other ducks, always on the lookout, diving beneath the water as soon as they see or hear anyone approaching, thinking it might be wicked Iktomi with a new bag of tricks. Better a live, ugly mud hen than a pretty, dead duck.

 # IKTOMI TRYING TO OUTRACE BEAVER

{Santee}

It was winter. It was cold. Iktomi was walking about. "It's hard to find anything to eat. I have been going on an empty stomach for days." Of course, that wasn't true. He had eaten a rabbit only a few hours before, but Iktomi is always ravenous, he is never satisfied. "Oh, my," he said, "listen to that poor stomach of mine growling." He was looking around. Not too far away he saw Beaver sitting on the ice of a frozen lake. Beaver was cooking. He was stirring a large pot resting upon two stones with a fire under it. Iktomi's nose began to twitch. He smelled the food. It smelled wonderful. "How can I get some of it?" he said to himself.

Iktomi went over to Beaver. "Elder brother," he said, *Toniktuka hwo?* How are you this fine morning?"

"I am well, *lila washtay*. Thank you. I can't complain."

"I see you are cooking up a fine meal. It smells very good. I hear you are a fine cook, and a great hunter, too. What's in the pot?"

"Oh, just some bear meat, cousin Spider."

"Elder brother, I was told that you are the fastest runner hereabouts. Yes, people are talking about what a great runner you are."

"People are always exaggerating, cousin Spider. You know how they are always speaking nonsense."

"No, not at all, elder brother. You are justly famous," said Iktomi. "But I have an idea. Why don't we have a race, you and me? I would consider it an honor to race against someone like you."

"Well, all right, cousin, I am game. In what way should we race?"

"We'll walk around the lake to the far side and then we'll race across the ice back to the pot here. And whoever reaches this pot first gets the bear meat."

"Well, all right, cousin, if that's what you want."

Iktomi thought to himself: "That slow, fat old fellow will be easy to beat. I can already taste that delicious bear meat."

They walked around the lake. They got to the far shore. "Now I'll count to three, elder brother. When I say 'three,' we start running."

"All right!"

The race began. The ice was very slick. Beaver, with his large, webbed feet, had the better hold on it. To Iktomi's surprise and dismay, Beaver was getting ahead of him. Then a crack opened in front of Iktomi and he fell into the lake. He swam underneath the ice to where Beaver was already gorging himself on the bear meat.

There was a small hole in the ice right there. Iktomi put his mouth up to this hole. "Elder brother," he begged, "please give me a little of the food." Beaver took a small piece and dropped it into Iktomi's mouth.

"*Pilamaya,* thank you, elder brother, let me have some more."
Beaver dropped another piece into Iktomi's mouth. "More, more," said
Iktomi. Beaver grabbed a big chunk of bear dung, which was there
within his reach, and dumped it into Iktomi's mouth.

"Is this a way to treat a relative?" Iktomi complained. He swam
under the ice to another crack, big enough to let him climb out. He
shook himself. He was frozen stiff. "That evil old fellow has played a
trick on me," Iktomi said to himself, "but this is not the end. Someday
I shall have my revenge!"

 # TOO SMART FOR HIS OWN GOOD

{*Sioux*}

Iktomi, the clever Spider-Man, is smart, sometimes too smart for his
own good. Iktomi was sitting on a log, one fine morning, sunning himself, when he saw Četan, the Hawk, flying about. "Brother," cried
Iktomi, "give me a ride!" The good-natured Hawk let Iktomi climb on
his back. Up in the air Iktomi enjoyed the flight and the fine view, but
soon he was bored. Iktomi is always bored, unless he can play a joke on
someone. He decided to have some fun at the Hawk's expense.

Whenever they encountered somebody—an eagle, buzzard, or
magpie—Iktomi made to them a gesture in sign language indicating
that Hawk was a stupid, no-account *hlete,* good-for-nothing. Thus he
played Hawk for a fool. He thought Hawk could not see him doing
that. He thought: "Hawks don't have eyes on the backs of their heads."

What Iktomi forgot was that Hawk could see their shadow on the
ground and could watch Iktomi making fun of him. "I'll get even with
that tricky Spider-Man," thought Hawk, and all of a sudden turned
over, flying upside down. Iktomi lost his grip and fell through the air,
landing inside a hollow tree.

Iktomi was still trying to find his way out when it began to rain. It
rained very hard. The tree was very dry. It soaked up the water like a
sponge and swelled up. Poor Iktomi was being crushed to death.

Poor Iktomi! In his pain and fear he began to pray. "Great Spirit, why did you make me so smart that I always try to fool everybody? In the end I am only fooling myself. Please save me! Have pity on me!" Thus Iktomi humbled himself. His former pride and wickedness made him feel very small, so small that he was able to crawl out of that tree. A little humility and prayer can be a good thing sometimes.

PART SIX

SPIDER-MAN
IN LOVE

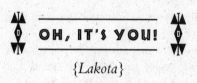

OH, IT'S YOU!

{Lakota}

Iktomi is always horny. He only thinks about copulating. There was a beautiful young girl in the village, with sparkling come-hither eyes, shining long raven hair, heaving bosoms, and the graceful, undulating movements of a cat. From the first moment he saw her, Iktomi thought only about how he could induce her to sleep with him.

He waited at the brook where the women went to fetch water, and when the beautiful girl came there with her water bag, Iktomi played love tunes on his *siyotanka,* the flute used for courting, and tried to beguile her with his tunes. But Iktomi was not at all good-looking, his figure was not in the least imposing, and his manners were deplorable. So the girl showed in the many ways that women have, without saying it in so many words, that she had not the slightest intention of letting him get close to her. The expression on her face made it obvious that Iktomi was repulsive to her.

Still Iktomi was after her, following her wherever she went, whispering suggestive words, saying what a great lover he was and what pleasures she was missing by rejecting his advances.

The beautiful girl was annoyed. She thought it was an insult that such a low, unappealing, unmannered fellow like Iktomi wanted to make love to her. So she went to Iktomi's wife. "Auntie," she said, "that lustful husband of yours wants to do *tawiton,* have sex, with me."

"Is that the only news you can give me? There is not a girl or woman in the village he doesn't want to do *tawiton* with."

"Well, what do you want to do about this?"

"That louse-ridden, lying *hlete,* good-for-nothing fellow. He no longer cares to make love to me. He says I am too old for him, he with his gray hair and potbelly! Too old, hah! I'm younger than he is. I wish I could catch him in the act and give him the beating he deserves."

"Auntie, what will you give me if I arrange it so that you can play a trick on him and, at the same time, catch him trying to commit *wawičihahahapi*, adultery?"

"I would gladly give you my best horse and my best beaded and quilled dance outfit."

"That sounds good to me, auntie. Here is what we will do. I'll invite that *wawičihaha* of yours to come to spend the night with me. Tomorrow there will be no moon. It will be very dark. You will take my place. When he comes, you'll pretend you are me."

"I can hardly wait," said Mrs. Iktomi.

So next morning the beautiful girl went to the brook, as always, to fetch water. And, naturally, Iktomi was already there with his love flute. "I'm beginning to warm up to you," the beautiful girl said to Iktomi. "Come to think, you are rather cute. My tipi is over there, the one with the sun design painted on it. I live alone, except for my grandmother, who is blind and deaf. She won't notice anything. But you must come after it is dark. I don't want people to see you. I don't like them gossiping about me."

"Why, well, of course, my beautiful *winčinčala*. You won't regret it. I am the greatest lover of them all! Oh, what a *yasinsin,* orgasm, I'll give you! It will leave you limp and panting with delight."

"I can hardly wait," said the beautiful girl.

That night Mrs. Iktomi took the place of the beautiful girl in the girl's tipi. "Don't mind *unci,* grandmother," the girl told Mrs. Iktomi. "She is blind and deaf and sleeps all the time. Thunder could not wake her. She won't notice anything."

"*Washtay,* good, let's get on with it."

Mrs. Iktomi was lying in the place where the beautiful girl used to sleep, waiting for her cheating husband. She did not have long to wait. As soon as it was dark Iktomi crept into the tipi. He went to where his wife was stretched out. He embraced her. "*Imaputake,*" he said, "kiss me!" And "*Washte chilake,* I love you. How sweet your breath is compared to my old woman." He felt her all over. "Oh, what a beautiful, firm little body you have, not lumpy and saggy like that of my wife. What a joy to make love to a young, beautiful girl instead of to an old, ugly hag!"

Iktomi felt between his wife's legs. "Ah, how pleasingly moist your *shan,* vagina, is compared to the dried, shriveled-up one of my wife." He panted. He mounted her. They did it. Iktomi fell asleep. When he awoke he saw that it was his wife he had done it with. "Oh, it's you," he said. "I knew it was you all the time. Wasn't it great?"

Mrs. Iktomi had a heavy club. She used it on her husband. She beat him black and blue. He howled with pain.

"I'll give you 'sagging breasts,'" she shouted. "I'll give you 'lumpy body.' I'll give you '*shan puza,* dried-up vagina.' This old hag will beat the shit out of you!"

"Ow, ow, have pity, wife! I'll never stray again."

Iktomi was very sore for quite a long time, but no beating could keep him from philandering. Soon he was at it again.

TOO MANY WOMEN

{*Lakota*}

Iktomi was traveling. He came to a village of about forty tipis. He saw many women in this camp, but no men. He asked one of the women: "Where are your men?"

"I don't know what men are," said the woman. "I don't know what *men* means."

"You are joking," said Iktomi.

"No," said the woman, "I am not. You ask too many questions. If you want to know something, you have to ask our two women chiefs."

"Where can I find them?"

"Over there, in the big tipi, right in the center."

Iktomi went there. Inside the big tipi he found the two women chiefs. Each of them was holding a cradleboard. In one cradleboard was a baby rabbit, in the other a baby fox. "What are these for?" Iktomi wanted to know.

"These are our children," said the women chiefs.

"Who are the fathers?" Iktomi inquired.

"We don't know what *father* means," said the women.

"Fathers are the ones who help make babies."

"These babies made themselves. They just popped out of us, from here." The women pointed to a place between their legs.

"Don't you have any men around here?" Iktomi asked.

"We don't know what men are."

Iktomi said to himself: "These women have never been with a man, that's why they give birth only to rabbits and foxes." Aloud he said: "I want to show you something."

Iktomi pushed his breechcloth aside and showed them his man-thing. It was standing up proudly. The woman with the rabbit looked closely at it. She looked at it for a long time. "This is a very strange thing," she said. "I have never seen one like it. How come I don't have a root like this?"

"Because I am a man and you are a woman. All men have it and it is not a root, it's a *wichasha-che.*"

"What is it good for?" the woman wanted to know.

"It's for copulating."

"What is copulating?" she asked.

"It means 'making babies.' "

"How?"

"You have a certain place in your body where you put this thing of mine. It fits perfectly. You put it in there and, after a while, you have a baby—not a little rabbit or fox, but a real human being."

"All right, where do you put it?" Iktomi was only too happy to show her. He slipped his penis into her vagina. "That feels good," said the woman. Iktomi started to move back and forth. "Now it feels even better," cried the woman. "Move faster, move harder! Don't stop!"

They finished. Iktomi withdrew. "What do you call what we just did?" the woman wanted to know.

"We did *tawiton,* we copulated."

"Oh, that's what it was."

Then the other woman-chief, the one with the fox baby, said: "I want to have a look at that strange root of yours." Iktomi showed it to her. It was flaccid. "It looks like a worm or a slug," said the woman. "It doesn't look as if it could do anything worthwhile."

"Just wait, and you'll see it standing up again."

"Well, go ahead, make it rise, hurry!" After a while Iktomo's *che* was standing up again. He put it into the fox-baby chieftess. "Ah, this is good indeed," she said. Thus the two women chiefs were satisfied.

Then the two women chiefs came out of their tipi and called out: "You women, do you want to know what a man is like? There is one in our tipi. Do you want to know what copulation is like? He'll show you. Do you each want to have a baby? He'll make you one. So come and meet the creature called MAN."

Then the women crowded into the tipi to *tawiton* with Iktomi. There were so many of them that most had to wait for their turn outside. "Have pity!" cried Iktomi. "This is too much of a good thing. What you admire so much cannot stand up all the time. It needs a long rest. Right now it's only good for making water."

The women would not listen. They said: "We'll beat you until you do *tawiton* with us." Then they hit him with sticks. He managed to satisfy a few of them, but then became totally exhausted. He almost fainted. But more and more women crowded in on him, shouting, "My turn now! My turn now!" and beating him unmercifully when he could not do what they wanted.

He said to himself: "I started something I cannot finish. Will I ever learn?" Aloud he said: "You wild women, if you want my *che* to rise up again, you must let me walk about a bit. That's the only way get it to rise."

"All right, go and walk about," they said. Iktomi walked about in

ever widening circles. When he thought that he had a sufficient head start, he began to run as fast as he could.

"Stop him!" yelled the women. "This good-for-nothing man is running away from us. After him!"

Iktomi got to a river ahead of them. He saw a single canoe there. He jumped into it and paddled furiously. The women could not follow. They stood at the riverbank wailing and shaking their fists.

Over his shoulder Iktomi cried out to them: "So long, women! Sometime I'll see you again. I enjoyed meeting you!" He got to the far bank and walked off. "Well. I taught them something new," he said to himself.

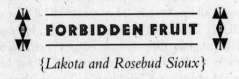

FORBIDDEN FRUIT

{Lakota and Rosebud Sioux}

When Iktomi was fourteen years old, he wanted to get married. His parents told him: "You are too young. Have you earned eagle feathers? Did you count coup on enemy warriors? Have you learned to be a good hunter and provider? Do you have many horses to offer to your future in-laws? Become a man first, then marry."

"No! No! I'm not too young," protested Iktomi, "and there's a girl I have my eyes on. If I wait, someone else will get her." Iktomi whined and wheedled. He used his considerable gift of glib talk to overcome all objections. He made his parents give in to his demands.

Dressed in all his finery, wearing his best beaded leggings and his father's war shirt, decorated with the scalp locks of slain enemies, bringing along a dozen fine horses his parents had given him for this purpose, he used his powers of persuasion to talk the girl of his desires to marry him. He won the girl's widowed mother's consent by offering her the horses as bride payment. So he assumed the role of a husband.

Before Iktomi took up married life in his own tipi, elders warned him: "Never talk directly to your mother-in-law. It isn't done. It is bad, particularly, as in your case, your mother-in-law is a widow without a husband. There is a reason. The worst thing a man could ever do is make love to his mother-in-law. It is worse than killing a fellow tribesman. Of course, such a horrible, evil deed has never been done since this tribe was founded, since the beginning of time. Still, there should not be even the smallest temptation, like getting too familiar with your mother-in-law or spending too much time in her company. We thought you should know."

"Such a thing is not even to be thought of," Iktomi answered them.

Married life agreed with Iktomi. He made love to his wife every day, sometimes twice. He learned to hunt a little bit, though mostly he scrounged meat from others. On the whole, Iktomi and his wife were satisfied with what they had. Thus things went on in a pleasant way for two or three years.

Early one morning, Iktomi went out to do a little hunting. He forgot to take the quiver containing his arrows. So, after a short time, he went back to his tipi. Then he remembered that he had left his quiver with his mother-in-law, who had promised to embroider it with porcupine quills. So he went to his mother-in-law's tipi. He surprised her as she came out naked from under her buffalo robe, before she had a chance to put on her dress. Iktomi liked what he saw. "Hmmm, she is rather pretty," he thought. "She is still young and pleasantly plump. Compared to her, my wife is skinny—scrawny, to tell the truth. Really, I think a fellow would be lucky if she'd let him sleep with her."

From then on, the image of his mother-in-law, crawling naked out from under her robe, became fixed in Iktomi's mind. In his dreams he imagined making love to her. Whenever he made love to his wife, he pictured holding his mother-in-law in his arms. He slept with his wife less and less often. She began suspecting him of carrying on with another woman. Life in Iktomi's tipi grew less and less satisfying. Iktomi was thinking about his mother-in-law all the time. It inflamed his senses. It caused a hot stirring in his loins. Then, doing the unimaginable, doing what had never been done since the beginning of time, occured to him. He made up his mind to sleep with his mother-in-law. He thought: "Her husband was a warrior. He must have been lusty and vigorous. He was killed by enemies a few years ago. She must be missing his embraces." He also thought: "How can I get under the same blanket with her? How can I do it without my wife noticing it? And will my mother-in-law let me do it? This is something very difficult to achieve."

Iktomi is a very clever fellow. He hit upon a scheme that would get him what he wanted. He began talking about becoming a warrior. "The one thing missing in my life," he told his wife, "is becoming a great fighter and horse stealer. I have not yet counted coup. I wish to earn eagle feathers and war honors. Sometime I will be a chief." He had never spoken that way before. Actually, he was afraid of fighting. The thought of facing an enemy made him tremble. But it suited his purpose to talk about going on the warpath. One evening he came home and told his wife: "I have been accepted as a member of the Tokala [Kit Fox] Warrior Society. It is a great honor."

The Tokala were the fiercest fighters. They never showed their backs to the enemy. They went into battle shouting: "It is a good day to die!" They were the bravest of the brave. Iktomi's wife was impressed. Some days later, Iktomi told her: "Wife, we will be going on a raid against the enemy soon. Our war chief has had a vision that each member of the party should take his mother-in-law along to cook and help carry weapons and provisions."

Iktomi's wife was incredulous: "But that has never been done before," she said. "It is against our traditions. It is forbidden."

"I know, I know!" said Iktomi. "I don't like it, either. But a vision has to be obeyed. If we don't, our medicine will be bad. We will lose the battle. We'll all be killed!"

Iktomi's wife told her mother, who said: "This is really unheard of, but if it comes from a vision, I guess I'll have to go." So the women prepared everything needed for Iktomi and his mother-in-law to go on the warpath.

A few days later, Iktomi came running. He was greatly excited: "Wife, mother-in-law, they have gone! They forgot to take me! All the warriors and their mothers-in-law have departed! They must be far ahead. After them! After them!" Of course, there was no war party to catch. It existed only in Iktomi's imagination, but the women believed him. Iktomi picked up his weapons, his mother-in-law her bundles, and off they went.

Night fell. Iktomi's mother-in-law said: "The Tokala must have gotten a really big head start."

"Yes, they must have," said Iktomi. "I hoped to have caught up with them by now." Iktomi put up a small brush and blanket shelter for his companion. He also gave her a buffalo robe to keep warm. "I'll sleep outside," he told her. "It wouldn't be fitting for me to be alone in the same shelter with you."

"It sure wouldn't," said his mother-in-law.

In the middle of the night Iktomi began scratching at the shelter cover: "Mother-in-law, it's so cold. I am freezing to death. May I come in and warm myself?"

"Well, all right," she said. "I don't want you freezing to death."

Iktomi made his teeth chatter. "Dear mother-in-law," he implored, "I can't get warm. Listen to my teeth chattering."

"Yes, they are really clicking away like a deer's hoofbeats."

"Mother-in-law, if I could get under the buffalo robe with you, maybe I could get warm."

"Well, all right, but keep your distance."

"I will, I will!" Once under the robe, Iktomi went on pretending to tremble with cold. His shiverings made the little shelter shake. "Dear mother-in-law," Iktomi suggested, "if I could snuggle up to you, the warmth of your body might stop my shivering."

"Well, all right, you really seem to have the shakes badly."

The body warmth, the snuggling and cuddling, awoke a long-slumbering desire inside the woman. She thought to herself: "How long has it been since I had a man lying by my side? I really miss it. And who's to know?" So when Iktomi started to grope underneath her dress, his mother-in-law did not resist *"Imaputake,"* she said, "kiss me!" So he slept with her.

The next morning, as Iktomi and his mother-in-law were getting up, he told her: "I think the Tokala are too far ahead of us now. We'll never catch up with them. Let's go home."

"Yes," she agreed, "let's go home."

"You know something?" he added.

"What?"

"Mother-in-law, it is so much nicer making love to you, lying so softly, than doing it with your skinny daughter. You are so much better at it."

"Thanks for telling me."

"Mother-in-law, when we get home, don't tell on me."

"Don't worry," she said.

THE SPIDERS GIVE BIRTH
TO THE PEOPLE

{Arikara}

There was once an old Spider-Man who lived by himself with his wife. One day the Wolf and his friend went to visit these old folks. The Spider-Man was dirty, his eyes were red, he had no hair on his head, he was dirty all over, and he emitted a bad odor. His wife was also very dirty; her hair was thin and very coarse. The Wolf had never seen people like these people.

The Wolf asked these people: "How do you copulate?"

The Spider-Man and his wife showed Wolf how they did it. They did it all wrong, Spider-Man sticking his huge penis into all the wrong places. Also both the Spider-Man and his wife emitted a big stink while doing it. So they copulated in the manner of Spiders.

Thereupon Wolf taught them the right way to copulate in a more beautiful position.

The Spider-Man and the woman were both willing to try it the new way. So the Wolf and his friend went and got some wild sage and fixed up some medicine. They dipped the wild sage into the water and rubbed it all over the two Spider people. As he rubbed the wild sage over them, they became different; they looked better, and they did not smell bad. Whereupon Wolf and his friend thoroughly taught the Spider-Man in what manner, by uniting their private parts, they could beget people. So Spider-Man and his wife produced people, and if Wolf had not shown them how to copulate in the right way, there would not be any human beings.

THE WINKTE WAY

{*Omaha*}

Winkte is the Sioux word for hermaphrodite or
transvestite. Such people were also known as Berdaches
in Indian literature.
Iktinike and Rabbit are always chasing women, but
sometimes, just for a change, they turn themselves into
winktes, *doing it the* winkte *way.*

Iktinike and Rabbit were ambling about. By chance they met. "*Hau,* uncle," said Rabbit, "I was just thinking about you—and here you are!"

"Yes, nephew, I am glad to see you," said Iktinike. "I have been thinking about you. Come along. Let's go someplace where nobody can see us."

"Why, uncle?"

"You're asking too many questions. Come along!"

They went into the woods. "Friend," said Iktinike, "bend over. Let me get on top of you. Let's do it the *winkte* way."

"No, uncle," objected Rabbit. "You bend over and I get on top of you."

"No, young friend, I am the older. I go first. Respect your elders."

"On the contrary," Rabbit insisted, "youth must be served. It is the younger who always goes first."

They argued for a while. At last Iktinike lost patience. "All right, get on top of me." Rabbit did. "Oh, it hurts!" cried Iktinike. "Your *che* is very big!"

"No, it isn't," said Rabbit. "Your *onze* is too tight." After only a few seconds, Rabbit got off Iktinike's back and ran off. Rabbit is very quick at that kind of thing.

As Rabbit was running off, Iktinike called after him: "Hey, come back! It's my turn now!" But Rabbit just continued running, laughing loudly. "That rotten, evil-smelling, bug-eyed fellow has played me false," Iktinike complained. "It's just like him. He always plays tricks on me and I fall for them."

Iktinike was furious. He would have liked to punish Rabbit, but Rabbit was too fast. He could not be caught. So all Iktinike could do was call Rabbit some very bad names. So Iktinike was walking toward home. He came to a place where some boys were playing stickball. Iktinike called out to them: "*Hokshila,* what's new?"

"Nothing much, uncle," one boy answered. "Only that Rabbit came by here, telling everybody that he mounted you."

"Oh, he shamed me," thought Iktinike. "He's bad-mouthing me already!"

Iktinike went on. He came to a place where boys were gambling with plum pits. "Young brothers," Iktinike inquired, "what's new?"

"Nothing much. Rabbit came through here and told everybody how he got on top of you."

"Oh, no! That no-good, lying, long-eared *hlete* is only spreading false rumors!"

Iktinike went on. He came to a place where boys were shooting with toy bows and arrows. "Hey, you kids, what's new?" Iktinike wanted to know.

"Only that Rabbit came through here, telling everybody that he used you in the *winkte* way."

"Oh, that split-nosed, stinking liar!" cried Iktinike. "Don't believe him!"

Iktinike hurried on. Suddenly he had to relieve himself. He squatted down, but instead of *chesli*, little baby rabbits popped out of his *onze*. "Oh, no! This is really too much!" cried Iktinike. "What next?"

Finally he arrived at his home. His wife greeted him lovingly. She was in an amorous mood. "Let's *tawiton*," she said.

"Not tonight," Iktinike declined. "I've got a headache."

PART SEVEN

THE VEEHO
CYCLE

HE HAS BEEN SAYING
BAD THINGS ABOUT YOU

{*Northern Cheyenne*}

Veeho encountered a man who had strange powers. He could command stones to turn over and the stones did this without being touched, even if the man ordered them to do this from a distance. Veeho watched this man using his powers.

"Uncle," said Veeho, "what you are doing is wonderful. You surely are the greatest medicine man I ever met. I wish I could command stones to turn over. Then people would admire me; then women would come to share my blanket. Then I would be no longer poor, because people would give me many gifts to see me doing this. Uncle, have pity on me, give me a little of your stone power."

"I pity you," said the man. "I will give you that power, but before I do, you must promise to do this in a certain way."

"I promise, I promise," said Veeho.

"You must command the stones to turn over only four times. If you do it more often, you will be in big trouble."

"I promise, I promise," cried Veeho, "only four times. Only four times!" Then the man gave him a little of his power. Veeho hurried back to his village. He called loudly to all who could hear him: "People, behold me! People, behold my powers!"

Then the people who happened to be there watched Veeho commanding stones to turn over. Then the people said to each other: "We have misjudged Veeho. We thought he was just a fool, but now we see that he is a great man." Then everybody began to respect Veeho.

Some days later Veeho cried again: "People, behold me! People, gather round and behold my powers!" This time the whole village came to watch Veeho commanding stones to turn over.

Then everybody was astounded. People stood in awe of Veeho. "Surely," they said, "Veeho is a great medicine man." They came to Veeho to be doctored, to be cured of their illnesses. They made Veeho gifts of horses even though he did not cure their sickness. They believed in him because he could make stones obey him.

Some time after this, Veeho again went into the middle of the camp circle, crying: "People, come and behold me! Behold my great powers!" And again, before the eyes of all the people, Veeho made stones turn over at his command, without Veeho ever touching them. Then people began to call Veeho "Chief." Veeho had been a poor hunter. Now he had to hunt no longer. Every day people brought him meat, more than he could eat—back fat, buffalo-hump meat, buffalo tongues, meat from different animals. People were saying: "Veeho is not only powerful, he is rich. He is sure to marry a great chief's daughter."

Some time passed. Then Veeho again called upon everybody to assemble, crying: "People, behold my powers! Behold Veeho, the great, the powerful!" And he again had stones turn over at his command. Then a great chief gave his daughter to Veeho in marriage. Then there was a big feast. Then the beautiful chief's daughter entered Veeho's tipi. Then he slept with her. Veeho said to himself: "I am truly a great man."

Time passed. Veeho once more called the people together to watch stones obeying him. Again he cried out: "People, behold me!" Veeho had forgotten that he was supposed to do his wonderful feat with stones only four times. He had forgotten the warning that he would be in trouble if he commanded stones to turn over a fifth time. There was a big Rock standing a little way beyond the camp. Veeho led the people to it. "Behold me doing something people will talk about forever!" He commanded: "You, big Rock, turn over!"

The Rock did not turn over. It began rolling toward Veeho, threatening to flatten him. Veeho got scared. He started to run. The Rock rolled after him. Veeho ran faster and faster, but the Rock kept after him. Veeho could not gain on the Rock. He could not outrun it. The Rock dogged Veeho's heels. It was already treading on them. Veeho ran until he could run no more. Then the big Rock rolled halfway over him, resting on Veeho's chest. Veeho could hardly breathe. The Rock was about to crush him to death. Out of the corner of his eye, Veeho noticed Buffalo standing nearby. "Brother." He moaned and groaned. "Brother, help me. Get this Rock off my chest!"

"I cannot do it," said Buffalo. "That Rock is too big and powerful."

Veeho craned and twisted his neck, seeing Bear walking on the left. "Brother," he cried. "Brother, help me. Get this Rock off my chest!"

"I cannot do it," said Bear. "This Rock is too big and powerful."

Veeho twisted his head toward the right, and saw Moose standing there. "Brother," he croaked. "Brother, get this Rock off my chest!"

"I cannot do it," said Moose. "This Rock is too big and powerful."

Veeho was looking up. He saw Eagle soaring above him. Veeho mustered what little strength he had left and cried aloud: "Brother Eagle, this Rock has been saying bad things about you. He said that you are ugly, that your beak is crooked, that you have a voice that makes people cover their ears. This Rock said that you stink of rotten fish and spoiled meat. I told this Rock that he was wrong, that you are beautiful, that your beak has just the right shape, that your voice is lovely, and that you smell good. I told this Rock that he was a liar."

Hearing this, Eagle flew into a terrible rage. He dove straight down upon the Rock and, with his beak, broke the Rock into tiny splinters, thereby freeing Veeho from its crushing weight.

But Veeho was in a bad shape. He was bruised all over. Some of his ribs had been broken. His appearance was pitiful. Painfully he dragged himself back to his lodge. His wife looked at him. She said: "I should not have married you. I shall be looking for another husband. You are not a great man. You are nothing but a fool."

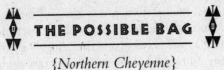

THE POSSIBLE BAG

{Northern Cheyenne}

*Four is the magic number among almost all tribes.
In many tales things are done four times and bad things
happen if they are done more often.*

Veeho was walking about. He had heard about a rich man who never
lacked food, though he did not seem to hunt much. Veeho said to himself: "That man is worth visiting." Veeho went there. The rich man's
lodge was surrounded by racks on which much meat was drying. Many
buffalo robes were hanging from the branches of nearby trees. "Yes,
indeed, this is a good man to know," thought Veeho. He entered the
man's lodge. The owner was at home. He seemed to live alone.

"Elder brother," said Veeho, "I am glad to meet you. I heard many
good things about you. May I stay a while?"

"Yes, you may," the man agreed. "Make yourself comfortable. Help
yourself to some of my buffalo-hump meat. There is more than enough
for the both of us."

Veeho gorged himself. He looked around. Hanging from a lodge-
pole in the back he saw a large possible bag. He wondered what could
be in it. The more he looked, the more curious he became. He could
not get the possible bag out of his mind.

The man told him: "You can stay the night if you wish."

"Yes, thank you, elder brother," said Veeho, "it is too late for me to
go on."

It grew dark. The rich man laid down on a buffalo robe. Veeho
waited until his host was sound asleep, then he took down the possible
bag, slung it over his shoulder, and crept silently out of the lodge. As
soon as he was outside, Veeho began to run. He was afraid that the man
would wake up and discover that his possible bag was missing. Veeho
ran as fast as he could. He did not want the man to catch him. He came
to a big lake. In order to go on, he had to run around the lake. This
seemed to take forever. Veeho thought: "This lakeshore has no end."

Veeho ran and ran until he could run no more. Then he laid down and fell asleep.

He woke up because somebody was shaking him by the shoulder. It was the rich man. He asked Veeho: "Younger brother, what are you doing with my possible bag?"

"Oh, elder brother, I needed it for a pillow under my head."

"But it's lying by your side."

"Well, it must have slipped while I was asleep," Veeho tried to convince him.

"You better leave this bag alone," said the man, tying it to a lodge-pole. "It contains medicine and should not be used for a pillow or for anything else."

Veeho looked around and saw that he had never left the lodge. The owner was so rich and powerful a magician that all the country round-about, from horizon to horizon, was contained in his lodge.

They spent the day chatting. They ate buffalo tongues and livers. Veeho asked his host: "Elder brother, what are you afraid of?"

"The only thing in the world I'm afraid of is Goose," said the rich man.

"Really? How strange," said Veeho. "I also am afraid of Goose. It's a very dangerous animal." After a while Veeho added: "Brother, I have stayed too long. I must go now."

Veeho left. Once outside the lodge, he changed himself into Goose. He had the power to transform himself. In the shape of Goose, Veeho went back into the rich man's lodge, crying: "Honk, honk!"

The rich man had one look at him and almost fainted. Terrified by what he thought was Goose, he fled in a great panic, grabbing the possible bag, but leaving everything else behind.

Veeho went back to his own lodge, where his wife and children were waiting. Veeho told them: "I went to a rich man's lodge. It is large, full of good things to eat and furnished with fine buffalo robes. I have frightened this man away. He won't come back. Come and let us live in his lodge and enjoy what he has left behind." Veeho and his family then went to the rich man's lodge and settled down there.

Soon after, Veeho said to his wife: "The man who owned all this has a large possible bag. I think that in this bag is what made him rich. I very much want to have this bag. I will track him down and take this bag away from him. There is enough food for you here to last until I come back." Veeho followed the man's footprints. He followed them for four days and nights. He caught up with the rich man. When Veeho saw him from afar, he quickly transformed himself once more into Goose. He overtook his prey, crying loudly: "Honk, honk!"

The man was very scared. Trembling and with chattering teeth, he begged Veeho: "Please, uncle, have pity. Don't kill me!"

Veeho asked: "What will you give me if I let you live?"

"Whatever you wish," answered the man.

"Give me the possible bag you are carrying with you," Veeho demanded.

"All right, all right, take it, but open it only four times. If you open it more often, bad things will happen." Veeho took the possible bag and let the man go.

Veeho hurried home to his wife and children. He showed them the possible bag, crying: "This is what I wanted!" He could not wait to untie the bag. As soon as he did, a fat buffalo cow jumped out. "This is what made that man so rich," cried Veeho. "Now we shall lack nothing. Now we shall have a feast every day. This is the way to live!" He quickly tied the bag shut. He fastened it to a lodgepole. It was hanging there. Veeho killed the cow. They butchered it. They had a big feast stuffing themselves with fat hump meat, delicious tongues, livers, and sweet kidneys. The meat lasted for many days.

When it was finally gone, Veeho said: "My wife and children, it is time to open that wonderful bag again." He did and another young, fat buffalo cow jumped out. Again they feasted. Whenever they ran out of food, Veeho untied the possible bag. He was about to open it for the fifth time when his wife warned him: "That man told you not to open this bag more than four times. He told you that bad things would happen if you did."

Veeho laughed. "That fellow was angry with me for taking the bag away from him. He does not want us to be rich forever. That's why he said this. This bag is bottomless. It will bring forth a young, fat cow every time I open it."

Veeho untied the possible bag for the fifth time. At once numberless buffalo tumbled out—bulls, cows, and calves, an unstoppable flood of animals. They trampled over everything. They almost crushed Veeho, his wife, and his children to death. They trampled down the lodge. They trampled Veeho's horse to death. They stampeded all over the village, running over women and children left and right, tearing down lodges, stampeding horses, crushing dogs under their hooves. There seemed no end of buffalo. Their drumming hooves resounded like thunder as they rushed off in all the four directions—north, east, south, and west. Their herds covered the whole prairie as far as the eye could see. Finally they all disappeared beyond the horizon.

The people were all shook up. Their village lay in ruins. Their lodges were destroyed, their belongings trampled to bits, their horses gone. "Who could have caused this great evil?" the people asked each other.

"It wasn't me," said Veeho.

So this is the way buffalo came into this world. The people soon forgot the devastation caused by the onrushing buffalo. They recovered. They were overjoyed to have buffalo to hunt. Now there was much food. Now there was an end of famines. The people were asking each other: "Who has done this great thing for us?"

Veeho was about to say something, but his wife stopped him short, telling Veeho: "Husband, keep your mouth shut!"

HAIR LOSS

{*Northern Cheyenne*}

Veeho was walking about. He came across two young, comely *tsis-tsis-tas,* maidens. He said to himself: "They are good-looking. I will talk to them. I will amuse them. Then maybe one of them will let me sleep with her. Maybe both will."

Veeho walked up to the girls. "Good evening, little cousins. I am lousy. Would you please be so kind as to pick these nits out of my hair? They make my scalp itch so bad." He laid down between them. The girls started to pick the lice out of Veeho's hair, one sitting at his right side, and the other on his left. This made him drowsy and he fell asleep.

Then one girl said to the other: "Do you know who this louse-ridden fellow is? I think it is that no-account Trickster, Veeho."

"I think it is, too," said the other girl, "he is always playing nasty tricks on people, particularly on women. Let's play a trick on him, for a change." The two girls covered Veeho's whole head with prickly, spiny burrs. Veeho slept through it all.

When Veeho woke up, he at once noticed that his head was covered with burrs. They had nested in his hair and tangled it all up. For hours Veeho tried to get the burrs out of his hair, but it was impossible. They had formed an impenetrable mass, making his head feel like the back of a porcupine. "Oh, this is bad!" said Veeho. For hours he tried to remove the burrs. His fingers were scratched and bleeding from the sharp, needlelike spikes. His scalp, too, was bleeding. "Oh, it hurts," wailed Veeho. He gave up.

Walking toward his home with his big, painful headdress of burrs, he encountered Mouse. "Oh, little brother, help me," said Veeho. "You see the sorry state I'm in. Please gnaw off this whole mess—hair, burrs, and all."

"Gladly," said Mouse. "Aren't we relatives and friends? What are relatives for?"

Mouse got busy gnawing, gnawing, gnawing. It was hard work, but finally Mouse got it done. He had gnawed off everything, leaving Veeho's skull bare, as if some enemy had scalped him. "Thank you, little brother," said Veeho, continuing on his way.

When Veeho arrived back at his lodge, his wife at first did not recognize him. She thought he was some kind of monster and cried out in fear. "Foolish woman," said Veeho, "don't you see it's me?"

"Oh, my poor husband!" lamented the wife. "What has happened to you? How did you lose your beautiful bushy hair?"

"Don't ask so many dumb questions, nosy woman," said Veeho. "What's for supper?"

BROTHER, SHARPEN MY LEG!

{Cheyenne}

There was a man whose leg was pointed, so that by running and jumping against trees he could stick in them. By saying *naiwa-toutawa*, he brought himself back to the ground. On a hot day he would stick himself against a tree for greater shade and coolness. However, he could not do this trick more than four times.

Once while he was doing this, Veeho, White Man, came to him, crying, and said: "Brother, sharpen my leg!"

The man replied: "That is not very hard. I can sharpen your leg."

White Man stood on a large log, and the other man, with an ax, sharpened his leg, telling him to hold still bravely. The pain caused the tears to come from his eyes. When the man had sharpened his leg, he told him to do the trick only four times a day, and to keep count in order not to exceed this number.

White Man went down toward the river, singing. Near the bank was a large tree; toward this he ran, then jumped and stuck in it. Then he called himself back to the ground. Again he jumped, this time against another tree; but now he counted one, thinking in this way to get the better of the other man. The third time, he counted two. The fourth time, birds and animals stood by, and he was proud to show his ability, and jumped high, and pushed his leg in up to the knee. Then coyotes, wolves, and other animals came to see him; some of them came to ask how he knew the trick, and begged him to teach it to them, so they could stick to trees at night. He was still prouder now, and for the fifth time he ran and jumped as high as he could, and half his thigh entered the tree. Then he counted four. Then he called to get to the ground again. But he stuck. He called out all day; he tried to send the animals to the man who had taught him. He was fast in the tree for many days, until he starved to death.

•

 # VEEHO HAS HIS BACK SCRAPED

{*Northern Cheyenne*}

Veeho was walking through the camp. He saw a man whose wife was scraping his back with an elk-bone flesher. She scraped off shavings as from a buffalo hide. "Elder brother, doesn't it hurt?"

"No," said the man, "it doesn't hurt at all."

"Why is your wife doing this?" Veeho asked.

"Watch me," said the man. He threw the scrapings from his back into a kettle of boiling water and, instantly, the scrapings turned into fat buffalo-hump meat. The man and his wife had a feast.

They shared their meal with Veeho. He told the man: "Elder brother, I wish I could do this. Then I could feed my family."

"You can have your wife scrape your back, and the pieces of skin will turn into buffalo-hump meat. But you must do it no more than four times."

The man was known to be very wise. Therefore Veeho trusted him. He went back to his tipi and told his wife to take a flesher and scrape his back.

"Won't it hurt terribly?" his wife asked.

"Woman, do as I say," answered Veeho. The wife scraped his back. It did not hurt. The pieces of skin from Veeho's back looked like scraps from a buffalo hide. "Boil water in your pot," Veeho told his wife. She did as told. Veeho threw the skin shavings into the boiling water. At once they turned into chunks of succulent hump meat. Veeho, his wife, and his children had a feast.

The next day Veeho again asked his wife to take her flesher and scrape his back. And, as on the preceding day, the scrapings turned into good, fat meat and again they filled their bellies. "Ah, this is the first time I am doing this," Veeho told himself. "Now I can do it three more times." He had forgotten that he had already had his back scraped once before. Veeho has a bad memory. He had his wife scrape his back two more times on the following days. He had now done this four times, but he thought it had been only three. Veeho told his wife: "Woman, this is the last time we can do this. Take your flesher and scrape my back real hard, as hard as you can. I am hungry. I want a great heap of fat buffalo-hump meat." He thought it was the fourth time, but it was really the fifth. The wife scraped hard. Veeho howled with pain. He was bleeding. Strips of flesh were dangling from his back.

Veeho went to the wise man. He said: "Elder brother, look what you have done to me. You told me this would not happen."

"Younger brother," the man answered, "I told you not to have your back scraped more than four times, but you did this more often than that."

"Really?" said Veeho. "I must have miscounted. I do not have a head for numbers."

"That's for sure," said the man.

Veeho sat down by the man's side before the tipi. The man said to his wife: "Take off your dress." The wife did so. The man took a sharp knife and cut his wife's dress into little pieces. He threw them into a pot of boiling water. Instantly the pieces were changed into delicious buffalo tongues, livers, and kidneys. The man and his wife ate these and invited Veeho to share their feast. When they had eaten all this good food, the man pulled his wife's dress out of the pot. It was no longer cut up into pieces. It was whole. It was as good as new.

"Elder brother," said Veeho, "I wish I could do that."

"And so you can," said the wise man, "but you must not do it more than four times."

"I won't," Veeho said, and went home.

As soon as Veeho arrived back at his lodge, he called his wife.

"Quick, woman, hand me your dress!" His wife took off her fine white buckskin dress decorated with quillwork and the eyeteeth of many elk. With a knife Veeho chopped the dress into pieces.

"Fool, what are you doing?" cried the wife.

"Be quiet and watch," said Veeho. He threw the chopped-up pieces of the dress into a kettle of boiling water and, in a flash, the pieces were transformed into good-tasting buffalo tongues, livers, and kidneys. Veeho, his wife, and his children feasted. They stuffed themselves until they were unable to swallow even the tiniest morsel. The snippets of buckskin formed themselves up into a dress again. It was like new when Veeho pulled it out of the kettle.

For four days in a row Veeho got rich food by cutting up and boiling his wife's dress. Again he miscounted. He thought he had done it only three times. "Well, wife, this is the last time we can do this," he said. "Take off your dress!" This time he did not chop up the dress but threw it whole, in one piece, into the pot. This time the dress did not turn itself into food but instantly shrank to the size of a tiny doll's dress.

Veeho took it and brought it to the wise man. "Elder brother," he said, "look what happened to my wife's fine dress. It would not even fit a mouse. You taught me the wrong way." He was not aware that he had done the dress magic five times.

"Little brother," said the man, "you have miscounted again. You are hopeless. You will never get it right. I will not teach you any more. My wisdom is wasted upon you."

"I guess you are right," said Veeho. Sadly he went home to his own lodge.

{*Cheyenne*}

Veeho was walking idly, as he always does. Then he saw a man, a very powerful man. This fellow was rooting up big trees, he was that strong.

Veeho went up to this man, saying: "My friend, why are you uprooting these big trees?"

"I need them for arrow shafts, cousin," this man answered.

"Friend, this is foolish," said Veeho, who always likes giving unasked-for advice. "It will take a long time and much labor to carve arrow shafts out of such big trees. You should take sticks of the right length for this."

"Cousin," said the strong man, "I do not mean to carve these trees up. I use the whole trunk for a shaft. All other, smaller kinds of shafts are too light for my taste."

"This is foolish talk," said Veeho, who was getting angry. "You are lying to me. I am too smart to believe such stories."

"Do you want me to show you how I use these trees for arrows?" said this strong fellow.

"All right, show me."

"Well, cousin, step back. I shall aim at you."

Veeho went back a little distance. "No," said the man, "farther." Veeho went farther backward. "No," said the man again, "you are

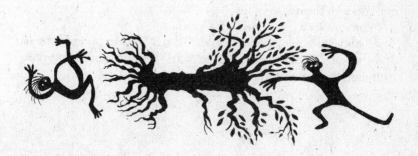

much too close for me." Veeho went back a third time. "Still too close," said the man.

"This fellow is trying to fool me," thought Veeho. "He is sending me a long way off, then he will run away." All the same he walked backward for a fourth time. He walked to the top of a hill. He stood there.

"This is far enough," shouted the strong fellow. He took up a huge tree trunk, roots pointing forward, and hurled it toward Veeho. He did not use a bow. The tree trunk flew straight as an arrow. Veeho saw it coming. As it came hurtling through the air toward him, it made a loud, whirring noise like a whirlwind. Veeho got scared. He looked around. He saw a fox hole. Veeho was diving into it, trying to hide himself, but he could not get all the way in. His buttocks were sticking out. The trunk hit Veeho with full force. It took his buttocks right off, knocking one to one side and the other to the other side. It knocked Veeho's buttocks pretty far.

The strong fellow walked over to see how he had done. He said: "Well, my arrow shaft flew straight."

Veeho was crying. "Friend," he wailed, "look what you have done! You have knocked my buttocks clean off. I need them. I need them for sitting upon."

"Don't make such a noise, cousin," said the man. "I will put you together again." He went looking for Veeho's buttocks. He found one. He went and slammed it against Veeho's backside. The buttock grew into its old place instantly. Then the man retrieved the second buttock and put it back where it belonged.

"I think you put my right buttock on my left side, and my left buttock on the right side," complained Veeho.

"Well, they are where I put them," said the strong fellow. "You must do with them as they are."

"You sure are a good shot," said Veeho.

Veeho went home, rubbing himself. It still hurt. In his lodge he sat down to eat. "Foolish one," said his wife, "why are you sitting there with this pained expression on your face?"

THE ONLY MAN AROUND

{*Northern Cheyenne*}

■

Veeho was roaming, according to his nature. He came to a village full of women, but without any men. When the women saw Veeho, they were very excited to see a man. They had lived all their lives without male company. So they crowded around Veeho, fighting to get close to him, crying: "Take me, take me!"

Veeho looked them over, one after the other, saying over and over to each: "You are very pretty, but not quite pretty enough for me." Finally he saw a dazzlingly beautiful woman wearing a white, decorated buckskin robe. "You are the one!"

"Come to my lodge," said the woman, taking Veeho by the hand.

Her lodge stood some distance apart from the village. It was a magnificent lodge made from sixteen large buffalo skins. The inner lining was covered with wonderfully quilled designs of many colors. Inside were two handsome backrests made of willow wands. Many painted parfleches were lying around, filled to bursting with pemmican and dried jerky meat. There was also a bed, large enough for two, covered with the softest, finest buffalo robes. The woman laid down on the bed. Veeho stretched out beside her. They made love. "Now you are my wife," said Veeho. He was quite happy about the way things had turned out.

Some blissful months passed. One day Veeho went out hunting. At first he found nothing. After a long while he saw a deer. He followed it, but could not catch it. The deer lured him farther and farther away, a great distance away, in fact. Then it disappeared. Veeho saw that he had happened upon a camp of some other tribe. He went there. He found that this camp contained only men. "Cousins, where are your women?" Veeho asked.

"Women?" said the strangers. "We've never met a woman in all our lives, but we sure would like to meet some."

"Then you are in luck," said Veeho. "I come from a village full of pretty women."

"Quick, quick, friend!" the strangers shouted. "Where's your village?"

"I'll lead you to it," said Veeho. "Just give me a chance. Don't stampede. Let me show you the way."

The men paid no attention to Veeho. They were soon way ahead of him. They just followed his tracks back to the women's village. In their eagerness to get to the women they were running as fast as antelopes. "Women," they were shouting, "we're coming, we're coming!"

Veeho is a very slow runner. He arrived at the village hours after the strangers. He at once went to his tipi. He entered it. Inside his wife was copulating with one of the strangers. The two of them were panting and sighing. They were so busy making love they did not even notice Veeho's presence. Veeho shook the man by the shoulder. "What do you think you're doing? This is my wife. Get out!"

"She is my wife now," said the man. "Get lost before I get angry."

The man got up. He was exceedingly tall and muscular. His face was ferocious, his expression fierce. He had his weapons with him. "Better get yourself another wife," said the man. "Get out of my lodge, or else!"

"I'm going," said Veeho. He went into the village, looking for another wife, but they were already taken up by the strangers, every one of them. There was not a single woman left for Veeho.

"I was stupid," said Veeho. "I should have kept my mouth shut."

PART EIGHT

THE NIXANT
AND
SITCONSKI
CYCLES

WHEN THE PEOPLE WERE WILD

{*Gros Ventre*}

The people before the present people were wild. They did not know how to do anything. Nixant did not like the way they lived and did things. He thought, "I will make a new world."

He had the chief pipe. He went outdoors and hung the pipe on three sticks. He picked up four buffalo chips. One he put under each of the sticks on which the pipe hung, and one he took for his own seat. He said, "I will sing three times and shout three times. After I have done these things, I will kick the earth, and water will come out of the cracks. There will be a heavy rain. There will be water over all the earth."

Then he began to sing. After he sang three times, he shouted three times. Then he kicked the ground and it cracked. The water came out,

and it rained for days, and over all the earth was water. By means of the buffalo chips he and the pipe floated.

Then it stopped raining. There was water everywhere. He floated wherever the wind took him. For days he drifted thus.

Above him the Crow flew about. All the other birds and animals were drowned. The Crow became tired. It flew about, crying, "My father, I am becoming tired. I want to rest." Three times it said this.

After it said so three times, Nixant said, "Alight on the pipe and rest." Repeatedly the Crow cried to him, and each time was allowed to alight on the pipe.

Nixant became tired sitting in one position. He cried. He did not know what to do. After he had cried a long time, he began to unwrap the chief pipe. The pipe contained all animals. He selected those with a long breath to dive through the water. First he selected the Large Loon. The Loon was not alive, but Nixant had its body wrapped up in the pipe. Nixant sang, and then commanded it to dive and try to bring mud. The Loon dived. It was not halfway down when it lost its breath and immediately turned back. It came up almost drowned at the place where Nixant was.

Then Nixant took the Small Loon's body and sang. Then the Small Loon dived. It nearly reached the mud at the bottom. Then it lost its breath and went up again and, nearly dead, reached the place where Nixant was.

Then he took the Turtle. He sang and it became alive, and he sent it and it dived. Meanwhile, the Crow did not alight, but flew about, crying for rest. Nixant did not listen to it. After a long time the Turtle came up. It was nearly dead. It had filled its feet and the cracks along its sides with mud. When it reached Nixant, all the mud had been washed away and it was nearly dead.

Nixant said, "Did you succeed in reaching the mud?"

The Turtle said, "Yes, I reached it. I had much of it in my feet and about my sides, but it all washed away from me before I came to you."

Then Nixant said to it, "Come to me," and the Turtle went to him. Nixant looked at the inside of her feet and in the cracks of its sides. On the inside of the feet he found a little earth. He scraped this into his hand. Meanwhile, the Crow had become very tired.

Then Nixant, when he had scraped the earth into his hand, began to sing. After he had sung three times, he shouted three times. Then he said, "I will throw this little dust that I have in my hand into the water. Little by little let there be enough to make a strip of land large enough for me." Then he began to drop it, little by little, into the water, opening and closing his hand carefully, and when he had dropped it all, there was a little land, large enough for him to sit on.

Then he said to the Crow, "Come down and rest. I have made a little land for myself and for you." Then the Crow came down and rested. After it had rested, it flew up again.

Then Nixant took out from his pipe two long wing feathers. He had one in each hand and began to sing. After he had sung three times, he shouted three times, *"Youh, hou, hou,"* and spread his arms and closed his eyes. When he had done this, he said to himself, "Let there be land as far as my eyes can see around me." When he opened his eyes, then indeed there was land.

After he had made the land, there was no water anywhere. He went about with his pipe and with the Crow. They were all that there was to be seen in the world. Now Nixant was thirsty. He did not know what to do to get water. Then he thought, "I will cry." He cried. While he cried, he closed his eyes. He tried to think how he could get water. He shed tears. His tears dropped to the ground. They made a large spring in front of him. Then a stream ran from the spring. When he stopped crying, a large river was flowing. Thus he made rivers and streams.

He became tired of being alone with the Crow and the pipe. He decided to make persons and animals. He took earth and made it into the shape of a man. He made also the shape of a woman. Then he made more figures of earth, until he had many men and women. When he thought he had enough persons, he made animals of all kinds in pairs. When he had finished making these shapes, he named the tribes of people and the kinds of animals. Then he sang three times, and shouted three times. After he had shouted, he kicked the ground, and there were living pairs of beings standing before him, animals and men. The reason why men are dark in color is that earth is dark.

Nixant called the world Turtle because the Turtle was the animal that had helped him to make the world. Then he made bows and arrows for men, and told them how to use them. The pipe he gave to a tribe that he called *haa'ninin,* Gros Ventre. Then he said to the people, "If you are good and act well, there will be no more water and no more fire." Long before the water rose, the world had been burned. This now is the third life. Then he showed them the rainbow, and said to them, "This rainbow is the sign that the earth will not be covered with water again. Whenever you have rain, you will see the rainbow; and when you see it, it will mean that the rain has gone by. There will be another world after this one." He told the people to separate in pairs and to select habitations in the world for themselves. That is why human beings are scattered.

THE TALKING PENIS

{Gros Ventre}

There was a man who had the power to call buffalo so that they could be hunted. Whenever there was no game, and the people were starving, this powerful man climbed to the top of a hill and sang: *"Hi-i-tana Wukatyii."*

Then the buffalo came and could be killed. Then the people had a feast. Nixant was jealous. He also wanted to be able to make buffalo come to him. He asked the powerful man to teach him the song. The

man did. He told Nixant: "Don't use it too often. Use it only once during the hunting months." Nixant would not listen. He used the song all the time. He wanted to show off. So many buffalo came that they ran all over the camp, trampling over tipis and people.

"Stop singing my song," the powerful man told Nixant. Nixant would not listen. He kept singing: "Come, buffalo, come to me!"

Nixant's penis was big. It stood up. It shouted: "Buffalo, do not come, stay away!" The buffalo did not come.

Nixant felt like copulating. He noticed some young women digging wild turnips. He called out to them: "You girls, come over here. I want to dance for you."

His penis stood up and shouted: "You girls, do not come. He only wants to abuse you! Stay away." The young women ran off. Nixant was angry and embarrassed.

Nixant sat among a circle of warriors. He boasted of the great deeds he had done.

The penis swelled up and said: "Nixant has not done these things. He is a liar. He never fights." The penis laughed. Then everybody laughed. Nixant was ashamed.

Again he sang the song: "Come to me, buffalo, come. We don't want to kill you for food. We want to dance for you."

The penis shouted: "Oh, you buffalo, don't believe him. Nixant is lying. He means to kill you. Teach him a lesson!" Then the buffalo came, crowded together, and shit all over Nixant, over his fine beaded war shirt, over his fine leggings, over his moccasins.

"This can't go on," said Nixant to his penis. "You shut up or I'll cut you off!"

The penis laughed. "You'll never do that. You're much too fond of copulating." The penis had a very good laugh. Everybody heard it.

A very ugly woman came to Nixant and said: "I can make your penis stop talking if you copulate with me every day."

Nixant had a good look at the woman. She was truly ugly. He said: "I'd rather not."

Nixant went to the powerful man. "Make my penis stop talking," he begged.

"Even I am not powerful enough to do that," said the man. "Only the ugly woman can help you. Go to her and do what she wants."

Nixant went to the ugly woman's tipi. He went inside. He stayed there for a long time. They did something in there. Nixant was not smiling when he came out of the ugly woman's tipi. He looked grim, but after that his penis never talked again.

"How did the ugly woman cure you?" a friend asked.

"I don't want to talk about it," said Nixant.

HAIRY LEGS

{Gros Ventre}

Nixant saw two women getting ready to cross a stream. He felt like having sex with them. But then, he always wants to do it. He decided to play a trick on them. He quickly put on a woman's dress and let his hair hang loose. He joined the two women. He pretended to be a woman himself. It was already getting dark; that is why he could get away with this. Crossing the stream, they all were hitching up their dresses, way up.

One of the girls said to Nixant: "I never saw a woman who had such hairy legs as you have."

"Oh," said Nixant, "it's just grass stuck to my legs." He made his voice sound like a woman's voice.

The light was fading. The other girl asked: "What's that dangling under your dress?"

"It's a love root," said Nixant.

They got to the other bank of the river. They laid down to rest. "This love root of yours," said one of the girls, "what do you use it for?"

"Oh, it's good for whatever ails you—aches and pains, a sickness. Even if you're not sick, it makes you feel good."

"Do you cook it or eat it raw?" the girls asked.

"No, no, it only works if you stick it up between your legs. Here, let me show you."

He showed it to them. He did this several times. "You are right," said the girls. "This root makes one feel good."

They went to sleep. At dawn, at sunrise, when the girls woke up, they discovered that Nixant had tricked them. They saw his hairy legs. They lifted his dress and saw what his "love root" was. They discovered that the person they had taken for a woman was Nixant. "He's put one over on us," they said, "but let's not complain. If we tell, people will only laugh at us."

SITCONSKI AND THE BUFFALO SKULL

{*Assiniboine*}

Sitconski used to walk along the bank of a river. He saw a buffalo skull lying there. Whenever he passed it, he kicked it into the water, but he invariably found it in exactly the same position next time. He wished to find out the reason. Once he burned the skull and pounded it into powder, which he threw away, but the next time he again found the head in the same old place.

"This is queer," he thought. He burned it up again and lay down to sleep a short distance from the remains. He heard something like a buffalo's footsteps. Looking about, he could not see anything. He went to sleep once more; again he heard the noise, but could not see anything on looking up. "I must be mad. I'll sleep and won't open my eyes until it is nearby." When the noise approached, he looked up, but saw nothing. The fourth time he heard the sound, he said: "I won't look anymore." He did not look. At last he heard snorting and felt something puffing in his face. Looking up, there was an old buffalo, preparing to hook him.

Sitconski fled, pursued by the buffalo, which nearly caught him. Sitconski cried for help. He saw a hard rock and ran toward it. It had a crack, which admitted him and then closed up. The buffalo began to lick the rock with his tongue until it was worn down to a small size. Then Sitconski fled to a stump and sought shelter in its hollow. The buffalo hooked the tree and split it apart.

Sitconski fled; once the tip of the buffalo's horns just caught him and he yelled. He asked a willow to help him, twisted its trunk into a swing, and swung back and forth, avoiding the buffalo's horns. Then the buffalo twisted the willow until it broke. Sitconski cried, "Let me go, brother!" and again ran away.

He came to a big lake and plunged in. The buffalo began to lap it up until Sitconski was left high and dry on the mud. He could not run, but only crawled on his hands and feet. The buffalo pursued him. Sitconski said, "I'll give you tobacco. Let me go."

"You kicked my skull every time you passed. Hurry up and get me tobacco."

"What sort of tobacco would you like to have?"

The buffalo told him. Then Sitconski cut some willow bark, made tobacco, and gave it to the buffalo, who lit it by holding it toward the sun. Then he let Sitconski alone.

SHE REFUSED TO HAVE HIM

{*Assiniboine*}

Sitconski wanted to marry the daughter of a chief, but she refused to have him. He planned a scheme to get back at her. The people had broken camp. He went to the old campsite and found a piece of white robe. Shaking it, he said, "I wish I had the whole robe." He thus secured a whole robe. He picked up some red cloth and similarly transformed it into a large piece. In the same way he got a weasel skin and an otter-skin headdress. He then tracked the people.

He met one of the chief's sons, who conducted him to his father's lodge. The chief's daughter liked Sitconski in his disguise. "I am going home soon," said Sitconski. "My people live far away."

The girl said she would get some wood. Sitconski waited for her. She called out to him, "I'll go with you."

He stood still and said, "Get your things and we'll go together."

The girl got her dress and ran back to Sitconski, but he was gone. She only found a weasel-skin legging on the ground, which turned into excrements. The girl returned to camp and told her father how Sitconski had fooled her.

The chief said to the people, "We had better move camp. My daughter is ashamed."

NI'HANCAN AND WHIRLWIND WOMAN

{*Arapaho*}

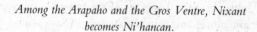

Among the Arapaho and the Gros Ventre, Nixant
becomes Ni'hancan.

Ni'hancan was traveling. He met Whirlwind Woman crawling.* He said, "Get out of my way." So Whirlwind Woman went away, and the dust spun in a circle. Soon he came to her again. "I do not want you, Whirlwind Woman, go away!" he said. Then she whirled off. Again he came to her and said: "There are some people that I like to have near me, but I do not like you." So she flew off, but came back in his path along the riverbank.

Ni'hancan came to her again. Then he began to like her. "I want you for my sweetheart," he said.

"No," she answered, "I am not used to remaining in one place. I travel. I would not be the wife for you."

"You are like me!" said Ni'hancan. "I am always traveling. Moreover, I have the same faculty as you," and he began to run, and turn, and spin about, raising the dust and throwing the dirt up into the air with his feet. But Whirlwind Woman refused him. Then he started again, running and spinning, stirring more dust and kicking it higher. Coming back to her he said: "There, I have the same power as you. I can throw the earth just as high!"

Whirlwind Woman started, whirled, caught him, and blew him over the bank, so that he fell headfirst into the water. "I was only joking, I was not intending to do anything to you," he called.

*In Arapaho the word for *whirlwind* is the same as for *caterpillar*.

Whirlwind Woman called back: "Such is my power." She was already far away.

 # NI'HANCAN AND THE RACE FOR WIVES

{Arapaho}

There was a party of young men going on the warpath. One of them carried the buttocks of a woman. While these men were walking, Ni'hancan came along and joined the party. "Say, young man, let me carry that, so that you may rest yourselves," said Ni'hancan.

"No, you might stumble and break it. We can't travel without it, for we brought it with us to use," said one of the party.

"We are always particular with it and it does not allow anybody else to carry it," said they.

"Yes! I shall be very careful and walk steadily," said Ni'hancan.

So these young men gave him the burden and he carried it. One day, while they were going fast, Ni'hancan struck his foot against a stick or rock and stumbled, dropping his burden and breaking it in the center into two equal parts. Ni'hancan got a scolding from the party and went off to another direction.

He came to a camp circle. When the women saw him coming, they started to catch him in a race. When they finally caught him, he told them that he was going to the painted tipi in the center, toward the west of the camp circle. "Leave me alone, for I am going over to the tipi that suits me best!" said he to the women. This tipi was beautiful and there was a pipe of peace hung outside of it above the door. Ni'hancan went in and found a woman all by herself. This woman wanted him to remain as her husband, for there were no men in the camp circle.

Still, Ni'hancan ran away and went back and reached the young men with whom he had recently journeyed. "When I stumbled and broke it into two parts you men scolded me for it. Now I have come over to tell you that I have found a camp circle consisting entirely of women. Now is your chance to be happy and become husbands. Because you men put the blame on me for breaking that object, and so putting an end to your fun, I came to tell you the truth, that there is not a single man in sight in that camp," said he.

"Well, then, Ni'hancan, we will have a race for wives. The one who runs the fastest gets the prettiest," said the young men.

"All right! That will do, but you must understand that I have already selected a tipi, which stands in the center of the circle and has a pipe of peace hanging over the door. You folks might outrun me and take a liking to that tipi. It belongs to me by right, because I got to this camp circle first," said he.

"Oh, pshaw! We can't beat you, for we know that you can run very swift. You can easily get to the tipi that you mentioned first," said the young men. So they all stood in a row and started. Ni'hancan was in the race.

Before starting, they agreed that all should slacken their speed to allow Ni'hancan to get in the lead. Consequently, he was in the lead just after they began the race after the women for wives.

"Oh, say, Ni'hancan, stop! You are too fast; this is not fair. We think that you ought to bear weights at your ankles and at your wrists, to give us some chance," said the young men. So these young men went out and searched for stones, which they took and fastened to his ankles and wrists.

Then the young men and Ni'hancan stood in a row again. Again

they started on the race. These young men agreed not to run fast, but to give the chance to Ni'hancan. Ni'hancan was in the lead again. "Oh, say, stop, Ni'hancan! You are too swift for us. We think that you are giving us a poor chance for the women. Had you not better put a heavier weight on your ankles and wrists?" said the young men.

"All right! You may fasten on the weights if you desire," said Ni'hancan.

"Oh, Ni'hancan is light and very swift, therefore he can surely outrun all of us," said the young men in earnest voices. So finally they began the race again to the camp, the young men taking the lead, while Ni'hancan stopped and began to untie the stones and rocks.

"Oh, partners, remember my tipi stands in the center and bears the painting outside of a pipe of peace, but you can run for the other places," said he in a loud voice. The young men, running as fast as they could, did not pay any attention to him.

When the young men had reached the tipis and selected every one, Ni'hancan came in panting. He went to the painted tipi and peeped in and saw the woman with a man. Ni'hancan told the man in the tipi that he once had been in the tipi but that he had run away. Then the owner of the tipi ordered Ni'hancan away. He was greatly disappointed and walked away to the east part of the camp and came to a well-tanned tipi, which was owned by an old woman. He went in and found the old woman sitting alone. "Well, grandson, where are you going?" said the old woman.

"Old woman," said Ni'hancan, "you have a nice tipi. You have much meat in your big pot. I am not going anywhere."

So, not getting his first choice for a wife, Ni'hancan married this old woman.

PART NINE

MAGICAL

MASTER

RABBIT

LITTLE RABBIT FIGHTS THE SUN

{*Ute*}

■

Ta-vwots, the Little Rabbit, was sleeping with his back to the sun. He got burned. His children saw that his back was smoking and cried: "Father, what is happening to your back?"

Little Rabbit woke up with a start. "Children," he rumbled, "why do you wake me up?"

"Father, your back is covered with sores. It has holes in it," cried his children.

Then Little Rabbit knew that it was Ta-vi, Sun, who had burned him. He got very angry. "My children," he said, "I must go and fight Sun." He left right away.

On his way to fight Sun, Little Rabbit came into a beautiful valley and in its middle stood a cornfield with the ears ready for roasting. Little Rabbit had never seen corn before. He looked at the ears of corn and

saw that they were covered with beautiful, silky hair. He opened one husk and inside found white grains covering the cobs in rows. Then he knew that this was corn and that it was good to eat. He roasted an armful of ears over a fire and ate until his belly was full. Then it occurred to him that the cornfield might belong to somebody and that he had been stealing. So he dug a hole in which to hide himself.

Now, Cin-au-av, the owner of the cornfield, noticed that his corn had been stolen and right away guessed who had been the guilty one. The owner got very angry and cried: "I will kill this thieving Rabbit, I will kill him!" He called all his warriors together and began looking for the thief, but could not find him, because Little Rabbit had gone underground. At last they found Rabbit's hole and shot arrows into it. But Little Rabbit blew them back. Cin-au-av's people were enraged and shot more arrows at Little Rabbit, but with his mighty breath he blew them all back against them.

Then they ran to grab him with their hands, but he nimbly side-stepped them so that they only caught each other's fists. Then they said: "Let's dig him out!" And they dug in a frenzy, but Little Rabbit had an escape hole through which he slipped out. From the top of a rock he watched Cin-au-av's people dig deeper and deeper until they almost vanished from sight. Then Little Rabbit hurled a magic ball, which he always carried with him, at the ground above the diggers. It made the earth cave in on top of them, and they were buried.

Little Rabbit said: "Why did these foolish people get in my way? I am in a killing mood; I am going to fight the Sun. I'll make an end of anyone trying to stop me!"

Then he saw two men making arrowheads out of hot rocks. He watched them for a while from behind a tree. Then he went up to them, saying: "Let me help you." He looked at the rocks, which were glowing red-hot, and said: "These rocks will not burn me."

They laughed at him, calling him a fool, saying: "Maybe you are some kind of a ghost?"

"I am not a ghost," said Little Rabbit, "but I am more powerful than you. Put me on these red-glowing rocks and if I do not burn you must let me do the same to you."

"This fellow is really a fool," thought the two men. Aloud they said: "We agree." They put Little Rabbit on the sizzling rocks, but he cooled them with his magic breath and did not burn.

Little Rabbit said: "Brothers, now it's your turn." He seized them and held them down on the red-hot stones, and they were consumed by heat and fire until only their ashes remained. "Lie there," said Little Rabbit, "until you can get up again!" He laughed, saying: "This is good practice for fighting Sun!" He went on, uttering fierce war cries.

Next day he came upon two women gathering berries in baskets. He sat down and the women brought him a basket of berries to eat. He saw that there were many thorns among the berries, and told the women: "Blow these thorns into my eyes, because it will make them feel good!" They did as told, thinking to blind him, but he blew the thorns away with his magic breath.

Then the women asked: "Are you a ghost?"

"I am not a ghost," he answered. "I am just an ordinary, everyday fellow. I guess you know that thorns cannot hurt your eyes. Let me show you." They agreed and he made them blind. "That will teach you offering a guest berries mixed with thorns," said Little Rabbit, and knocked them dead. "Aha," he said, "I am learning how to kill. This is good practice. I am going to kill Sun." He went on, whooping and hollering.

The next day he saw some women standing on the top of a high cliff. They saw him coming. "It is Little Rabbit," they said to each other. "Let us kill him by hurling rocks at his head as he passes." He heard them. He stopped a little short of them, took some dried meat mixed with chokecherries. He ate some of it with great relish.

The women on the cliff became curious. "What have you got there?" they asked him.

"Something very sweet and good-tasting. Come to the edge and I will throw some of it up to you."

The women went to the brink of the cliff. Little Rabbit threw lumps of the jerk meat up to them, but so that they could not quite reach them. He kept throwing it up again and again, until the women came to the cliff's very edge, leaning way over trying to catch the meat. They leaned so far over that they toppled from the cliff and fell to their deaths. "You got what you deserved for your greed," said Little Rabbit. "I am on my way to kill Sun." He went on, uttering war cries.

The day after, Little Rabbit saw two women making willow baskets lined with pitch. He was still a good way off, but he heard them talking, for he had a wonderful ear. He heard them saying: "Here comes that no-good Rabbit. Let's kill him."

He went up to them and said: "What were you talking about?"

"Oh, we were only saying: 'Here comes that good-looking grandson of ours.'"

"Is that so? Well, let's see whether I can fit into one of your water baskets." He got in. "Now braid the neck," he told them.

"Gladly," they said. They wove the basket's neck really small, thinking: "Now he's trapped. He can't get out." But with his magic breath Little Rabbit burst the basket open, and stood there smiling. "You must surely be a ghost," said the women.

"I am no ghost," he said, "just a common little no-account Rabbit. But why do you wonder? Don't you know that such a basket can hold water, but never a human being?"

"You are smart and know everything," said the women.

"Try it out for yourselves," he told them. They jumped into baskets lined with pitch and got stuck. "Why don't you jump out?" he taunted them. Then he rolled them around, and kicked them about, and made fun of them. Finally he killed them with his magic ball. "I am getting better and better at this killing business," said Little Rabbit. "I am going to fight Sun." He uttered a war cry and went on.

The next day Little Rabbit came upon Kwiats, the Great Bear. Kwiats was digging in the ground, making a huge hole. "What are you doing?" asked Little Rabbit.

"Brother, I am digging a hole so that I can hide myself from Little Rabbit, the Great Slayer of all who stand in his way."

"What a coincidence," exclaimed Little Rabbit, "I am trying to hide myself from this same terrible killer. Let us dig together." While Kwiats scooped out huge amounts of earth, Little Rabbit quickly made himself a secret passage out of this den. He slipped out. After a while, Kwiats wondered where his companion had gone. "I wonder where the little fellow is at?" Kwiats grumbled. He found the secret passage all the way to the exit, but he could not get through because he was much too big. He could only squeeze his head through. At the exit Little Rabbit was waiting. He shattered Kwiats's skull with his magic ball. "I am really getting the hang of it now," said Little Rabbit. "Now I go on to fight Sun." He uttered a war whoop and continued his journey.

Next, Little Rabbit came across Tarantula. Tarantula was very smart.

He had already heard about Little Rabbit and his deeds. Tarantula had a magic club that could not hurt him, but could hurt others. "I shall be using it to kill Little Rabbit," Tarantula said to himself. Aloud he said: "Brother, I have a terrific headache. It is caused by an evil spirit inside my skull. Please beat it out of me with this club."

Little Rabbit pounded Tarantula's head with the club but could not hurt him. Little Rabbit was smarter than Tarantula. He figured out what Tarantula was up to. He quickly exchanged the club for his magic ball and with it pounded Tarantula's head to bits. "I am on my way to kill Sun," Little Rabbit cried. "Now I know I can do it!" He uttered his piercing war cry.

Little Rabbit came to the edge of the world in the east. He was careful not to fall over the edge into bottomless nothingness. He waited for Sun to come up. As soon as Sun did, Little Rabbit shattered his face into a thousand fragments. They were scattered all over the world, setting the earth on fire. The flames burned Little Rabbit's toes, then his legs, body, and arms, until only his head was left. It rolled on all by itself until the terrible heat burst his swollen eyes, which exploded in a flood of tears that covered the whole earth and put out the fire. It took a long time until Sun and Little Rabbit had re-created themselves. "It seems killing is not the answer," said Little Rabbit.

THE LONG BLACK STRANGER

{*Omaha*}

Rabbit lived alone in his tipi—alone except for his grandmother. Every morning Rabbit went out to hunt with his bow and arrows and always someone long and black followed his footstep. Whenever Rabbit looked back, the long black one was there. Rabbit could not shake him. It seemed as if he were stuck to Rabbit's heels.

Rabbit was scared of whoever was following. He said to himself: "I will get up very early, before that long, black fellow." But it was no use. The stranger kept dogging his trail. This went on day after day. Rabbit was angry. One evening, after he came home, he made himself a snare out of his bowstring.

"Why are you doing this?" his grandmother asked.

"Because someone is always following me," Rabbit answered. "I am fed up with this. I will trap him." He put the snare along his footprints.

In the morning, when Rabbit checked his snare, he saw that he had caught something. It was blindingly bright and very hot. He ran back to his tipi. "Grandmother," he said, "I have caught something terribly bright and scorching. I am afraid of it. But I want to get my bowstring back." He took his knife and went to where his snare was.

The thing he had caught in his trap was very angry. It shouted: "You no-good fellow, how dare you set a snare for me? Cut me loose at once or I'll burn you to ashes!"

Rabbit wanted to obey but was afraid to come too near. The thing was so hot that already the grass around it was smoldering. "Who are you?" Rabbit asked.

"They call me Sun," the glowing thing answered. "Why do you keep standing there with your mouth open? Miserable oaf, use your knife to cut me loose. Hurry!"

Rabbit crept near to the thing on his belly, stretching his arm, holding the knife as far out as he could. Quickly he cut the bowstring. At once Sun rose into the sky and lit up the world. Of course, the

somebody who had followed his footsteps had been his own shadow. Coming so near to Sun, Rabbit had been burned between his shoulder blades. Ever since then he has a dark, reddish spot there.

WHY THE POSSUM'S TAIL IS BARE

{Cherokee}

The Possum used to have a long, bushy tail, and was so proud of it that he combed it out every morning and sang about it at the dance, until the Rabbit, who had had no tail since the Bear pulled it out, became very jealous and made up his mind to play the Possum a trick.

There was to be a great council and a dance at which all the animals were to be present. It was the Rabbit's business to send out the news, so as he was passing the Possum's place he stopped to ask him if he intended to be there. The Possum said he would come if he could have a special seat, "because I have such a handsome tail that I ought to sit where everybody can see me." The Rabbit promised to attend to it and to send someone besides to comb and dress the Possum's tail for the dance, so the Possum was very much pleased and agreed to come.

Then the Rabbit went over to the Cricket, who is such an expert hair cutter that the Indians call him the barber, and told him to go next morning and dress the Possum's tail for the dance that night. He told the Cricket just what to do and then went on about some other mischief.

In the morning the Cricket went to the Possum's house and said he had come to get him ready for the dance. So the Possum stretched himself out and shut his eyes while the Cricket combed out his tail and wrapped a red string around it to keep it smooth until night. But all this time, as he wound the string around, he was clipping off the hair close to the roots, and Possum never knew it.

When it was night the Possum went to the lodge where the dance was to be and found the best seat ready for him, just as the Rabbit had promised. When his turn came in the dance he loosened the string from his tail and stepped into the middle of the floor. The drummers began to drum and the Possum began to sing, "See my beautiful tail." Everybody shouted, and he danced around the circle and sang again, "See what a fine color it has." They shouted again, and he danced around another time, singing, "See how it sweeps the ground." The animals shouted more loudly than ever, and the Possum was delighted. He danced around again and sang, "See how fine the fur is."

Then everybody laughed so long that the Possum wondered what they meant. He looked around the circle of animals and they were all laughing at him. Then he looked down at his beautiful tail and saw that there was not a hair left upon it, but that it was as bare as the tail of a lizard. He was so much astonished and ashamed that he could not say a word, but rolled over helpless on the ground and grinned, as the Possum does to this day when taken by surprise.

RABBIT ESCAPES FROM THE BOX

{Creek}

The Rabbit had so often deceived mankind that a council was held to try him and, being found guilty, he was condemned to death by drowning. A box was made and he was put into it, carried to the banks of a stream, and left there for a while. A little child came to the box during the absence of the people and, discovering the Rabbit, asked him what he was doing there.

"Oh, I am listening to the sweetest music in the world," said he.

"Let me get in there, too," begged the child. So the Rabbit told the child how to open the box, and once Rabbit was out and the child was fastened in, away he ran into the forest.

When the people returned they lifted the box and threw it into the stream and said: "There, we will never be troubled by the Rabbit again." The next busk came, when every criminal is free to return, and hardly had the dancing ground been swept clean when in jumped the

Rabbit, all dressed in red, and danced with the pretty girls, while all the people stood amazed.

"Did we not drown him?" they said. "We put him in a box and threw him into the water, yet here he is."

Asked how he came back, the Rabbit replied: "I am glad you threw me into the water. I did not die, I went to a beautiful place, where there were thousands of pretty girls who begged me to stay, and I am now sorry I came away from them." The young warriors crowded around him and did not tire of hearing about such a lovely land. They begged him to show them the way, and he selected those he most envied and told them to prepare boxes in which they could be placed. When all were ready, their friends carried them to the stream and the Rabbit ordered them thrown in.

Again the busk rolled around and anxious friends awaited the return of the young warriors, but they did not come. At last the boxes were found on an island and in the boxes were the bodies of the ill-fated young men. A little box was also found containing the bones of the child. Then it was known that the Rabbit had deceived them again. On being questioned, he said: "I told you I was the only one who had ever returned from that beautiful country. I warned the warriors, but they would have me show them the way, and no one can be blamed except themselves."

RABBIT AND POSSUM ON THE PROWL

{Cherokee}

■

The Rabbit and the Possum each wanted a wife, but no one would marry either of them. They talked over the matter and the Rabbit said, "We can't get wives here; let's go to the next settlement. I'm the messenger for the council, and I'll tell the people that I bring an order that everybody must take a mate at once, and then we'll be sure to get our wives."

The Possum thought this a fine plan, so they started off together for the next town. As the Rabbit traveled faster, he got there first and waited outside until the people noticed him and took him into their home. When the chief came to ask his business, the Rabbit said he brought an important order from the council that everybody must get married without delay. So the chief called the people together and told them the message from the council. Every animal took a mate at once, and the Rabbit got a wife.

The Possum traveled so slowly that he got there after all the animals had mated, leaving him still without a wife. The Rabbit pretended to feel sorry for him and said, "Never mind, I'll carry the message to the people in the next settlement, and you hurry on as fast as you can, and this time you will get your wife."

So he went on to the next town, and the Possum followed close after him. But when the Rabbit got to the town he sent out the word that, as there had been peace so long that everybody was getting lazy, the council had ordered that there must be war at once and they must begin right in the town. So they all began fighting, but the Rabbit made four

great leaps and got away just as the Possum came in. Everybody jumped on the Possum, who had not thought of bringing his weapons on a wedding trip and so could not defend himself. They had nearly beaten the life out of him when he fell over and pretended to be dead until he saw a good chance to jump up and get away. The Possum never got a wife, but he remembers the lesson, and ever since, he shuts his eyes and pretends to be dead when the hunter has him in a close corner.

TAR BABY

{*Biloxi*}

The Rabbit and the Frenchman were two friends. The Rabbit aided the Frenchman, agreeing to work a piece of land on shares. The first season they planted potatoes. The Rabbit, having been told to select his share of the crop, chose the potato vines, and devoured them all. The next season they planted corn. This year the Rabbit said, "I will eat the roots." So he pulled up all the corn by the roots, but he found nothing to satisfy his hunger."

Then the Frenchman said, "Let us dig a well."

But the Rabbit did not wish to work any longer with his friend. Said he to the Frenchman, "If you wish to dig a well, I shall not help you."

"Oho," said the Frenchman, "you shall not drink any of the water from the well."

"That does not matter," replied the Rabbit. "I am accustomed to licking the dew from the ground."

The Frenchman, suspecting mischief, made a tar baby, which he stood up close to the well. The Rabbit approached the well, carrying a long piece of cane and a tin bucket. On reaching the well, he addressed the tar baby, who remained silent. "Friend, what is the matter? Are you angry?" said the Rabbit. Still the tar baby said nothing. So the Rabbit hit him with one forepaw, which stuck there. "Let me go or I will hit you on the other side," exclaimed the Rabbit. And when he found that the tar baby paid no attention to him, he hit him with his other forepaw, which stuck to the tar baby. "I will kick you," said the Rabbit. But when he kicked the tar baby, the hind foot stuck. "I will kick you with the other foot," said the Rabbit. And when he did so, that foot, too, stuck to the tar baby. Then the Rabbit resembled a ball, because his feet were sticking to the tar baby, and he could neither stand nor recline.

Just at this time the Frenchman approached. He tied the legs of the Rabbit together, laid him down, and scolded him. Then the Rabbit pretended to be in great fear of a brier patch. "As you are in such fear of a brier patch," said the Frenchman, "I will throw you into one."

"Oh, no," replied the Rabbit.

"I will throw you into the brier patch," responded the Frenchman.

"I am much afraid of it," said the Rabbit.

"As you are in such dread of it," said the Frenchman, "I will throw you into it." So he seized the Rabbit, and threw him into the brier patch.

The Rabbit fell at some distance from the Frenchman. But instead of being injured, he sprang up and ran off laughing at the trick that he had played on the Frenchman.

DON'T BELIEVE WHAT PEOPLE TELL YOU

{*San Ildefonso or San Juan*}

One day Rabbit Boy was nibbling on some nice green plants. He was so busy nibbling that he did not notice Fox Man creeping up on him. Fox Man grinned at Rabbit Boy. "What a coincidence. I was just thinking how nice it would be to have a fine, fat, juicy rabbit for dinner, and here you are. This is my lucky day."

Fox was about to leap upon Rabbit Boy and eat him up, but Rabbit Boy stopped him. "Wait a minute, friend, not so fast. Don't you know that it is very unhealthy to eat rabbits without having a drink of water first?"

"I guess I forgot it," said the Fox Man. "Thanks for reminding me."

"The brook is right over here," said Rabbit Boy.

While Fox Man was slurping up water, Rabbit Boy quickly picked up a big round stone, as heavy as he could lift it. Fox Man had just about finished drinking, but before he could turn around, Rabbit Boy told him: "Dear friend, if you close your eyes and open your mouth wide, I'll jump right in and save you the trouble of bending over and picking me up."

"You are really very considerate," said Fox. "I am almost sorry for making a meal of you, but as you know, one has to eat."

"Certainly, one has to eat," said Rabbit Boy.

Fox Man was sitting up, his eyes closed and his mouth wide open, waiting for his treat, and Rabbit Boy threw the big round stone down Fox Man's throat. The stone knocked out all of Fox Man's teeth. The stone was stuck in his throat. Fox Man was choking, sputtering, struggling, trying to cough up the stone.

"You don't have to always believe what people tell you, such as it being unhealthy to eat rabbits without drinking water first," said Rabbit Boy as he was running away.

PART TEN

NANABOZHO AND WHISKEY JACK

NANABOZHO AND THE FISH CHIEF

{*Great Lakes Tribes*}

Nokomis was Nanabozho's grandmother. "Grandson," she said, "my hair is falling out because I have no oil to preserve it. The oil that your dead grandfather had given me has run out. I want you to get me some oil for my hair."

"Grandmother," said Nanabozho, "where can I get this oil?"

"You must go to the Great Lake in the North. This lake is the home of Meshena-Magwai, the Chief of All Fish. Go and kill him. Bring him to me. Then we will boil enough oil from his body to last to the end of time."

"Grandmother," said Nanabozho, "you make the fish line and the fishhook. I shall make the canoe."

Nanabozho went to a lonely place on top of a hill. There he stayed for four days and nights, fasting and praying to Gitchee Manitou, the Everywhere Spirit, to bless his enterprise with success. Then he made his canoe out of birch bark. He made the paddle from oak. It took a whole big oak

tree to make it. Then his Nokomis gave him the fish line and the fish-hook. Then Nanabozho set out on the river that led to the Great Lake.

Nanabozho paddled out into the middle of the Great Lake. He threw out the line and the baited hook. In a loud voice he called out: "Meshena-Magwai, Chief of All Fish, take my bait!"

Way down at the bottom of the lake, the Chief of All Fish heard him. He told Trout: "Swim up and see who it is who dares to call me in this manner."

Up on the surface, Nanabozho felt someone immensely strong tugging at his line. "It must be Meshena-Magwai," he thought, "the Chief of All Fish. No one else could do such tugging." Trout had taken the bait. He pulled at the line with such force that Nanabozho's canoe was pulled halfway down, standing upright. Nanabozho was stronger than Trout. He managed to drag him into his canoe. He looked at Trout. He said: "You ugly, puny thing, you are not the Chief of All Fish. I think Meshena-Magwai is afraid to come up and fight me."

Trout was angry to be called "puny" and "ugly." He dove down to the bottom of the Great Lake and told the Chief of All Fish: "It is Nanabozho who is up there. He has no manners. He called me bad names. He says you are afraid to come up and face him."

The Great Chief of All Fish said: "Is that so?" He called the Giant Pike. "Nephew, go up there and teach Nanabozho some manners."

Giant Pike swam to the surface. He heard Nanabozho shouting: "Meshena-Magwai, Chief of All Fish, take my bait."

In his canoe Nanabozho felt a tugging at his line. The pull was so strong that it made the canoe swirl around in circles, again and again. It made the whole Great Lake foam and swirl. The waters rushed about Nanabozho's canoe in dizzying circles, making it spin wildly around its own axis. The waves formed an eddy that almost sucked Nanabozho and his canoe down to the lake bottom. But Nanabozho was mighty above all others. He succeeded in pulling Giant Pike into his canoe, though it took all his enormous strength.

When Nanabozho saw what he had caught, he was disgusted. "You insignificant, slimy thing," he shouted. "You are not the great Chief of All Fish. Is Meshena-Magwai trembling in fear of me? Is that the reason he does not come up to face me?" With a mighty heave, Nanabozho flung Giant Pike back into the water.

Giant Pike at once dove straight down to the bottom of the lake, telling the Chief of All Fish: "Nanabozho says that you, O Great Chief, are afraid of him. He insulted me, calling me 'slimy' and 'insignificant.' Will you let him get away with this?"

"I guess I must take care of this matter myself," said the Great Chief of All Fish, and he began slowly to rise to the surface.

Way above, Nanabozho was shouting: "Great Chief of All Fish, take my bait."

Meshena-Magwai broke the surface, making a huge wave that made the lake overflow in all directions, covering the whole country around about with man-high water. He made the waters boil. The Great Chief of All Fish was so big that there was no word that could describe this bigness. With one mighty gulp, Meshena-Magwai swallowed up Nanabozho, canoe, paddle, and all.

Inside Meshena-Magwai's body it was dark. Nanabozho heard a loud, reverberating *thump, thump, thump*. It echoed from the walls, which were the lining of Meshena-Magwai's stomach. Every thump shook his body like an earthquake. Nanabozho discovered that this great thumping came from the heart of the Great Chief of All Fish. Nanabozho had a war club dangling from his belt. He never went anywhere without it. He took the club and used it to beat the giant heart. After he had done this for a while, the heartbeat got weaker and weaker. At last it stopped altogether. Meshena-Magwai, the Great Chief of All Fish, was dead. Nanabozho had killed him by hitting his heart with the war club. The waves carried Meshena-Magwai's body to the shore. It was lying on the sand.

Nanabozho had won his battle, but Meshena-Magwai's mouth was clamped shut. Nanabozho found himself trapped in the Great Chief of All Fish's body. What was he to do? "Maybe I shall die in here," said Nanabozho. "Maybe I shall die of starvation." Then he heard a faint gnawing sound. It was made by a Squirrel that tried to make a hole through the Chief of All Fish's side. Nanabozho did not know how Squirrel had gotten inside the Fish Chief's body. It turned out that Squirrel was not strong enough to bore its way through to the outside. Then Nanabozho shouted loudly—so loud that it made the earth tremble: "This is Nanabozho, calling from within Fish Chief's body. If there is a friend of mine about on the outside, let him help me to get out!"

There was a scratching outside, on Meshena-Magwai's skin. It grew louder and louder. The squirrel continued to gnaw from the inside of the Great Chief of All Fish. From the outside, someone tried to scratch his way in. Finally the squirrel's teeth met the claws of a Seagull. They had made a hole in the Great Chief of All Fish's side. Squirrel and Seagull widened the hole until it was big enough to let Nanabozho squeeze through with his canoe. For their help, Nanabozho gave his two rescuers honoring names. He named Squirrel "Little Mighty Gnawer." He named Seagull "Winged Mighty Scratcher."

Nanabozho took leave of his two helpers. He tied the body of the Great Chief of All Fish to his canoe and paddled upriver to the home of Nokomis, his grandmother. He and Nokomis cut up Meshena-Magwai's body and boiled it down to oil. They got so much oil that it formed a whole lake of oil, enough to treat the hair of every woman to the end of time.

 ## WHY WE HAVE TO WORK SO HARD MAKING MAPLE SUGAR

{*Menomini*}

When Manabush came home empty-handed from a hunting trip, his grandmother, Nokomis, told him: "Go into the woods and collect birch bark for me. I am going to make sugar."

Manabush did not know what she meant. He did not know what sugar was. Nobody did. He collected birch bark, which Nokomis stitched together into cups. Nokomis then went from maple tree to maple tree, cutting a small hole into the trunk of each and putting into every hole a small stick over which the sap ran down into the birch-bark cups fastened below.

Manabush went from tree to tree, looked into the cups, and saw that they were full of maple syrup. He stuck his finger into the syrup and licked it. The syrup was sweet. Manabush said: "I never knew that anything so good existed." There were many maples and many birch-bark cups and all were full of thick, sweet syrup. In this way maple sugar came about.

Manabush told Nokomis: "Grandmother, this maple sugar is wonderful, but the making of it is too easy. The syrup makes itself. No effort is needed to produce it. People will become too lazy to do any work. They will just sit on their haunches and eat maple syrup. This won't do."

Manabush climbed to the top of one of the trees and sprinkled water over it. This made the syrup into thin sap, which dribbled down into the cups drop by drop. Thus Manabush made sugaring hard work. Wood must be cut, birch bark must be collected and stitched into cups, the sap must be collected, and it must be boiled down into maple sugar for a long time. This way nobody would be idle. Would it have been better to make sugaring easy, the way Nokomis did at first? Who knows?

 # WHO IS LOOKING ME IN THE FACE?

{*Menomini*}

Nanabozho was walking along. On the way he met Buzzard. They stopped to chat. "Brother, I envy you," said Nanabozho. "You can fly, while I have to remain always down here on the ground. How I wish to be able to soar up into the sky, as you do. How I wish to be able to view the earth from high up among the clouds."

"Yes, it is wonderful to be able to fly," said Buzzard. "I pity you because you cannot do it."

"Brother, why don't you let me climb on your back?" begged Nanabozho. "Then you could take me with you up into the sky. Then I, too, could view the world from above."

"What a good idea!" Buzzard agreed. "I will take you up there with me so that you can enjoy flying as I do, looking down at forests and mountains, valleys and hills, with all the animals moving about, everything spread out before you, to feast your eyes at the wonders below."

Nanabozho climbed eagerly upon Buzzard's back but noted that it was very smooth—too smooth, maybe. "The feathers on your back are

----

very slick, brother," Nanabozho told Buzzard. "I'm afraid to lose my grip and slide off you, falling to my death."

"Don't worry, brother," Buzzard reassured Nanabozho, "just hold on. There's nothing to it. I won't let you fall."

"Will you fly smoothly and evenly, without too much flapping of wings, without banking and jerking, without going too fast?"

"Trust me, brother," said Buzzard. "Stop worrying. I will fly very slowly and carefully. I won't show off, tumbling and diving and swooping. You won't slide off my back." But secretly Buzzard planned to play a trick upon Nanabozho.

Buzzard carried Nanabozho aloft, way up into the sky. At first he flew straight, without any sudden movements or fits and starts, letting Nanabozho enjoy the flight. "This is wonderful, brother," said Nanabozho. "I thank you for letting me experience this." Nanabozho's enjoyment did not last long. Suddenly, without warning, Buzzard swept the sky in dizzying circles, banking steeply to left and right, spiraling upward and downward at ever-increasing speeds, tumbling wildly toward the earth below.

Nanabozho could not hold on. He fell off Buzzard's back and plummeted straight down, crashing headfirst into the ground. The fall knocked Nanabozho senseless.

When he came to, the first thing Nanabozho noticed was a kindly-looking fellow with plump cheeks looking him in the face. "Who can this be?" he thought. "I don't know him." Then he discovered that the kindly-looking fellow was his own buttocks, because he was lying there all doubled up. He heard somebody laughing high above him. It was Buzzard, mightily pleased with the trick he had played on Nanabozho.

Still weak and addled by his fall, Nanabozho managed to unscramble himself and get on his feet. He limped away into the forest. "Buzzard has treated me badly," he said to himself. "I will repay him in kind. The joke will be on him."

Buzzard is a scavenger. If anything dead is lying somewhere, Buzzard will come and gobble it up. He loves carrion. Because of this Nanabozho transformed himself into the rotting carcass of a deer, lying in a place where it could be seen from far off. Nanabozho had the power to assume any shape he wanted. So he was lying there. Soon all the flying, creeping, crawling, and hopping carrion eaters came to feast on the dead deer—wolverines, crows, magpies, turkey vultures, and such like.

Flying high above, Buzzard saw all these scavengers converging upon the same spot. "There must be something good to eat there," he thought. He flew a little lower. He saw the deer. "I must get my share of it," he said to himself. "I must get it while something is left." He swooped down. He squeezed himself through the crowd of the other dead-meat eaters. But then he stopped. He was thinking: "Nanabozho is so clever. He has the power of transforming himself. Could he have turned himself into this dead deer in order to play a trick on me? Could he deceive me in this way as part of a scheme to avenge himself?"

Buzzard was hopping around, very close to the dead deer's body. The rotting meat smelled delicious to him. He longed to sink his crooked beak into the bloody, oozing carcass. "This surely is a dead animal," he assured himself. "Even Nanabozho could not fake this enticing stench. Even he could not manage to change himself into this putrid mass. No, this is the real thing; it can't be Nanabozho. I shall help myself to some of this meat. It is ripe, just as I like it."

Buzzard plucked out one of the deer's eyes. "Ah, how good this tastes!" he croaked. The deer's mouth was wide open. Buzzard stuck his head deep into it, pecking at the tongue. Suddenly the deer's jaws snapped shut. Buzzard's head was caught between the teeth. The deer had come alive again. It was Nanabozho.

"How are you, friend?" said Nanabozho, talking through his teeth. "Why don't you try to pull your head out of my mouth? Is this not a great and convincing disguise? I fooled even a smart fellow like you."

Buzzard pulled and pulled, but could not free his head, which was held as by a vise. He struggled for a very long time. Finally, Nanabozho opened his jaws just a tiny bit, so that, with one great effort, Buzzard could yank his head out, but not without stripping all the feathers from his head and neck.

"That's for throwing me off your back, friend," said Nanabozho, assuming his real form. "And for playing that trick upon me you shall be forever bald, and you shall stink always on account of the food you eat, so that everybody shall shun your company." And so it has been ever since—Buzzard has remained bald. His once beautiful head feathers are gone for good. His scrawny neck is ugly, red, and shriveled. He smells so bad that nobody can stand to be around him. Nanabozho went away laughing.

WHY WOMEN HAVE
THEIR MOON-TIME

{*Menomini*}

Manabush went out every day to hunt. When he came home one evening he found Nokomis sitting on her mat in her finest decorated deerskin dress, wearing a necklace and earrings made from pieces of seashells, her hair neatly combed and braided. He had never seen her in such a splendid state before. He asked her: "Grandmother, you are all dressed up. Did you entertain a visitor?"

"Who would visit me?" said Nokomis.

Manabush said to himself: "Someone has been seeing her, but she does not want me to know it."

The next day Manabush went out again to hunt with his bow and arrows, and when he returned, Manabush once again found Nokomis sitting on her mat in all her finery, wearing her best leggings and finest quill-decorated moccasins. And again Nokomis's hair had been neatly combed, and the partition, where her hair parted, had been painted vermilion red. Manabush thought: "Somebody surely must have been here to see Nokomis." Aloud he said: "Grandmother, has somebody been here to see you?"

"Who would come to see me?" said Nokomis.

On the third day Manabush went into the forest as usual and upon coming home again found Nokomis sitting on her mat, all dressed up. This time he did not bother to ask Nokomis whether she had entertained a visitor. He said nothing.

On the fourth day Manabush went out as always, but he only pretended to go hunting. He came right back and, from behind a tree, watched the wigwam. Soon he heard somebody crashing through the bushes, making a great noise, grunting and snorting. Presently the maker of all that racket appeared from among the trees. It was Bear. He was huge and he waddled straight to the wigwam and went in. Manabush waited for a little while and then lit up the end of a piece of birch bark until it was burning. He crept up to the wigwam, pushed aside the entrance cover, and looked inside. He saw Bear making love to Nokomis.

Manabush took his firebrand and thrusted it between Bear's legs. Bear howled with pain. His fur caught fire. Growling ferociously, Bear tore open the wigwam's side and burst through it. Howling, he ran off into the forest. Manabush ran after him with his bow and arrows. He caught up with Bear. He shot arrow after arrow into Bear's body. One of them pierced his heart. Bear died.

Manabush dragged Bear's body back to his wigwam. He threw it at Nokomis's feet, saying: "Here, Grandmother, I have killed a bear. Now we shall feast on bear meat."

"How did you kill him?" asked Nokomis.

"With my arrows," answered Manabush.

He cut up Bear, roasted the meat, and offered a piece to Nokomis. "No, no!" cried Nokomis, horrified. "That was my husband and lover. I cannot eat it."

Manabush then picked up a clot of Bear's blood and flung it between Nokomis's legs, crying: "Take this!"

Nokomis said: "Grandson, on account of what you have just done, from now on, all women will always have trouble every moon, and every moon will bring forth clots of blood like this one." And so it has been ever since.

 ## WHISKEY JACK WANTS TO FLY

{Cree and Métis}

Wesakaychak, Whiskey Jack, was sitting on a hilltop watching a flock of geese splashing in a lake or flying above it. They soared and dipped, honking loudly, having a good time. Wesakaychak watched their graceful movements and effortless winging across the sky. He said to himself: "Why should these geese have the power to do this, and I do not have it? I want to be able to fly like those birds. I deserve to have this power."

Wesakaychak went down to the lake, calling to the geese: "Little brothers, come over here! I have something to discuss with you."

"Oh, no," said the geese. "We know you. You're the one they call Whiskey Jack. You are the one who tricked us before. We'll keep our distance, because all you want is to knock us dead, pluck us, and eat us."

"No, no, no!" protested Wesakaychak. "You got me wrong. I'd never do such a thing. I love you as my little brothers. Trust me."

Finally the biggest, bravest gander went over to Wesakaychak. "All right, what do you want to discuss?"

"My little brother," said Wesakaychak, "I have put things to rights down here on earth. I killed the harmful animals who ate up all the others, I protected the weak. I brought order into the world down here. So now I have time to attend to the sky and to all who fly in the clouds. I want to do good things for you. If you lend me a pair of wings, I shall fly around and see whether there are any problems to be fixed."

The geese talked this over among themselves. Then the gander told Wesakaychak: "Elder brother, if you really mean to do good things for us, I guess we can lend you a pair of wings, but you have to be very careful. Flying is dangerous, even for those who are born to it. You must not be foolhardy but fly with caution."

"I will be careful," Wesakaychak promised.

The geese gave him an extra-large pair of wings. "Do not use them at once," they warned him. "Wait four days and nights until the wings

have grown solidly to your shoulders. Do not try to fly until four days have passed."

"I promise," said Wesakaychak. "I'll do as you say. These wings are sacred to me. Thanks, little brothers, for lending me a little bit of your power."

Wesakaychak could not curb his impatience to fly at once. He could not wait. He took off right away. He soared up into the sky, crying loudly like a goose: "Honk, honk!" He flew up and down, delirious with joy, and then one of his wings broke off and he tumbled headfirst into the lake. He almost drowned. He looked very bedraggled as he scrambled out of the water.

"That's Whiskey Jack for you!" said all who saw it.

The geese were very angry. They scolded Wesakaychak for his rashness. "I will be good from now on," said Wesakaychak, "I will behave myself. Only give me another pair of wings." He begged so earnestly that the geese relented and gave him a new pair of wings.

"Well," said the geese, "we have eaten all the fish, minnows, frogs, and toads around here. We must fly to another lake for food." The geese flew away in their usual arrow-point-shaped formation, honking loudly and merrily.

Wesakaychak flew at their head, crying, "Honk, honk!" as if he were a gander.

They saw a camp with people in the distance. "Don't fly near there," the geese warned him. "These people are dangerous. They are hunters. They would like nothing better than having roast goose for dinner." Wesakaychak paid no attention to them. He wanted to show off. He swooped down low over the camp, honking mightily. The people came running out of their wigwams, crying: "Geese, geese, enough to feed the whole village!" They shot their arrows at Wesakaychak and at the flock of geese.

The geese were honking: "Oh, my, oh, my, Wesakaychak, what have you done? You put all our lives in danger!"

"Don't make a fuss over nothing!" Wesakaychak shouted back. Just then an arrow hit one of his wings and broke it off. Wesakaychak fell to the ground. He fell hard. He was all shook up. The people came running, yelling: "Let's get that goose. Let's have a feast!" But then they saw who it was. "It's only that fool, Whiskey Jack," they told each other, "playing another one of his silly pranks. Will he never learn?"

This time the geese gave Wesakaychak a tremendous tongue-lashing. "You are not worthy to fly," they told him. "No more wings for the likes of you!"

Wesakaychak fell to his knees. "Have pity, little brothers," he wailed. "I'll never disobey you again! Give me another chance. Let me have another pair of wings." Wesakaychak wept a flood of tears.

The good-natured geese felt pity for him. They gave him a new pair of wings. "Use them wisely this time," they admonished him.

"I will. I will," promised Wesakaychak.

The geese had eaten up everything edible in their new location. "We must fly on to find more food," they said. They flew on, Wesakaychak in the lead, crying: "Honk, honk!" They were flying over some woods. There was a big forest fire.

"Don't fly near it," cried the geese, "or you'll be burned!"

"It's cold up here," Wesakaychak shouted back. "I'll just fly down to warm myself a little." He swooped down. He got too close to the fire. His wings burned up and he fell down all the way amid the burning trees. He almost burned to death. He was badly singed. He barely escaped the flames. There were some people living near that place. They hurried to see the big bird that had fallen from the sky. They saw that it was Wesakaychak. They were disappointed. "It's only that half-wit, Whiskey Jack," they said, "up to his old foolish tricks again. This dunderhead plays at being a bird. What will it be next?"

Wesakaychak hurt all over. His skin was blistered and hanging in shreds where the flames had reached it. "One more chance, little brothers!" he cried, before the geese had a chance to say anything. "Just one more chance. I'll be good from now on." He carried on so much, weeping and wailing, that the geese gave him a fourth pair of wings.

"But this is the last time," they told him. "If you mess up again, there will be no more wings!"

"I won't mess up. I won't mess up!" cried Wesakaychak.

The geese had eaten up all the fingerlings, pollywogs, worms, grubs, and caterpillars they could find in their new place. "We must fly to another lake to find food," they said.

They flew on with Wesakaychak in the lead. He was crying: "Honk, honk!"

They came to an inlet of the sea. There was a giant clam lying on the beach. The geese warned Wesakaychak: "Don't fly close to that clam. It is big and wicked. It could swallow you up."

"I'll be careful," Wesakaychak answered. But he was curious and flew down to the clam to look it over. "What can that clam do to me?" He thought. "It can't move, but I can fly." He flew too close to the giant clam and it snapped him up. Luckily, Wesakaychak had his strike-a-light, his steel, flint, and tinderbox. He lit a fire inside the clam, which got burned and opened up so that Wesakaychak could jump out. His hair was singed, his clothes burned.

When the people saw him like that they laughed at him, saying: "There goes that fool Whiskey Jack, who got himself snapped up by a clam!"

"I guess I was not meant to fly," said Wesakaychak as he staggered off. "From now on I walk."

WESAKAYCHAK, THE WINDIGO, AND THE ERMINE

{Cree and Métis}

There lives a fearful creature in the northern woods called Windigo. Some of the Métis call him the Loup-Garou. He lives on human flesh. He devours people. The Windigo's scream is so fearful that it paralyzes and renders helpless all who hear it. Nobody knows exactly what the Windigo looks like because those who have the misfortune to encounter him are instantly killed and eaten.

Wesakaychak was wandering through the forest one day when he suddenly found himself face-to-face with the Windigo. He was numb with fear. He was unable to move. He trembled. His teeth chattered. He thought: "This is the end of me." But he made up his mind to try outwitting the Windigo. He addressed the terrifying creature: "Elder brother, I am glad to see you. I always wanted to meet you." "Likewise," said the Windigo, grinning, baring his huge fangs and smacking his lips. "I, too, am glad to meet you. Hurry up, little fellow, and make a fire. I am hungry and I want to cook."

"There is no food here to be cooked," said Wesakaychak.

"Don't worry, there will be," said the Windigo, with his wolfish grin. "Hurry up, collect wood, make a good, hot fire!"

Wesakaychak gathered wood, very slowly, stick by stick. "How can I escape winding up in this monster's stomach?" he thought. He was desperate. At this moment he saw an Ermine coming along. Ermine was small. He had dark fur that blended in with the ground. The Windigo did not see him. "Friend, friend, come here," whispered Wesakaychak. "Save me. The Windigo is going to kill me and gobble me up. If you help me, I'll make you into the most beautiful animal in the world."

"How can I help?" asked Ermine.

"When the Windigo opens his mouth," Wesakaychak told him, "jump into it; jump down his throat. Compared to him, you are so tiny, he won't even notice it. Little brother, once you are inside, you'll find a big red round thing pumping away—thud, thud, thud. That is the Windigo's heart. You have such fine, sharp teeth, little friend, use them. Bite deep into the heart. Tear it to pieces!"

In the meantime the Windigo kept growling fearfully: "Hurry up with that fire! I am hungry!"

"I am working as fast as I can," said Wesakaychak, gathering wood as slowly as possible.

"You're stalling," the Windigo shouted, opening his mouth wide.

Ermine jumped in. Ermine is small, but fierce. He has the sharpest teeth in the world. He gnawed his way into the Windigo's heart; he bit deeply into it. The Windigo groaned, shuddered, and died. Ermine hopped out of the dead monster's mouth. He was covered with the Windigo's blood.

"Little friend," said Wesakaychak, jumping with joy and relief, "let me clean you up." He washed the blood out of Ermine's fur.

"Elder brother," Ermine reminded Wesakaychak, "you promised to make me beautiful."

"And so I shall," answered Wesakaychak. He took some white clay and used it to paint Ermine's body as white as snow. He left only a tiny bit of black around Ermine's eyes and at the tip of his tail, just to remind people of how Ermine had looked before Wesakaychak had beautified him. Ermine, his fur glistening like silver, was now the prettiest animal in the world.

"Thank you very much for doing this," he said to Wesakaychak.

"Oh, it was nothing, don't even mention it, little brother," answered Wesakaychak. "It was the reward for the small service you rendered me." Gracefully, his silvery body moving like a snake, Ermine went home.

Wesakaychak addressed the people: "Friends, behold me! It is entirely due to my courage and wisdom that you no longer have to be afraid of the terrible Windigo."

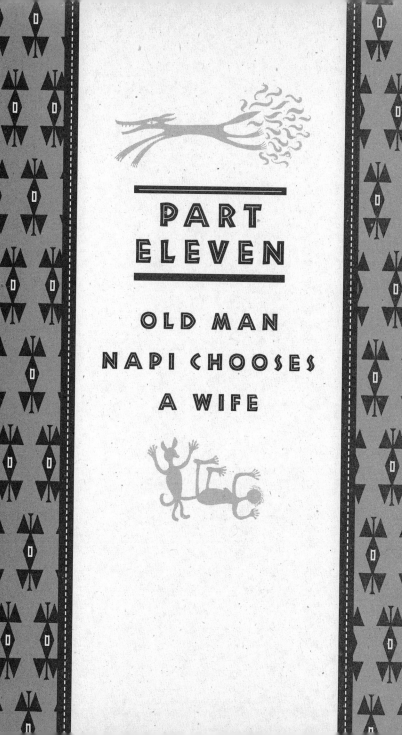

PART ELEVEN

OLD MAN NAPI CHOOSES A WIFE

CHOOSING MATES

{Blackfoot}

Having created the world, the animals, grass, trees, all life upon it, Old Man realized that by having men live by themselves, and women by themselves, he had made a mistake. He saw that they should live together. The camps of the two sexes were far apart: The women were living here at the foot of the mountains, in Cutbank Valley, and the men were away down on Two Medicine River. Each camp had a buffalo trap and subsisted wholly upon the buffalo that were decoyed into it.

As I have said, Old Man saw that he had made a mistake by keeping men and women apart. In fact, he found that he himself wanted a woman, so he went to the men and said: "You shall no longer live by

yourselves. Come! We will go up to the camp of the women, and each of us get one of them."

The men were more than glad to do that; it was what they had been hoping to do for a long time. So they hurried to put on their best clothes, and neatly braided their hair, and then started off with Old Man to the women's camp. When they came in sight of it, Old Man told them to stop right there and he would go ahead and plan with the women just what should be done. They sat down, and he went on to the women's camp. Himself he had no his old, soiled clothes; his fine clothes he had left behind with the men.

Arrived in the camp, he found only two or three women there; the women's chief and all the others were down at the buffalo trap, butchering the animals that they had that morning decoyed into it. When he told the few women that he found why he had come, he greatly excited and pleased them, and they started at once to run and tell the others to hurry up from the trap and meet the men.

"But wait. Not so fast. I want a word with you," Old Man called out; and when they came back to him, he asked: "What kind of a woman is your chief?"

"Everything that is good and kind and brave, that is our chief," one answered. And another said: "Ai! She is all that, and more; and she is the most beautiful woman of us all!"

This pleased Old Man. He said to himself: "That is the woman for me. I must have her." And to the waiting women he said: "It is right

that chief woman should mate with chief man. You women are to come to us, and each select the man you want. Now tell your chief woman that the chief man is brave and kind and handsome, and that she shall select him for her man. She will know him by the way he is dressed. He wears a buckskin shirt and leggings, embroidered with porcupine quills, and a cow-leather robe with a big porcupine-quill-embroidered sun in the center of it. You tell her to take him for her man!"

"We will do so!" the women cried, and started off for the buffalo trap as fast as they could run.

Old man hurried back to the waiting men and hurriedly put on his fine clothes, the ones he had described to the women.

Trembling with excitement, and out of breath from their long, swift run, Old Man's messengers arrived at the buffalo trap and told their wonderful news—that men had come to marry them; that each woman was to choose the man that she thought would best suit her. The butchering of the animals ceased at once, and the women started for their camp to put on their good clothes and recomb their hair. They wanted to appear as neat and clean and well dressed as possible before the men. Yes, all ran for their camp, all except the chief woman. Said she: "I cannot leave here until I finish skinning this spotted medicine calf. Go, all of you, and I will join you as soon as I can."

The work took more time than she thought would be required, and when she arrived in camp with the valuable skin, she found all the other women dressed and impatient to go and choose their men. "Oh, well, it doesn't matter how I look," she said. "I am a chief, I have a name; I can choose my man dressed just as I am. How did you say the man chief is dressed?"

They told her again what he wore, according to what Old Man had told them, and she said: "I'll choose him. Chief, I suppose, must mate with chief."

And so she went right with the others, wearing her butchering dress, all stiff with blood and grease from the neck down to the bottom of the skirt; and her moccasins were even more foul than the skirt. Her hands were caked with dry blood, and her hair was not even braided.

Their chief leading, the women approached the waiting men, all standing in a line and singing a song of greeting. Old Man stood at the head of the line, very straight and proud, and of fine appearance in his

new, porcupine-embroidered clothes. By these the chief woman recognized him from afar, and said to herself: "He is a fine-looking man. I hope that he will prove to be as good of heart as he is good to look at." And, leading her women, she walked straight up to him and laid a hand on his arm: "I will take you for my man," she told him.

But Old Man shrank back, his face plainly showing his loathing of such a bloody and greasy, wild-haired woman.

"I take you for my man," the woman chief repeated.

Then he broke away from her hold and ran behind his men: "No! No! I do not want you, bloody, greasy woman," he cried, and went still farther off behind his men.

The woman chief turned to her followers: "Go back! Go back to that little hill and there wait for me," she told them. And to the men she said: "Remain where you are until I return. I shall not be gone long." And with that she turned and hurried to her camp. Her women went to the hill. The men remained where they were.

Down at her camp the chief woman took off her old clothes and bathed in the river. Then she put on her fine clothes, a pair of new moccasins, braided her hair, scented herself with sweet grass, and returned to her women. She was now better dressed than any of them, and they told Old Man the truth when they said that she was beautiful of face and form; she was the most beautiful of them all.

Again she led her women to the line of waiting men. Again Old Man stood first, stood at the head of them. But she passed him by, as though she did not see him, and he, with a little cry, ran after her, took her by the arm, and said: "You are the woman for me! I am the chief of the men. You must take me!"

She turned upon him, and her eyes were like fire. She tore his hand from her arm and cried: "Never touch me again, good-for-nothing, proud-and-useless man. I would die before I would mate with you!"

And to her women she said: "Do not, any of you, take him for your man." And with that she turned and chose a man. The others, then, one by one, took their choice of the men. When all had chosen, there was one woman who had no man; all had been taken except Old Man. She would not have him, and became the second wife of one of the men.

The choosing over, all started for the women's camp. Old Man, now very sad-hearted, was following them, but the chief woman turned and motioned him off. "Go away. There is no food for you, no place for you in our camp," she told him; and he went away, crying by himself.

And that is what Old Man got for being so proud.

 # NAPI RACES COYOTE FOR A MEAL

{*Blackfoot*}

■

Old Man Napi was up to his usual tricks again. He came to a place where Deer and Elk played the game follow the leader. Napi watched them for a while. He asked those animals: "Can I play?"

The oldest, biggest Elk said: "Yes, you may."

Napi took the lead. He was singing: "Follow me, follow me!" He ran all over the place. The Elk and Deer ran after him. He led them to the edge of a high cliff called Buffalo Jump. Old Man Napi jumped over the edge. He fell all the way down. He fell hard. He was knocked unconscious. When he came to, he called to the Elk: "Jump over the edge also!"

"No," they said, "we won't. We might get hurt."

"You won't get hurt," Napi yelled up to them. "The earth down

here is very soft. I just took a little nap." Then the Elk hurled themselves over the cliff and fell to their deaths.

Napi called upon the Deer, shouting: "Jump, it's your turn now."

"No, we won't," said the Deer. "The Elk jumped and now they are
dead."

"They are not dead," called Napi. "They are resting. They are lazy.
They are asleep. They are fine." Then all the Deer jumped over the
edge and fell to their deaths.

There were some female Elk about to give birth. They told Napi:
"In our condition it is not good for us to jump." Then he let them off.

There were also some female deer who were pregnant. They also
told Napi: "With our bellies so big, jumping would be bad for us."
Napi told them not to jump. Had he not done so, there would be no
Elk or Deer in the world.

Old Man Napi said: "Now I will have a feast." He cut up the bodies
of the Deer and Elk who had fallen to their deaths. He hung up the
meat to dry. Coyote smelled it from a long way off. He came, limping
badly. "Old Man Napi," he said, "my leg is broken. I cannot hunt. Let
me have some of this meat." Coyote was only pretending. There was
nothing wrong with his leg.

Napi was stingy. He did not want to give Coyote any of his meat. He thought: "Coyote's leg is broken. He cannot run." Aloud he said: "Brother, let's have fun. Let's race for the meat!"

"Old Man Napi," said Coyote, "I am hurt. I cannot race."

"If you don't want to race," said Napi, "then you won't get anything to eat."

"It isn't fair," complained Coyote, "but what can I do? All right, we'll race. I will run for a hundred paces."

"No," said Napi, "we will run a thousand paces. We will run to that faraway tree over there and then race back here to where we are standing."

At first, Coyote hobbled along pitifully, crying: "Not so fast! Not so fast!" But on the backleg, after reaching the tree, he stopped pretending. He overtook Old Man Napi and left him far behind. Coyote came back first to the starting point, long before Napi. Coyote called all the other animals—Wolves, Cougars, Foxes, Bears, and Bobcats—to come and eat. He asked even little Weasels and tiny Shrews to come and help themselves.

At last Coyote heard Old Man Napi coming along, huffing and puffing, crying: "Have pity, leave me some of the meat, leave me some of the meat!" But there was nothing left when Napi arrived.

MAGIC LEGGINGS

{*Blackfoot*}

Old Man Napi was traveling. He arrived at Sun's tipi. Sun invited him in, saying: "Stay awhile. See what it's like around here. Make yourself at home." So Napi moved in with Sun. One day Sun told him: "We are short of meat. Let's go hunting. Let's go after deer and antelope."

"Good," said Napi, "I like deer meat. I also like antelope."

Sun put on his special leggings. They were beautiful, made of soft, tanned buckskin, wonderfully decorated with feathers and designs made from quillwork. "Why put on your best leggings, brother?" asked

Napi. "Hunting in rough country will ruin them. Such fine leggings should only be worn at a ceremonial dance."

"Don't speak of things you know nothing about," said Sun. "These leggings are big medicine. They are my hunting charms. Wearing them, I stamp my foot, and that starts a grass fire. Then the deer will jump out of the brush and we can easily shoot them with our arrows."

These leggings are indeed big medicine," said Napi. "If you would offer them to me as a gift, I would not refuse them."

"Oh, no," said Sun. "I need my hunting leggings. I shall never part with them."

"I must have these wonderful leggings," thought Napi, "even if I have to steal them." They went out hunting. Sun stamped his feet and the leggings started a brush fire. They burned all the bushes and tall grasses near them. Many white-tailed deer burst from out of the bushes. Sun and Napi each shot one. They went a little farther. Again Sun stamped his feet, and many pronghorn antelope jumped out of the bushes. Sun and Napi again each killed one with their arrows.

Sun and Napi butchered the game they had shot. They brought the meat to Sun's tipi. They had a big feast. The warmth of their fire and their full bellies made them drowsy. Sun took off his medicine leggings and placed them by his side. Then he fell asleep. Napi only pretended to doze off. In the middle of the night he tiptoed over to where Sun was sleeping, grabbed the wonderful leggings, and ran away with them.

He hurried to get as much distance as possible between himself and Sun's tipi. "How happy I am," he said to himself, "to have these big-medicine leggings. I will run as fast as I can. By the time Sun wakes up, I'll have a head start so that he can never catch up with me. He won't know where to find me. How I will enjoy these magic leggings!" Napi ran on and on until he was exhausted and could go on no farther. Then he lay down, put the leggings under his head for a pillow, and fell asleep.

When Napi woke up, he heard someone talking to him. He rubbed his eyes and saw that it was Sun. He also discovered that he was still inside Sun's tipi. He was unable to figure out how this could have happened. He did not know that all the world was contained in Sun's lodge and that, no matter how far he ran, he would never be able to leave it.

Sun asked him: "Old Man, why are my leggings under your head?"

"Oh, your tipi's floor is so hard," stammered Napi, "I used them as a pillow. I was sure you wouldn't mind."

As night fell again, Sun once more placed the leggings by his side and went to bed. This time Napi did not even wait until midnight to steal the leggings. As soon as he was sure that Sun was asleep, he seized the leggings and ran off with them. Napi still had not grasped the fact that the whole universe was inside Sun's tipi and that, even if he ran to the end of the world he would still find himself inside Sun's lodge. He at last fell down, utterly spent, and went to sleep with the leggings under his head.

Napi was again awakened by Sun asking: "Old Man, what are my leggings doing under your head?"

He opened his eyes and found himself at the place he had started from. He did not know what to say. Sun told him: "Old Man, if you like them so much, I make you a present of these leggings."

"Well, thanks," Napi mumbled, joyful but embarrassed. "Well, I'll be going home now." He crept away without looking back.

Sun thought: "Napi can't help stealing. It's in his nature."

When Napi got home, he said: "The big-medicine leggings are mine. Now I shall be a greater hunter than Sun. Now I shall never be hungry again." Napi put on the leggings. He walked to someplace covered with bushes. He stamped his feet. He cried: "Deer, come out!" The brush caught fire, but no deer appeared. Instead the flames swept toward Napi with terrifying speed. He fled, but the fire kept pace with him. It overtook Napi. The flames licked at his heels, singed his pack, and burned his hair. The leggings caught fire. Napi ran on, shrieking with pain and fear. He ran fast, but the flames ran faster. At last Napi came to a river and jumped in. Napi swam to the far bank. The flames could not follow him there. He was badly burned. His clothes had been reduced to cinders, the leggings to a heap of ashes scattered to the winds. His body was sore and his skin was covered with blisters. This was Sun's way of punishing Napi for his treachery.

PART TWELVE

GLOOSKAP THE GREAT

HOW THE LORD OF MEN AND BEASTS STROVE WITH THE MIGHTY WASIS AND WAS SHAMEFULLY DEFEATED

{Penobscot}

Now, it happened that when Glooskap had conquered all his enemies, even the Kewahqu, who were giants and sorcerers, and the M'teoulin, who were magicians, and the Pamola, who is the evil spirit of the night air, and all kinds of ghosts, witches, devils, cannibals, and goblins, that he thought upon what he had done and wondered if his work was at an end.

And he said this to a certain woman, but she replied, "Not so fast, Master, for there yet remains One whom no one has ever conquered or gotten the better of in any way, and who will remain unconquered until the end of time."

"And who is he?" inquired the Master

"It is the might Wasis," she replied, "and there he sits; and I warn you that if you get involved with him you will get into trouble."

Now, Wasis was the *baby*. And he sat on the floor sucking a piece of maple sugar, contented, troubling no one.

As the Lord of Man and Beast had never married or had a child, he knew nothing of how to handle children. Therefore he was quite certain that he knew all about it. So he turned to the Baby with a bewitching smile and told him come to him.

Then Baby smiled again, but did not budge, and the Master spoke sweetly and made his voice like that of the summer bird, but it was of no avail, for Wasis sat still and sucked his maple sugar.

Then the Master got angry, and ordered Wasis to come crawling to him immediately. And Baby burst out into crying and yelling, but did not move for all that.

Finally the Master had recourse to magic. He used his most awful spells, and sang the songs that raise the dead and scare the devils. And Wasis sat and looked on admiringly, and seemed to find it very interesting, but all the same he never moved an inch.

So Glooskap gave it up in despair, and Wasis, sitting on the floor in the sunshine, went, "Goo! goo!" and crooned.

And to this day when you see a baby well contented, going, "Goo! Goo!" and crooning, and no one can tell why, you know that it is because he remembers when he overcame the Master who had conquered the world. For of all the beings that have ever been since the beginning, Baby alone is the only invincible one.

GLOOSKAP TURNS MEN INTO RATTLESNAKES

{*Passamaquoddy*}

■

There was a certain tribe. Its people were rowdy and lecherous. Whatever they wanted to do, they did. They were disrespectful. They thought about nothing but copulating and gorging themselves with food.

Glooskap told those people: "A great flood is coming."

They said: "We do not care."

He told them: "The water will be so high it will go way above your heads."

They said: "We are good swimmers."

"The flood will sweep you away," Glooskap told them.

They said: "We like to take baths."

Glooskap told them: "This will be a really tremendous flood."

They said: "We don't mind."

Glooskap told them: "Be good and pray!"

They said: "Don't bother us. Go away!"

These people decided to have a big feast of eating, singing, and dancing. They made rattles out of turtle shells filled with pebbles. They danced in rhythm with their rattles. It began to rain, but these people kept dancing. It thundered, but still they danced. Lightning struck the ground around them. They only laughed and kept dancing.

Glooskap became angry. He did not drown them in the flood. He turned them into rattlesnakes. So now, when the snakes hear somebody coming, they rise up and lift their heads, while their bodies sway as if in a dance. And they shake their rattles as they did when they were still human beings.

"I like this kind of music," said Glooskap.

 # KULOSKAP AND THE ICE-GIANTS

{*Passamaquoddy*}

At Saco, Maine, there lives a man with his two sons and a daughter. All are great wizards; all are Kiwa'kws, Ice-Giants, who eat people—men, women, and children. Everything they do is wickedness, horrible deeds, and in the world people are tired of them and their evil acts.

Once, when they were young, Kuloskap was a friend to them; he made their father his father, their brothers his brethren, their sisters his sisters. But they grew older and he has learned of their evil deeds. Kuloskap says: "Now I shall go. I shall seek the truth; if this is true, I shall go do it. They must die. No one will I spare who eats people. It makes no difference who it may be."

This family lives at Saco on the sandy field in the bed of river of Saco at Elnowebit, or Ogyagwchh, between Kearsarge and the big rock where the water fairies live.

This old man, the father of the wizards and the father adopted by Kuloskap, is one-eyed and half gray. Kuloskap now makes himself like him. One cannot distinguish which is which. He enters the wigwam and sits down by the old man.

These brothers who kill hear someone talking. Slyly they look in; they see a newcomer so like their father that one can know that it is not the same. They say: "A great wizard this, but he must be tried or he goes."

Their sister takes a whale's tail and cooks it for the stranger. She puts it on birch bark newly peeled. One of the brothers enters; he takes it. This one says: "You are eating too well." He removes it to his house.

Kuloskap says: "What was given to me, that is mine. So then I shall take it back." But he only sits still; he wishes it to return. Back it comes on the newly peeled birch bark to where it was before.

They say: "This indeed is a great wizard, but he must be tried or he goes."

After they eat, they fetch in a great bone, a whale's jaw. The oldest Indian tries to break it with both hands, but it bends only a little. He gives it to Kuloskap. He really breaks it, using only his thumb; like a pipestem it snaps.

Again the brothers say: "He is a great wizard, but he must be tried." Then they fetch a great pipe filled with strong tobacco. No one who is not a wizard can smoke it. This they pass around; everyone smokes. The brothers swallow the smoke. Kuloskap fills it full and burns out all the tobacco with a single puff.

They say: ""He is a very great wizard, but once more he must be tried." They all try to smoke with him still. The wigwam is closed; they must smother him with smoke. He puffs away, as if he were sitting on top of a mountain. They cannot bear it any longer. They say: "This is not worthwhile; let us play ball."

Where they play is near Saco where it bends in the river. They begin to play ball. Kuloskap finds that the ball is a hideous skull alive, which snaps at his heels. If he were another man and it bit him, it would cut off his foot.

Kuloskap then laughs and says: "You then are playing such a game; it is well, but let us all play with our own balls." So he goes to where a tree stands. He breaks off a bough. He turns it into a skull more hideous than the other. The wizards run away from it, as when a lynx chases rabbits; they are really completely beaten.

Then Kuloskap stamps on the ground. The water, foaming, rushes down, coming from the mountains; all the earth rings with the roar. Then Kuloskap sings a song such as can change the form of everyone. These brothers and their father become fish. They rush off together where the water foams; they are as long as men. Then they go to the sea where it is deep. There they dwell forever.

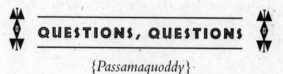

QUESTIONS, QUESTIONS

{*Passamaquoddy*}

Glooskap asked Master Rabbit: "Why is it that you can walk on top of the snow?"

"Because my feet are like snowshoes."

"How come you have no tail?"

"Because I am always sitting on my ass nibbling plants. So it withered away."

"Why are your eyes so red?"

"I looked once too often into the sun."

"Why do you have a groove in your nose?"

"Because I am always sniffing, sniffing to the right and sniffing to the left. I sniffed so hard it split my nose."

"Why are your ears so long?"

"Because I like to eavesdrop. I am nosy. I strain so hard to listen to what other people are saying that my ears get longer from day to day."

"Why is your shit round?"

"Because I like to eat berries. They are round when they go in, and they are round when they come out."

"Why is your piss red?"

"Because I drink a lot of brandy. I learned drinking from a white man."

Then Glooskap stopped asking questions.

A NEW WAY TO TRAVEL

{Micmac}

Some Glooskap tales are strongly influenced by contacts with Europeans. This story reflects memories of the so-called French and Indian Wars of the eighteenth century, which ended in tragedy for the natives.

Once, Glooskap was sitting by the seashore eating a meal. You can still see the bones of the animals and fish he ate there. They have turned to stone. He walked along the beach. Because Glooskap is ten times as big and heavy as an ordinary man, with every step he took, he sank into the ground up to his ankles. His sunken footsteps can still be seen today.

They have turned into stone. Walking along this beach, Glooskap came upon a stranded whale. The whale could not get off. With a mighty push Glooskap shoved him back into the sea where it was deep enough for the whale to float. The whale then opened his mouth wide and Glooskap walked in. The whale swam away with Glooskap inside his belly. He was swimming toward England. "A good way to travel," said Glooskap.

When he came to England's shore the whale opened his mouth again and Glooskap walked out. He had landed in a place where trees were so tall one could not see their tops. The King had heard of Glooskap's arrival and he sent men to find out what kind of man this Glooskap was.

The men asked Glooskap: "Where do you come from?"

He pointed to the West, across the ocean, and said: "I come from over there."

They asked: "Do you plan to stay here?"

"Yes," said Glooskap, "I like this country."

The men went back and told the King: "This stranger, Glooskap, is a big and powerful fellow."

The King sent his men back to see Glooskap. They told him: "The King wants to see you. We have come to bring you to him."

Glooskap said: "I don't feel like seeing the King right now. I'll see him when I feel like it."

The men went back to the King and said: "Glooskap doesn't feel like seeing you."

The King grew angry. He said to his men: "Go, tell Glooskap to come, or I shall punish him. I am the King. Who does Glooskap think he is?"

The men went back to Glooskap and said: "You better come along now or there will be trouble."

Glooskap answered: "I'm not ready yet. I shall see the King when I am ready."

When the King heard this, he was mad, very mad. He sent his soldiers to punish Glooskap. The soldiers bound Glooskap's hands and dragged him to the King's castle. They gathered wood and stacked it up into a big pile. They put Glooskap on top of it. They told him: "The King has ordered us to burn you alive for having insulted him." Then they set fire to the woodpile. When the wood had burned down to ashes and the smoke had lifted, Glooskap could be seen, alive and well, sitting calmly in the black ashes, smoking his pipe.

The King, who had watched this, was frightened. He told his men: "Put a double charge of powder into that cannon over there. Then stick Glooskap into the barrel. Ram him down tight. Then fire him off. Shoot him back across the sea to his own country. I don't want him here."

The soldiers did as they were told. They put a double charge of powder in the barrel. They rammed Glooskap down after it with a big ramrod. They put a match to the touch-hole. They fired off the gun. There was a big flash and a big bang. Then Glooskap came out of the cannon, smiling.

The King said to his men: "I must humble myself to this fellow, because he is powerful." The King went to Glooskap and said: "Let's shake hands."

Glooskap would not take the King's hand. He told him: "You are no good. You tried to kill me. You have sent soldiers to my country across the sea and they have done evil."

The King was afraid of what Glooskap might do to him. He fell down on his knees, imploring Glooskap: "Be merciful."

Glooskap said: "Get up. I don't want people kneeling before me. I'm going now. I don't care for you, I don't care for your people, I don't care for your country."

He went back to the seashore. He went to the water's edge. The whale was already waiting. He opened his mouth wide and Glooskap walked in. This time the whale had to swim only a short distance. He brought Glooskap to France. Glooskap landed. He put up a wigwam. He sat in it smoking his pipe. He waited.

Some men went to the King of France. They told him: "Glooskap is here. He has put up a wigwam on the beach." The King had already heard of Glooskap and his great powers. "I must be polite to this fellow," he told his men, "I don't want to, but it can't be helped." The King mounted his horse and, together with his men, rode all the way to see Glooskap in his wigwam.

When the French King arrived Glooskap did not even bother to get up. The King got down from his horse and sat down beside Glooskap. They had a talk. The King could not speak Micmac. It did not matter because Glooskap speaks all languages spoken in this world. The King told Glooskap: "I would be very honored if you came to visit me in my castle."

"No, I have better things to do than that," said Glooskap, "I don't care for castles."

The King got angry. He shouted: "You impolite fellow, how dare you speak that way to me? Am I not the King?"

"Younger brother," said Glooskap, "I don't like Kings, either. What are they good for? Kings are of no account to me. The English King tried to kill me."

"But I am French!" answered the King.

"French or English, what does it matter?" said Glooskap. "They are all the same. All they want is to steal our land. Well, I am going now. Better watch your step or I shall make you sorry."

The King fell down in a faint, because Glooskap had frightened him.

Glooskap went to the water's edge. The whale was already there. "Let's go home," said Glooskap. The whale opened his mouth. Glooskap walked in. They swam off toward the West.

GLOOSKAP GRANTS FOUR WISHES

{*Micmac*}

Glooskap lived on an island shrouded in fog. The fog was the smoke from his great pipe. Glooskap sent out Rabbit with the message that those who could find and reach his island would be granted a wish.

Rabbit brought the message to four men. The first, who was short, wished to be taller than any other man alive. The second wanted to be rich. The third wanted to live forever. The fourth was a poor man who longed to become a good hunter so that he could feed his family.

These four men launched their canoes upon the sea, paddling into the direction where they hoped to find Glooskap's island. It was hard going. The waves were high. They tossed the canoes backward, threatening to sink them. The man who wanted to become taller than anyone else knew a song to calm the waters. The waves abated.

Then arose a great wind blowing the canoes back toward the shore. The man who wanted to be rich and own many things made a tobacco offering, and the winds ceased to blow.

Then up came a great white whale, swimming around the canoes, churning the sea into white foam, threatening to smash canoes and men with his mighty fluke. The man who wanted to live forever had a whale charm carved from a whale tooth. He cast it into the swirling foam and at once the great whale swam away.

Then the four men in their canoes encountered a fog bank stretching from horizon to horizon. They knew that somewhere, inside this impenetrable mist, Glooskap's island had to be. But how to find it inside that seemingly endless fog? The poor man who wanted to be a good hunter had a pipe. He lit and smoked it, and as he puffed the smoke into the fog, it dissolved and Glooskap's island was revealed. Thus the four men appeared before Glooskap.

"I imagine," said Glooskap, "that you have come to have a wish fulfilled."

"That is why we have come," said the four men.

Glooskap addressed the first man. "Tell me your wish."

"I am short," said the man, "I am puny. Women laugh at me. None of them wants to marry me. I wish to be taller than any man alive."

Glooskap gave him a small, fringed rawhide bag. "In this pouch," he said, "is contained what will make you tall. Take it, but under no circumstances open it until you are back in your own home."

"I will do as you say," answered the man.

Glooskap addressed the second man. "Tell me your wish."

"I want to be rich and to possess many things," said the man. "If one is rich and owns many possessions, it is easy to get a beautiful chief's daughter for a wife."

Glooskap gave him a small, fringed rawhide bag. "In this pouch are contained the riches you desire. Under no circumstances open it before you are back in your own home."

"I will do as you say," said the man.

Glooskap turned to the third man. "Tell me your wish."

"I want to live forever," said the man. "I am afraid of death. I cannot bear the thought of dying."

Glooskap handed him a small, fringed rawhide bag. "In this pouch," he said, "is a medicine that will make you immortal. Take it, but under no circumstances open it until you are back in your own home."

"I will do as you say," said the man.

Finally Glooskap addressed the fourth man, saying: "Tell me your wish."

"I am poor," said the man, "I am a bad provider. I wish to become a good hunter so that I can feed my family."

"Your wish is granted," said Glooskap, giving the man a small, fringed rawhide bag. "This pouch contains what will make you a great hunter. Do not open it until you are back in your own home."

"I will do as you say," answered the man.

The four men paddled their canoes back toward the shore. The man who wanted to be rich steered his canoe so that it was soon out of sight of the others. "I cannot wait to find out what is in this little bag," he said to himself. "How can it contain all the riches I want?" His curiosity got the better of him. He opened the bag. At once many things turned out of it: fine buckskin coats decorated with quills, rich furs, beaver pelts, beaded moccasins, bags filled with corn, tobacco, and jerky meat, shell ornaments, wampum belts—everything a man wanting to be rich could desire. The things piled up in the canoe and their weight threatened to sink it. Desperately, the man tried to close the pouch and prevent more things from pouring out. He could not do it. The canoe sank and the greedy man, who wanted to be rich, drowned.

Of the others, the short man, who wanted to be tall, landed first. "I cannot wait to become taller than any man alive," he cried. "I cannot stop myself from opening this pouch. It is sure to contain some medicine that, once eaten, will make me tall." He opened the pouch and at once was changed into a pine tree, the tallest in the land.

The third man, who wanted to live forever, landed next. He set out for home. He was halfway there when curiosity overcame him. He said

to himself: "Glooskap ordered us not to open our little bags until we were back inside our homes. But as I am to live forever, what can happen to me if I open it?" He opened the pouch and at once was changed into a huge rock. It is still standing at the spot where he opened his bag. It will stand there forever.

The fourth man, the one who was poor and wished to become a great hunter, did not open the pouch Glooskap had given him. He joined his wife and children. He told them: "The little bag I am holding here was given to me by Glooskap. It contains a medicine that will make me a great hunter. But I will not open it. I think a man should become a skilled hunter by his own efforts." At once he heard the voices of all the game animals—deer, elk, moose, beavers, rabbits, the fish in the sea, and the birds in the sky, telling him their secrets, telling him the best way to catch them. And so this poor man became the mightiest hunter in the land and his wigwam was always full of good food and his wife's cooking fire was always burning.

If Glooskap tells you not to do a certain thing, don't do it!

A PUFF OF HIS PIPE

{Micmac}

Glooskap was a mighty smoker. No one else loved smoking as much as he. One puff from his pipe became a huge cloud covering the whole sky. Glooskap himself had a large field of fertile earth upon which he grew tobacco. He raised so much tobacco that he could have given a bag full of it to every man living in this world.

Now, one day, came to Glooskap a shaman, an M'teoulin, who was an evil sorcerer who wished to kill Glooskap, but Glooskap could read what was going on in another person's mind, as if it had been a string of wampum. He saw and read the evil thoughts in that M'teoulin's mind.

"I hear that you are a mighty smoker," the M'teoulin said to Glooskap, "but I think I am mightier than you."

"Maybe so," said Glooskap.

"Let us have a smoking contest," said the M'teoulin.

"If that's what you want." The evil M'teoulin took out of his bag an enormous pipe, bigger than any ever seen before, filled its bowl with a mountain of tobacco, and lit it. Then the evil M'teoulin sucked and burned up the whole contents of his pipe bowl with one big pull, blowing the smoke out through his nose with one gigantic puff. "Behold my power!" he said to Glooskap.

Glooskap did not answer, but only smiled. He pulled out of his bag

the mightiest pipe in the world. Its stem was a hundred paces long. Its bowl was so large that four ordinary human beings could hide themselves in it. He filled it with a whole year's harvest from his vast tobacco fields. He made a forest fire to light it. Then he sucked mightily and puffed the evil M'teoulin right out of this world into nothingness.

PART THIRTEEN

SKELETON MAN

WHILE THE GODS SNORED

{Hopi}

At the beginning of time a number of gods emerged into the world. We don't know from where they came. They took council together at the foot of a mountain peak. They tried to share out the land between them, but could not agree to who should get what, or how much. They quarreled about this.

Masau'u traveled south, then he came full circle back to the place from where he had started. Everything within the circle he had thus made he called his land. It was very large, maybe ten times as large as Hopi land is now, maybe a hundred times. This was the land of the Hopitu then.

Masau'u is a god, a creator, a boundary-maker. He is also a thief, a liar, and a lecher who plays tricks upon men, animals, and inanimate

things. He plays jokes even upon his fellow gods. He makes trees grow crooked and makes the faces of humans look ugly or ridiculous so that he can laugh at them.

From a hilltop he would watch the gods meet in council and per-form their rituals. From his vantage point he would mimic and make fun of them—ape their movements and songs until the angry gods had to stop whatever they were doing. Often they chased Masau'u in order to punish him, but he could never be caught.

One day all the gods came together to sing and dance, as was their custom. They were surprised when Masau'u joined them, and were suspicious, fearing that he would play a trick on them, but he sweet-talked his way into their confidence and was on his best behavior, so that the gods thought he had reformed himself and let him stick around. He had brought a bundle with him, but nobody paid any attention to it. The day and the dances came to an end. Then Masau'u sang to the gods. He sang so sweetly and soothingly that the gods became drowsy and fell asleep.

Still continuing his song, Masau'u watched the gods snoring, dead to the world, oblivious to what was happening around them. Then Masau'u took out of his bundle an image of himself, which he placed in the attitude of someone sleeping like the rest of the gods, with the legs drawn up under the chin and the head resting on the knees. Masau'u then climbed a nearby hill and started to roll boulders down its side.

The crashing noise woke up the gods, who cried: "This must be Masau'u at his usual tricks, flinging rocks at us."

"No," said others. "Look, he is among us, fast asleep."

They did not know what to think. One god tried to wake up the hunched-over figure, thinking it was Masau'u. Then they discovered that it was just a lifeless image. The gods got very angry and became even more enraged when they saw the real Masau'u on the hilltop rolling down boulders. Then they all tore up the hill to seize Masau'u and punish him. Masau'u did not wait for them but ran away. For many days the gods chased after him, but Masau'u was too fast and could not be caught.

At last Masau'u got tired. He thought himself so far ahead of the other gods that he thought it safe to lie down for a short rest. But the gods were much closer to him than he thought. Hard on his heels, they heard him snoring and found him asleep in the shade of a large rock.

The angry gods grabbed Masau'u, stripped him, took away everything he had on his person, and administered a severe beating. Masau'u limped away, naked and hurt. But, being very resourceful, he was soon his old self again. Then he thought how to revenge himself. He went to see Sun, saying: "I am one against many. I need a friend to help me. I need a brother to fight by my side against my enemies."

Sun said he was too busy with his daily traveling from East to West, making daylight, but suggested that Masau'u go to Shotukinunwa, the God of the Sky, for assistance. Masau'u followed Sun's advice. Masau'u made many promises to the Sky God, telling him of what he would do for him in return for his help. Then Shotukinunwa gave to Masau'u a brother and comrade to help him in his fight. So Masau'u and his new friend each got himself a club and a round stone and set forth to take vengeance. And any enemy they encountered they clubbed down and robbed. And, likewise, any Hopitu who were lazy and did not want to plant corn for Masau'u, they also beat. They did this for many years.

Today, Masau'u comes to visit the people in daytime, and shows them by his gestures how he used to beat his enemies and that he would punish them in the same way if they grew lazy and did not plant corn. This ceremony takes place in the afternoon, after the people have planted Masau'u's corn, and continues until dark. Then Masau'u lets the people go and returns to his home in the rocks, where he stays for a year. Then he comes back to the people at the end of corn-planting, when they renew their promise not to be lazy and the ceremony is repeated.

HOW MASAAW SLEPT WITH
A BEAUTIFUL MAIDEN

{*Hopi*}

■

Aliksa'i. It is said Musangnuvi was settled. There, on the east side of the village, lived an old grandmother with her granddaughter, a most beautiful girl.

It so happened that their supply of fuel had been exhausted, so the old woman made plans to collect wood down on the plain to the west of Musangnuvi, where greasewood bushes were plentiful. She picked up her walking cane, along with rope to bind the wood together, and descended to the area north of Toriva. There, along the bank of a wash, she shuffled about, picking up dry sticks.

She had not even gathered a large bundle when someone strode up and struck her a blow that immediately knocked her unconscious. The one responsible for this deed was Masaaw. He had evidently been spying on the old woman and now, after stunning her, he started to flay her. That accomplished, he slipped into the old woman's skin, transforming himself into her very likeness. Then he picked up her walking stick, shouldered the bundle of wood, and trudged slowly off, imitating her very movement. Masaaw had evidently been studying the old woman's gait as she approached the area.

When he finally turned the corner of the mesa, he came upon the old woman's home and tapped on the ladder with her stick. Each time the old woman returned from hauling wood, she was wont to strike the ladder in just that way. And indeed, no sooner had he struck the ladder than the young girl came out onto the roof. "Thanks," she shouted to her grandmother. "You are home already?"

"Yes, I have arrived," Masaaw replied, speaking Hopi.

The young girl hoisted the bundle of wood up to the rooftop, whereupon the old woman clambered up, untied the load, and stacked the wood along the edge of the house where the wood was usually piled up. Then both went indoors. By that time it was evening and getting dark. The girl had already prepared bean soup and *somiviki,* and these the two had for supper. After they had eaten, the old lady said: "I'm already sleepy. I got so weary that I'm already drowsy. I think we'll go to bed," she suggested to her grandchild.

"By all means. Surely you must be worn out," the girl replied. "After all, you hauled the wood a long way."

And so the girl spread out the bedding where the two usually slept and both of them lay down. Quite some time later the old woman suddenly turned over to face her granddaughter and embraced the girl. And then, while grasping her with both hands, she little by little worked her way on top. "Dear me," screamed the girl. "Why on earth are you doing such a thing?"

"Why, my granddaughter, it seems to be a fact that when a woman gets as old as I, she grows a penis," the old grandmother explained. "That's exactly what happened to me. I have grown a penis, and that's why I am climbing on top of you," she declared.

The poor grandchild had no wish to suffer such an act, but Masaaw mounted her all the same and started to copulate with her. Oh, how he rammed into the maiden. After he had finished, he muttered: "There, let it be thus. Apparently this happens when you grow as old as me. Wait till you reach old age. You'll most likely grow a penis, too."

Following Masaaw's intercourse, the two fell asleep. Next morning the old woman announced: "Well, I'm going after fuel again." With these words Masaaw left and shuffled off to gather wood. He was, of course, still garbed in the old woman's skin. When Masaaw arrived at the same place as the day before, he saw the old woman still lying there stripped of her skin. The wretched creature was nothing but a hump of red flesh. Masaaw now sloughed off the woman's skin, rolled it into a ball, and flung it at her. Lo and behold, the skin stretched back on the woman just as before. Next Masaaw revived her, however not before he had gathered wood for her. He bundled up about the same amount as she had collected herself, and then left.

The old woman soon came back to life, slung the sticks on her back, and trudged homeward with her wood. Arriving at her house, she banged on the ladder several times in rapid succession. Once more the girl quickly emerged and shouted: "Thanks! You have come back?"

"Yes, I've come home," said the grandmother.

"All right, come on up." With that the young girl pulled up the fuel wood. Then the old woman climbed up, untied the sticks, and stacked them in a pile. As before, the girl had already prepared a meal ahead of time, so the two ate supper. When they were done with their meal, the old woman showed no sign of sleepiness. She was not the least tired, so grandmother and granddaughter sat around until night fell. When the two were ready to go to bed, the girl once more spread their bedrolls out. But as they lay down together, the old woman showed no intention to touch the girl.

The girl was restless. Finally she turned to her grandmother and asked: "Why did you copulate with me last night, grandmother?"

"Oh dear, that can't be so, for I have no penis," the old woman exclaimed.

"But you certainly did make love to me last night," the girl retorted. "According to you, a woman grows a penis when she reaches old age."

"Never in my life did I have intercourse with you," the old woman replied, vehemently denying the accusation.

The young girl just lay there.

"Oh, my poor grandchild, it must have been that evil old man who had the gall to do that to you. He came up to me, knocked me out, and then carried my bundle of wood here." The old woman was referring to Masaaw. "It could only have been him. He's such a nasty one that he made up this story as an excuse to make love to you. I certainly don't have a penis," the grandmother insisted. "But Masaaw is a man and thus surely possesses one. That's why he copulated with you. Oh, my poor, poor grandchild!" the old woman kept muttering out of sympathy for her granddaughter.

This was how Masaaw came to sleep with another female, and here the short story ends.

Aliksa'i. People were living at Orayvi. Not far from the village, at Mat-supatsa, was Masaaw's home, where he lived with his grandmother. Every night when the villagers went to bed, he inspected the area around Orayvi. In this way he guarded the Orayvis.

One day when he was returning from his inspection tour around the village, he heard something just as he reached his house. It sounded as if someone were having a good time, and the shouting and laughing seemed to be coming from Orayvi. So he went a little distance toward Orayvi and listened once more. Evidently some people were making a great deal of noise in Orayvi. As soon as he realized this, he returned to his house. He entered and blurted out to his grandmother, "Some people at Orayvi really seem to be very happy."

"That's for sure, and I am aware of it. Boys, girls, men, and women play *sosotukpi* there in the kiva every night. It's getting so bad that they go to bed late. At first they used to go to bed right away, but now it's usually very late. So I am well aware of what is going on."

Thereupon Masaaw replied: "I'd very much like to be there together with the others one of these days. I have no idea how to play *sosotukpi*."

"That's out of the question," his grandmother replied. "You can't do that. They are afraid of you, so don't count on anything like that!" Her words made it clear that she would not give him permission to go under any circumstances.

From that day on Masaaw kept mulling it over as he made his nightly rounds in Orayvi. One day when he returned home, he said to his grandmother, "It's always on my mind to visit Orayvi when I'm inspecting the area there. So tomorrow, after I make the rounds, I will go there."

"Well, if you recall, I forbade you to do that. On the other hand, I have a hunch that you don't intend to obey me. So why don't you go. But if you do go, be sure to cover yourself tightly with your blanket and don't let it slip off, for the people are very much afraid of you. For once, listen to me and don't reveal your face!"

Now at last he had her consent. Masaaw started looking forward to the following evening. And once more he made his inspection rounds. But as soon as he got home, he grabbed his blanket and headed toward Orayvi. Once again his grandmother warned him, "You must not show your face under any circumstances. Take just a quick look at them and then come back."

He arrived at Orayvi and, sure enough, in one kiva they were playing *sosotukpi*. Since there were a lot of boys and girls on the kiva roof, he did not climb up on the roof but stood at the corner of a house and watched. The people were in a happy mood. There was shouting and laughter in the kiva.

After he had stood there for a long time, the people watching from the roof one by one got tired and departed. Eventually only one person remained on the top of the kiva. Thereupon Masaaw thought: "I'll go up there and peek in. Then I can see for myself what the game is like. I have no idea why they are carrying on so happily."

Saying this, he climbed up to the kiva. He lay flat on the top of the roof alongside the one remaining person. He kept his head tightly covered and let only his eyes show a little bit. Then he started watching the players below. They were enjoying themselves tremendously.

After a while his neighbor took a look at him. Now, Masaaw had been having such a good time watching the players that he stopped paying much attention to his blanket. He had uncovered his head and when the person lying next to him saw his face, the poor soul passed outright away. Masaaw was by now just as excited as the others down in the kiva. He was completely unaware that he had dropped his blanket. In the end he got so worked up that he didn't even notice that he had entered the kiva.

But someone had apparently heard him come in and announced to the others: "A stranger has come in." However, the players paid no attention to him. Again and again the man tried to point it out to them. Finally they heard him. Their game stopped immediately and then all of them started running toward the northern wall base of the kiva.

Masaaw, too, ran there with them. He had hardly reached them when they started running back to the southern base. And again he ran with them. Thus they kept running back and forth. They headed for the northern part, but he ran there, too. They tried to run away from him, but he kept running along beside them.

According to him it was awfully spooky. Because he, too, had become scared, he kept fleeing back and forth with the others. After a while all the players had fainted and he stood there all by himself. Next to him people lay scattered on the floor.

He ran out, snatched up his blanket, and ran all the way home. He entered the house so fast that he more or less tumbled in. Excited and nearly out of his mind, he gasped: "How horrible! How dreadful!"

"What is it?" his grandmother asked.

"Well, I was in Orayvi, and I entered the kiva where they were playing and competing with each other. All of a sudden something happened and all the players started dashing back and forth in the kiva. It was dreadful for me! Let me tell you, I will never go back there. Something white hovered over the men's heads. It frightened me out of my wits. I really was scared stiff of that white thing, whatever it was. It was awful!"

Thereupon his grandmother spoke: "So you entered the kiva?"

"Yes, the people were having such a good time that I went in. And then, when I had been in there only for a few minutes, they all went crazy and started running from it, wherever it was."

"It was quite the contrary," his grandmother interjected. "They were afraid of you because you look like a skeleton—and so they took to their heels when you scared them. That's why you must never go there again. What you said scared you were only the white eagle feathers they wear in their hair. They can't do you any harm." With these explanations his grandmother chided him.

In the kiva, meanwhile, as soon as somebody gained consciousness, he just got up and ran away home. Thus those boys and girls and men and women who tempted Masaaw to Orayvi got frightened to death. Again did they gamble in the kiva at night.

From that day on Masaaw guarded Orayvi again. I suppose he is still making his inspection tour there somewhere. And there the story ends.

PART FOURTEEN

RAVEN LIGHTS THE WORLD

HUNGRY FOR CLAMS

{Hoh and Quileute}

Long ago Raven was a man, a human being. He was lazy and he was a thief. He stole rather than fend for himself. He was always trying to scavenge, to get something without working for it. He was living at the end of a long rocky beach. A certain woman lived at the other end. This woman went down to the shore, saying: "I will dig clams while the tide is low." She dug up a lot of clams. She had a basket. Each time it was full she went up on the beach and emptied it upon a reed mat. Whenever her basket was full she did this. The clams piled up. "This is good," she said, "because I am very hungry." She was digging clams the whole time during which the tide was low.

Raven was walking along the beach. He happened to come across the woman's pile of clams. "What a big heap of fine clams!" he exclaimed. "What luck to find clams without having to dig for them. How pleasant to get food without having to work for it!" He saw the woman digging clams in the distance. "She is far away," he told himself.

"She won't see me." Raven smacked his lips. Quickly he ate up all the clams. Then he hurried off with a full belly.

The woman came back with another basket of clams. She discovered that all the clams she had piled up on her reed mat were gone. "I know who has done this," she cried. "It was that no-good, thieving Raven who has stolen my clams!"

The woman was very angry. She decided to get even with Raven. She had great powers, which she used to punish him. She fixed it so that Raven could not get a drink of water anywhere. The weather was hot. Raven was thirsty. He went to the stream to drink, but as soon as his lips touched the water it receded. He went to a pond. He cupped his hands to scoop up some water, but when he put his hands to his lips the water disappeared. His throat became parched for lack of moisture. His mouth was dry and his lips cracked. He was dying of thirst. He did not know what to do.

Raven hit upon a plan. "I am going to fool this powerful woman," he said. "I shall disguise myself." He covered his body with feathers to make himself look like a bird. He made himself a bag from bird skins. He went to a stream to fill this skin-bag with water, but as soon as he lifted it to his lips to drink, all the water in the bag evaporated. He could do nothing to quench his awful thirst. He had not fooled the powerful woman.

Raven saw his reflection in the stream. "With all those feathers stuck on me," he said to himself, "I look like a bird. Well, I might as well be one." And so Raven changed himself into a bird. He flew all over the country to find a place where he could get a drink of water. When he was far enough from the powerful woman (and her powers reached very far), he at last found such a place. Raven has been a bird ever since. But his nature did not change. He is still a thief and he is still lazy.

GIVE IT BACK! GIVE IT BACK!

{Haida}

Yehl, the Raven, was a cheat, a thief, a selfish scrounger. What some-body else had, he wanted. Whatever he himself had, he kept. He was the most covetous and stingy fellow on earth. When people were talking, he always eavesdropped. Maybe he could snatch up a piece of information here and there that could be of use to him.

There was a group of men coming back from fishing. They had beached their canoes and stood talking in a circle. Yehl crept up on them unseen. "Maybe they will reveal where the fish are biting," he told himself.

One man was relating a strange tale—he was saying: "Out there, beyond the lonely spruce tree, at the mouth of the river, way beyond, there is an island. It is always shrouded in fog. I don't think anybody has gone there for years. A gale swept me there, swept my canoe high up on the beach. I found a village there of big houses with tall totem poles in front of them. These houses were filled with many treasures. One was full of many kinds of food—smoked salmon, halibut, dried fish, jerky meat, cured deer, elk and moose meat, fish roe, seal blubber—so many kinds of food I can't remember them all. The house next to it is filled with objects made from copper, and the house after this is filled

with objects made from iron. Then there is a house full of carvings made from walrus ivory, and finally a house stuffed with the finest furs—otter, sable, silver fox, beaver, soft deerskins, and warm blankets made from animal pelts. And nobody lives there. The island is abandoned. It is very strange."

When Yehl heard this, he became terribly excited. His heart pounded. His brain heated up. "I must get to this island," he cried. "I must get all these wonderful things!" In his mind he already owned them. He flew and hopped back to his home as fast as he could. He screeched, he rasped, he sputtered, he raved: "Wife, wife, come quickly! Hurry, hurry, hurry! Help me get our canoe into the water. Be quick!"

"What is the matter, husband?" asked Yehl's wife. "It is already afternoon. It is too late to go fishing."

"Who's talking of fishing?" croaked Yehl. "There is an island out there with a whole village full of wonderful treasures. I must have them. Hurry, hurry, before anyone gets there first!"

"That would be stealing," said his wife. "These wonderful treasures must belong to someone."

"How could I have married such a stupid woman?" screeched Yehl. "That stuff belongs to nobody. It belongs to whoever finds it! The people who lived there died long ago. Or they moved away. Or, if they should still be around, they don't deserve those wonderful things, because they don't take proper care of them. Hurry, hurry!"

They pushed the canoe into the water. They paddled in a frenzy. They paddled far out into the sea. Yehl steered the canoe into a fog bank and in it found the island. Yehl beached the canoe. He jumped out and, in his eagerness to get his hands on the wonderful things, ran toward the houses faster than he had ever done before. What he found in the seemingly abandoned houses surpassed his expectations. Here was wealth beyond imagination. The thought of possessing these things made Yehl giddy. He jumped with joy; he capered and frolicked like the fool he was. He screamed for his wife to come and help him pack and load the goods. "Lazy woman!" he shrieked. "Hurry, hurry, pack, pack, load, load!"

Yehl is just about the laziest person in the world. He always lets his wife do all the work. But this time it was different. He toiled like a slave. Feverishly he gathered goods, tied them up in bundles, carried them to the boat, hurrying back to the houses for more. He panted. He was drenched in sweat. He urged on his wife to follow his example: "Pack, pack, load up, carry, carry, faster, faster!"

His wife finally collapsed from exhaustion. She sat down in the middle of the largest room of the largest house and refused to move. "Husband," she said, "I am almost dead from my exertions. I will sit here until you are finished. I don't want these things that, I am sure, belong to somebody."

"Sit there, lazy one!" croaked Yehl. "I would beat you, but I don't have the time for it." He continued frantically to load his canoe with loot. His greed had no bounds. "I am rich!" he croaked. "Oh, how I will enjoy my wealth! Kaw, kaw, kaw!"

At last Yehl was done. He had emptied the houses of whatever was valuable or edible. He called his wife: "Useless woman, get going. We are leaving."

"Husband, I can't get up," his wife called back. "Invisible hands are holding me down. Invisible hands of invisible people. I can't move!"

"Don't make up silly stories, you old, no-good hag!" Yehl shouted. "Get a move on! Hurry, before it gets dark."

"I can't," wailed his wife. "Invisible people won't let me go!"

"Don't lie to me, stupid woman!" Yehl shouted. "Stay there till you rot. I'm going." He ran to his canoe, sagging under the weight of so many goods, trying to shove it back into the sea. The canoe would not move. Yehl pushed and pushed with all his might, but the canoe would not budge.

Then, to his horror, Yehl felt invisible hands grabbing hold of his arms, his legs, his wings, even his hair, gripping him with suffocating, supernatural strength, as a hundred voices whispered: "Give it back, give it all back!"

For a while Yehl resisted. "These treasures are mine, mine, mine! I will keep them. I won't give them back!"

But immensely strong arms, belonging to unseen people, held him in a deadly embrace, squeezing the breath out of his body while he heard his wife wailing: "Husband, I beg you, don't leave me behind!"

"All right, all right," Yehl croaked at last. "Whoever you are, you can have these things back, you stingy people." And, at once, the invisible hands let go.

Then Yehl's wife came running, saying: "Husband, the people one cannot see released me. Here I am. Let's bring all these things back to where they belong and let's get out of here. This place makes me shudder."

All night, and most of the next day, Yehl and his wife labored to carry the ill-gotten things back. Then they shoved off in their canoe, paddling ever so slowly, bone-weary and tired. "I could weep," said Yehl, "thinking of all those wonderful things we had to give back."

"And I could weep," said his wife, "for having married such a greedy, foolish fellow like you."

RAVEN STEALS THE MOON

{Haida}

There was a tribe dwelling on the coast. They lived by fishing. They were nurtured by the sea. They were fish eaters. Now, Raven, the Trickster, was a very lazy bird. Instead of going fishing or hunting for himself, he followed the boats of the people, begging them to give him some of their catch. "Caw, caw, caw," he screeched with his hoarse, raucous voice. "Gimme, gimme, gimme." He was always hungry. He was insatiable.

The people were kind. From time to time they threw him a fish, but it did not matter how many times they fed him; it was never enough. "Caw, caw, caw," he screeched. "More, more, more." He grew even more demanding.

The people got tired of his unending begging. "This bird is a pest," they said. "He is a big nuisance. He is getting too overbearing. He does not leave us in peace for a moment. He gorges himself on half of what we catch. It is too much. We won't feed him anymore!"

Then they told Raven: "Enough is enough, never-full Trickster! No more fish!"

Raven threw a tantrum. His eyes were glowing red with rage. He screeched: "Caw, caw, caw, you stingy people. I'll get your fish all the same!"

Then Raven began to steal the fish from the people. He snatched them right out of their nets, from their fishhooks, out of their boats. "Hah, hah, hah," he croaked. "I told you!"

Then the people began throwing stones at Raven. They even shot at him with their bows. Raven screeched: "Caw, caw, caw! At the time of the next full moon I'll avenge myself. At the time of the next full moon I'll get even with you!"

The people were uneasy. "Raven has all kinds of power," said the women.

"He's a trickster; he could make trouble," said the men.

"We're afraid of Raven," said the children.

"He's just a nasty bird," said the chief. "He can't do anything."

One night, at the time of the new moon, the people were sitting in a circle around the fire, eating smoked salmon and telling stories. Now and then one of the men said: "I wonder what Raven is up to now," or one of the women would say: "I hope Raven is not up to any mischief."

"We are afraid," said the children.

"Stop it," said the chief. "Raven is just a dumb, thieving bird. He has no power."

Then they all heard a mighty croaking and cawing, and the beating of wings. Raven came flying, circling over them: "Caw, caw, caw, now I'll teach you a lesson!" Then Raven soared high into the sky, way, way up, and snatched the silvery moon, carrying it away, nobody knew where, leaving the people awestruck, cowering in darkness. Then there was loud wailing and lamenting.

"What shall we do?" said the people the morning after. "How can we go on living without moonlight?" They were all very sad, but four days later they heard a loud croaking once more, and the beating of flapping wings. Raven had come back.

"Caw, caw, caw," he screeched. "Will you feed me again, if I put the moon back where she belongs? Wouldn't that be worth a lot of fish?"

"I guess so," answered the people. "What can we do? It's a bargain." Then Raven got the moon out from wherever he had been hiding her and, grasping the moon with his beak, flew way up into the sky and put her where she belonged so that she could bathe the night with her silvery light.

"I thought Raven was just a pesky, good-for-nothing bird," said the chief, "but now I have to admit that Raven is powerful."

YEHL, THE LAZY ONE

{Haida}

Yehl was hungry. He was too lazy to hunt or fish for himself. He was always freeloading, letting other people feed him. He came to a hut. In it lived an old woman and her daughter. The daughter was beautiful. Yehl said, "I have traveled all day. I could do with some refreshment."

The old woman was kind. She roasted up a salmon for him and also gave him some deer meat. The whole hut was full of every kind of food—dried meat, smoked salmon, all sorts of good things. Yehl said to himself: "This is a good place to stay for a while." To the old woman he said: "I want to marry your daughter. I am a great hunter and fisherman. Also I am a tireless and skilled worker. I am a wood-carver and boat builder."

"That is just the kind of man I want for my daughter," said the old woman. The daughter agreed. So they were married. Yehl was happy. He gorged himself on the old woman's food. Every night he made love to his wife. However, Yehl did not do any work. He just lay around, taking naps, singing a song, patting his full belly. The old woman and Yehl's wife did all the fishing and trapping.

The old woman told Yehl: "Son-in-law, you made us many promises of all the great things you would do for us. But you have not kept them. It is high time that you provide for your wife and myself."

"Mother-in-law," said Yehl, "I noticed that you have only a very small canoe. I shall build you a really big boat, one to be proud of, a boat that can go far out into the ocean. A boat with which to catch whales and walrus. I will do this. You women go on catching salmon, trapping and snaring."

"We could use a bigger boat," said the old woman.

Every morning, not too early, Yehl took the old woman's tools, as he said: "To work on this big boat." Every evening he came back, saying: "Mother-in-law, cook up a big salmon for me because I work so hard." Or he would say: "Wife, roast me up a big moose liver. I need strength to do my work." So he lived like a big chief.

Every morning he went a good distance to a point jutting into the sea. There he would lie down, sunning himself, watching the sea otters playing, listening to the birds. The one thing he did not do was work. Now and then he would get up and give an old tree trunk a few whacks with his ax. The sound carried far. He wanted his mother-in-law and his wife to hear it to make them think he was working.

When Yehl came home in the evening he would say something like: "Today I got more cedar wood for our big boat," or "Today I have been working on the paddles," or "Today I began carving the figure-head for the bow." Every time the old woman or his wife would ask him, "When will the boat be finished?" he would say, "Soon, very soon."

One day, after Yehl had "gone to work," the old woman told her daughter: "I do not trust that husband of yours. Follow his tracks. See what he is doing." Yehl's wife did what her mother told her to do. She followed Yehl's tracks. She came near the point where Yehl was always loafing. She heard him snoring. He was sound asleep. There was no sign of someone being at work, no sign of a boat or even the beginning of a boat. The wife slipped away silently. Yehl had not woken up. He kept snoring.

That evening, as he approached the hut, Yehl whistled and shouted: "A hardworking man is coming, a great boat builder arrives. What have you women cooked for me?" There was no answer. He went inside. The hut was empty. His wife and his mother-in-law were gone. There was no fire, just cold ashes. There was not a scrap of food left. The place had been emptied out. The women had made sure of leaving nothing behind.

"I guess they caught on to my game," Yehl said to himself. "I am so hungry. Women can be mean."

RAVEN AND HIS SLAVE

{Tsimshian}

*Slavery occurred among some Northwest Coast
tribes, such as the Haida, Tlingit, and Nootka.
Slaves are usually prisoners from enemy tribes
or their descendants. The lives of these slaves were
not much different from those of their owners, but
during potlatches an opulent chief might show his
contempt for wealth and property by casually slaying one
of his slaves with a special club called "slave-killer."*

Raven was very hungry. He scrounged around for food but found nothing to eat. He flew along the seashore and came to rest near a large village with many people. A huge whale was lying on the beach. Raven thought of how he could have it for himself. He put on his raven blanket and flew over to the spot where the whale was lying. He screeched loudly. He used raven language. The villagers heard him. They could not understand his screeching but worried about what he meant.

The following day some men in the village got together to gamble. Raven joined them. He sat down among the gamblers. He had disguised himself as a human being. He had the power to do this. The men did not recognize him for what he was. They talked among themselves about Raven. They said: "We would have liked to understand what Raven said. Maybe it was something important. Maybe he has the power to foretell the future."

Raven said: "I heard what he said. I understand raven language. He was warning us that in a few days a deadly disease would come and kill many people."

Then the men were very much afraid. The chief of that tribe was told about this.

The next morning the chief said to his slave: "Go tell the people to pack up and leave."

The slave went from house to house, crying: "A deadly disease is

coming. It will kill everybody. You people, pack up and leave! Hurry!"
Then the whole tribe ran off in a panic.

Raven was happy. He moved into the chief's big house. He cut
up the whale. He filled four houses with whale meat. He ate the meat
and the fat. It lasted him for a long time. When the meat was gone,
Raven prepared to leave. He took the chief's fine dancing outfit and
put it on. He threw his own raven blanket away. It was the one his
father had given him. He was proud of his new outfit, but it turned into
moss and lichens.

Raven felt bad about this. He went back, picked up his discarded
raven blanket, and put it on again. He went on. He saw a very beautiful
dancing blanket hanging on a tree. He took off his raven blanket and
tore it up, throwing the pieces away. He put on the beautiful dancing
outfit. He laughed. He cried: "Now I look like a young chief!" But his
new garment turned into dry, wilted grass.

Raven wept. He went back, picked up the pieces of his raven
blanket that he had thrown away, and somehow stitched them together
with plant stems. Then he went on feeling sorry for himself. Then he
saw once more a nice dancing outfit and a blanket made of marten fur
hanging from a tree. He laughed. He dressed up in the dancing outfit
and put the marten blanket over it. "Now I really look like a big chief,"
he said to himself. He made out a village in the distance. He thought:
"The people in that place will admire me. Do I not look every inch a
chief?" But as he thought this, his garments once again turned into
rotten moss and lichens.

Again he felt sorry for himself. He went back for his old raven
blanket, put it on, and flew toward this new village. He landed at some
distance from this place. He said to himself: "I must arrive as a great
man." He took a pair of clamshells and made them into ear ornaments
for himself. He shaped them like the ear ornaments big chiefs used to
wear. Next he took a stick of rotten spruce wood and transformed it
into a living slave, whom he named Lgum. Raven told Lgum: "Go into
this village and tell the people there: 'Behold, do you know that a great
chief is about to visit your tribe?' "

Lgum did as told. He went ahead, going from house to house,
shouting: "Great tribe, do you know that a big chief is about to visit
you? He is coming! He is here! He is wearing shiny abalone ear ornaments. Behold him!"

Raven was strutting about on the beach. Lgum kept shouting: "A great chief is walking on the beach in front of your village. Come and behold him!" Then the whole tribe came running to meet Raven, who was honoring them with his presence. The tribe's chief invited Raven into his house and set before him rich food of all kinds.

While he was enjoying his meal, Raven looked around him and noticed that the chief's house was filled with dried codfish. Raven thought that it would be good to have all this codfish for himself. He whispered to his slave: "When I leave the house, you must follow me." Aloud he said: "I have eaten so much rich food that I have to relieve myself."

Lgum said: "I also have to go and relieve myself."

They left and went someplace behind the house. Raven asked his slave: "Did you see that great number of dried codfish?"

Lgum answered: "I saw it."

Raven told him: "I want to have this codfish for myself. After we go back into the house, I shall pretend that I am stricken with a deadly disease. You must say: 'Raven just died. He is dead.' Then you must put me in a burial box. But do not close the lid too tight. Then tell the people to move away at once to avoid dying from my sickness."

Raven and Lgum went back into the house. Raven pretended to fall sick. He was writhing on the floor. He moaned and groaned. He croaked: "This is the end of me." Then he lay still.

Lgum cried: "Great tribe, the mighty chief is dead. He died of a fatal disease. Let us put him into a grave box!" Lgum put Raven into the box. He tied the lid to the box with cedar-bark rope. He pulled the rope tight. He closed the lid firmly. Then he cried: "Great tribe, leave at once. Let everyone move away quickly, or you will all die of this chief's sickness!" Then all the people fled in a great hurry, leaving all their belongings behind.

After a while Raven called out from inside his burial box: "Lgum, is everybody gone?"

"No, master," answered his slave, "there are still some people around. Be patient." Then Lgum went into the chief's house and ate up the best of the codfish. Raven tried to get out of the box, but he could not free himself because the lid was bound so tightly. After Lgum had eaten as much as he was able to, he untied the box and let Raven out, saying: "The people are gone now." Raven noticed at once that the best of the codfish was gone and he guessed that Lgum had played a trick upon him. But he did not say anything. Raven and his slave stayed at that place until the rest of the codfish was gone. Then they left.

Raven and Lgum came to another village. Again Raven told his slave to announce the coming of a great chief—namely himself. Lgum went from house to house, shouting: "Oh, great tribe, do you know that a mighty chief is approaching? He is wearing wonderful ear ornaments of abalone shell. He is coming! He is here! Behold him!"

Then the whole tribe rushed to meet Raven and to honor him. The chief of this place invited Raven to partake of a feast. Raven and Lgum went into the chief's house. He set before them rich food—broiled salmon, whale meat, and seal blubber. There was also a dish of mouth-watering crabapples.

Raven longed to eat this sweet delicacy, but Lgum told the chief: "My master has been sick lately. Eating these crabapples could kill him."

Then the tribe's chief said to Lgum: "In that case, you may eat them."

Raven had to watch as Lgum ate up all the crabapples. He was very angry, but could not do anything about it. So he bided his time.

Raven took leave of the chief and his tribe. He wandered off, followed by Lgum. Raven walked ahead and his slave walked behind him.

They came to a deep canyon. It was so deep they could not see its bottom. Raven placed a dried-up skunk-cabbage stalk across the canyon to serve as a bridge. Raven walked across. Lgum was afraid. He said: "This bridge is not very sturdy."

"This bridge is very strong," Raven replied. "It could hold ten like you. It could hold a whale."

Lgum walked onto the bridge. When he came to the middle of the skunk-cabbage stalk, it broke and Lgum tumbled down to his death. As he hit the canyon floor, his stomach burst open.

Raven swooped down after him. He said: "I made this man out of a rotten spruce stick and how has he thanked me? He cheated me and played tricks on me, but nobody cheats Raven and remains unpunished. So there he lies dead on the ground." Raven saw that Lgum's open stomach was filled with the best of the codfish, the broiled salmon, and the whale meat. He also saw the sweet crabapples. Raven smiled and ate up the contents of his dead slave's stomach. Then he flew away, thinking: "What comes next?"

A LOUSY FISHERMAN

{Haida}

Yehl gives himself airs. He imitates the manners of those who are better and nobler than himself. He wants to be like them, but never succeeds.

Yehl was hopping along the river. He saw many salmon swimming upstream to their spawning grounds. He tried to grab them with his claws, but could not catch a single one. He tried to dive down upon them and spear them with his beak, but could not do it. He is a very bad fisherman. He is a bad provider. His wife is always hungry, but not as hungry as Yehl, who is always ravenous, who can never get enough.

Yehl said to himself: "Why tire myself out catching these nimble, leaping salmon? It is hard work. Let someone else do it." He hopped and flew to the river's mouth, where Eagle has his home. It took him quite a while to get there. He saw Eagle perched on top of a tall pine tree. He pretended not to see him. He pretend to be just accidentally passing by. He sang loudly, "Kaw, kaw, kaw," in his rasping, croaking voice. Yehl was not a very good singer. He might not be a fine singer, but he was a loud one. He wanted Eagle to notice him. He knew that Eagle was a very generous person who would never let a wanderer pass by him without inviting the stranger to share his meal.

It went as Yehl had planned it. Eagle heard Yehl's kawing and croaking. He looked down and saw the raven hopping along below him. "Good day, friend," Eagle called down from his perch. "Come to the house and have something to eat."

"If you insist," said Yehl.

They both went into the house. Eagle's wife was serving smoked salmon. It was delicious. Yehl wolfed down the food. He gorged himself. He stuffed himself so that his belly's weight made him unable to fly. He could not even hop. He had to take a long rest, digesting all this food, before he could finally take his leave. Yehl had eaten so much that he barely left a mouthful for his hosts, who were too polite to comment upon it.

Saying good-bye, Yehl wanted to show Eagle what a big fellow he was. "I, too, am a great fisherman," he told Eagle. "I, too, am generous. I invite you and your good wife to dine with me tomorrow. I shall also invite many friends. It will be a feast to be remembered for years."

The next evening the guests arrived, including Eagle and his wife. Yehl's wife already had a fire going, but the Raven had not caught a single salmon. All day he had tried to get one, without success. "These fish are too fast," he said to himself, "they leap, and jump, and wiggle. How can one catch fish like these? I need a big, fat, and very slow one."

Then Yehl saw a whirlpool forming in the river, and below it a huge, dark fish who seemed not to move at all. "That's the one for me!" cried Yehl. He dove down with all his might to spear this big salmon with his beak. But as he crashed into that huge, dark fish, it turned out to be a rock! It broke Yehl's beak and knocked him senseless. He floated down the river and would have drowned had Eagle not seen his mishap. Eagle swooped down, grabbed Yehl by the scruff of his neck, and carried him to safety.

Back at his house, when Yehl came to, his beak hurt badly and he croaked with pain. His wife tied up his broken beak. The guests departed hungry, without having eaten even the tiniest bit of fish. Eagle remarked: "I don't think Yehl is as great a fisherman as he claims to be." Yehl's sense of self-esteem suffered for a while—but not for long.

RAVEN LIGHTS THE WORLD

{Tlingit}

Raven was there first. He had been told to make the world by his father, but we do not know who this father was or how he looked. There was no light at that long-ago time, a time of beginning. Raven knew that far away in the North was a house in which someone kept light just for himself. Raven schemed, thinking of how best to steal the light to illuminate the world.

Light's owner had a beautiful daughter. Raven made himself into a small piece of we know not what. The girl swallowed it and it made her pregnant. When she was about to give birth, her father scooped out a hole in the earth and lined it with moss. Squatting above it, the girl brought forth a baby boy whose eyes were very bright and sparkling. After some time the baby began crawling around. There were some bags hanging on the wall. The baby cried and cried. His grandfather said: "He wants one of the bags. Give him the one at the end, the nearest one." The baby rolled the bag around. It opened. It was full of stars. The stars flew up into the sky through the smoke hole and settled in their appointed places. That was why that baby was born. It kept crying. So they gave him another bag. Little boy rolled it around and it opened. Out flew moon, ascending into the sky through the smoke hole.

There was one bag left. It contained daylight. The baby boy kept crying. His grandfather said: "Give him the last one." The baby seized it and uttered the Raven cry: "Gaah." It took on the form of Raven and, clutching the bag, flew out through the smoke hole. The baby was Raven who had reborn himself.

Raven traveled on. He knew that Petrel had a spring that never dried up. Petrel guarded it jealously. He kept a lid on it. He wanted to keep its water for himself. There was, at that time, no water in the world, not a single drop of it. Raven went to visit Petrel. Raven said: "Brother, I have been wandering all day. I am tired. I think I will stay with you overnight."

"Well, all right," said Petrel. He kept an eye on his spring.

"Let's go outside and watch the moon," said Raven.

"I never go outside," said Petrel.

They went to sleep. Raven only pretended to be dozing. As soon as he heard Petrel snoring, he got some dog dung from the outside and smashed it all over Petrel's buttocks. In the morning Raven told Petrel: "Brother, you have beshitted yourself." Petrel believed him. He went outside to clean himself with moss. As soon as Petrel was outside, Raven uncovered the spring and drank it dry. He cried, "Gaah," and tried to fly away through the smoke hole. He got stuck there.

Petrel built a fire underneath the smoke hole. "You are a thief," he cried. "I will burn you up." Up to this time Raven had been white. The smoke and the fire, which singed his feathers, turned him black. He has remained black ever since.

At last, Raven managed to squeeze himself through the smoke hole.

He had not dropped any of the water. He flew through the air and let water fall down from his beak. Thus he made the oceans and the great rivers. When Raven had only a few drops left he used them to make lakes and ponds. When he had finished he cried, "Gaah."

Raven traveled on. The world was still dark, because he had kept his daylight bag closed. He came to a village full of different kinds of beings. Raven opened his bag just a little to give them a bit of light, but they all cried: "Stop, you are blinding us!" Raven got angry and opened the bag all the way. Then sun jumped out and flew up into the sky. His brightness frightened the village people. Those of them who wore scales and seals or otter skins jumped into the ocean. Those with the skins of land creatures ran off into the woods. So now there were sea animals and land animals. Raven cried, "Gaah," and traveled on.

Raven found a piece of jade. He made a beautiful ax out of it. Ever since people have made pretty things out of jade. Raven saw Salmon swimming in the water. He called out to the fish: "Brother, come here." Salmon did not trust Raven. He did not come. Raven said to Jade: "Tell Salmon to come!" Then Raven hid himself. Jade called to the big fish: "You fellow with the slimy back and the filthy gills, come over here!" Salmon swam to the shore. Raven came out of hiding, cried, "Gaah," and killed Salmon with his jade club.

Raven flew along with his big fish. He got all kinds of birds, big and small, to perform all sorts of tasks for him. He told them, "Friends, go get some skunk cabbage." They brought it. "This is a good place for cooking," Raven told the birds. He put the salmon in a pit lined with skunk cabbage, and put hot coals on top of it. "Get some more skunk cabbage from beyond that mountain. When you come back the fish will be done." The birds did as they were told. While they were gone, Raven dug up the salmon and ate it. When the birds came back, Raven said, "Let's dig up the fish and see whether it's done." They dug, but there was nothing left but the bones. "How could this have happened?" said Raven. "It puzzles me. But, friends, I will do something for you." Then Raven gave every bird something different—a color, a crest, a longer or shorter tail, a straight or hooked beak. Then he named them. So now we have all these birds. When he was finished, Raven cried, "Gaah," and flew off.

Raven journeyed on. He encountered Bear and Cormorant. "Friends," he said, "let's go fishing. I know a place where we can find much halibut." Cormorant had a canoe. They got in. Raven sat at the stern. "I will steer," he said, "because I know the spot where the halibut are." Bear sat in the middle. Cormorant seated himself at the bow, acting as a lookout.

Bear asked: "What shall we use for bait?"

"I will find something," Raven answered. When Bear was not looking, Raven quickly cut off his testicles with one swoop of his copper knife. Bear died instantly. Raven used Bear's testicles for bait. They caught many halibut. They paddled the canoe back to shore.

"Brother," said Raven to Cormorant, "you have a louse crawling on your head. Open your beak wide and I will put the louse in for you to eat." When Cormorant opened his beak, Raven reached inside and tore Cormorant's tongue out. He did this so that Cormorant could not tell Bear's wife what had happened. So from that time on Cormorant cannot speak. He can only make a gurgling sound.

Raven and Cormorant went to Bear Woman's house. "Where is my husband?" Bear Woman asked. Cormorant made a gurgling sound. "What is he saying?" Bear Woman asked.

"He is saying that Bear is making fishhooks by the shore," Raven answered. Raven had filled a halibut with red-hot, glowing coals. He handed it to Bear Woman: "Here, swallow this whole." She did. The fire inside her belly killed Bear's wife. Raven then skinned her. He and Cormorant went back to the shore where Raven skinned the male. Cormorant gobbled. Raven struck Cormorant across the buttocks, saying, "You are a nuisance. Stay away. Swim to the rocks over there." Ever since, Cormorants have lived on the rocks sticking out from the sea. Raven stayed at that place until he had eaten up all the bear meat. Then he cried, "Gaah," and flew off.

Raven came to a place where many people were busy fishing. "What do you use for bait?" he asked.

"Fat," they told him.

"Let me taste it," Raven begged.

They gave him a piece. It was delicious.

Later, whenever the people were fishing, Raven swam under the water and picked off the bait from their hooks. The people felt something tugging at their lines, but when they pulled them in there was nothing on the hooks. They caught no fish. There was one among them who was a clever fisherman. When he felt something tugging on his line he jerked it, quick as lightning. It took Raven by surprise. His nose was caught on the hook. It broke off. The clever man pulled in his line. Raven's nose was stuck on the hook. "I have caught a wonderful thing," said the fisherman. He brought the nose to the chief who said, "This is indeed a wonderful thing."

Raven came ashore. He pulled his hat way over his face so that no one could see that his nose was missing. He went to one of those people's houses and asked, "Has someone caught a wonderful thing?"

They told him, "Our chief has it."

Raven went inside the chief's house. He saw his nose hanging on the wall so that people could admire it. He quickly snatched it up, put it back into place, and flew out the smoke hole, crying, "Gaah." The people never found out who he was.

Raven paddled along in his canoe. Mink came to the shore and shouted, "Take me along?"

"What can you do, friend?" asked Raven. "What can you contribute to our journey?"

"I can make a big stench," said Mink.

"How?" asked Raven.

"By breaking wind," was the answer.

"Show me," said Raven.

Mink demonstrated his powers. The gust was so strong it made a hole in the canoe's side.

"Better stay away," said Raven. He plugged the hole and paddled on. He came to a place where an old woman lived. He asked, "Can I stay here overnight?"

The old woman said, "Yes."

While the old woman slept, Raven pulled up her dress and stuck sea urchins all over her buttocks. When the old woman awoke in the morning she cried, "Oh, oh, my backside hurts. It stings. Something sharp is sticking there." She begged Raven, "Pull it out, please, pull it out!"

"Will you do me a favor in return?" Raven asked.

"Whatever you want," cried the old woman, "only pull the sharp things out of my buttocks!"

Raven pulled the sea urchins off. "What I want from you in return," he told the old woman, "is to make the tides ebb and flow. There must be tides. I put you in charge of this." Then he cried, "Gaah," and flew off. The old woman started right away to make the tides rise and fall.

She has done it ever since. Also, since that time, the older women get, the more black spots they get on their buttocks.

Raven paddled on. He met Petrel's canoe. He called out, "Petrel, when were you born?"

Petrel answered, "Long, long ago, when the Great Whale arose from the ocean."

"That is only minutes ago," said Raven.

Then Petrel asked, "Raven, when were you born?"

"Before there was a world," was the answer.

"That is only a few seconds ago," said Petrel.

They argued. They quarreled. Raven tried to catch Petrel and kill him. Petrel put on his fog hat. Instantly he was wrapped in white mist so that Raven could not find him. "Brother," Raven shouted, "I won't hurt you. Let's stop quarreling. Throw away your fog hat." Petrel threw it away. Fog came out of it. It hovered above the sea. It swirled around mountains. So, now there was fog. Raven called, "Gaah," and traveled on.

Raven came to a place where he saw something bright and flickering in the darkness. He told Chicken Hawk: "Go, get this bright thing for me." Chicken Hawk picked up the thing. It was very hot and burned half of his beak off. That's why chicken hawks have such short bills. The thing he brought was fire. "This might be very useful," said Raven. He distributed fire to all the people in the world. They were grateful. So, now there was fire.

Raven traveled on. He saw a huge whale swimming in the ocean, his mouth wide open, sucking up fish. Raven flapped his wings and flew through Whale's open mouth. He was inside the whale. He caught all the fish Whale was sucking in. He dragged them to the middle of Whale's belly and made a big fire. He roasted the fish on it. The fire reached up to Whale's fat, which lined his stomach. Whale cried with pain and died. Whale's fat had turned to oil. So, now there was oil in the world. Raven now wanted to leave but found that, in his death struggle, Whale had clamped his mouth shut. Raven could not get out. Whale's body was swept ashore. From inside Whale's head Raven heard people talking. He shouted, "Let me out, let me out!"

The people on the shore said to each other, "Someone is crying inside this whale." They made a hole at the top of Whale's head. Since then these huge animals have blowholes. Raven got out through this hole on top of Whale's head.

The people held a big feast eating whale meat. As soon as the feast was over, Raven told the people, "A great mud slide is coming which will bury your village. Whoever stays here will be killed." Then all the people ran away, leaving all they owned behind. Raven took possession of these things and flew off with them, crying, "Gaah."

Raven went on. He came to a place that was strewn with human vaginas. He gathered them up in a bag and continued on his way. He came to a village. The women there seemed to be very sad. "Why are you so sad?" Raven asked.

"Because we have no genitalia," the women complained.

"I can help you," said Raven, and distributed the vaginas among them. He showed the women where to put them. The women were very grateful and gave Raven a Chilkat blanket. Raven cried, "Gaah," and journeyed on.

Finally Raven made a pole to hold up the world. It was the last thing he made. He saw a man coming out of a house. The man took a little club from a hiding place and said, "Little Club, do you see the fat seal over there, sunning himself on that rock? Knock him dead!" The little club knocked the seal over the head, killing him. The man dragged the seal back to his house and put the little club back in his hiding place. Then he went off on some errand. As soon as the man was gone, Raven came out from behind some trees. He ate up the seal and then made off with the little club. The next day he said, "Little Club, go over to that walrus sunning itself on the shore, and knock him dead!"

Little Club refused, saying, "I don't know you. You are not my master."

Again and again Raven told Little Club to knock Walrus dead, and again and again Little Club refused. Then Raven got very angry and smashed Little Club to pieces. Raven said, "I am powerful, I made the world, but I could not force this small thing to obey me. It is time for me to take a respite from work." Then he cried, "Gaah," and sat down for a long rest.

APPENDIX

Algonquian

The Algonquian (or Algonkin), are possibly the largest group of linguistically related tribes in North America, scattered over the whole continent from the Atlantic to the Rocky Mountains. They include the Algonkin of Ottawa proper, the Cheyenne, Arapaho, Ojibway, Sac and Fox, Pottawatomi, Illinois, Miami, Kickapoo, and Shawnee. However, if an Indian legend is said to be of Algonkin origin, it generally means that it comes from an East Coast tribe, such as the Pequod, Mohegan, Delaware, Abnaki, or Micmac.

Apache

The name *Apache* comes from the Zuni word *apachu,* meaning "enemy." Their own name for themselves is N'de or Dineh, the People. In the early 1500s, a group of Athapascan-speaking people drifted down from their original home in western Canada into what is now Arizona, New Mexico, and the four-corners area. They were split into smaller tribes and bands, including the Lipan, the Jicarilla (from the Spanish for "little basket," referring to their pitch-lined drinking cups), Chiricahua, Tonto, Mescalero, and White Mountain Apaches.

The Apache were a nomadic people and lived in conical brush shelters (wickiups) to which they often attached a ramada—four upright poles roofed over with branches. They hunted and gathered wild plants; much later they also began to plant corn and squash. They usually dressed in deerskin and wore their hair long and loose, held by a headband. Men also wore long, flapping breechcloths. Their soft, thigh-high moccasins were important in a land of chaparral, thorns, and cacti, since they were primarily runners of incredible stamina rather than riders (though they acquired horses early and were excellent horsemen). Their main weapon was the bow, and it was used long after they had guns.

Apache women wove particularly striking baskets, some made so tightly that a needle could not be inserted between their coils. They carried their babies on cradleboards. Women played an important role in family affairs; they could own property and become medicine women.

The Lipan Apache at first kept peace with the whites, whom they encountered in the sixteenth century. Fierce nomadic raiders, the Lipans roamed west Texas and much of New Mexico east of the Rio Grande, and eventually became the scourge of miners and settlers, particularly in Mexico. Their great chiefs included Cochise and Mangus Colorado, as well as Goyathlay, the One Who Yawns, better known as Geronimo. Apache attacks on whites were not unprovoked, for these tribes had often been victims of treachery, broken agreements, and massacres by white Americans and Mexicans. They were not finally subdued until the 1880s.

The Jicarillas, now numbering fifteen hundred to two thousand, live on a 750,000-acre reservation high in the mountains of northern New Mexico. The White Mountain Apaches (also called Sierra Blancas or Coyoteros) live in Arizona and New Mexico, including about six thousand on the 1.6-million-acre Fort Apache Reservation in Arizona. In 1905, there were only twenty-five Lipan survivors left, and they were eventually placed on the Mescalero Apache Reservation.

Arapaho

The Arapaho, belonging to the Algonquian language family, were one of the hard-riding, buffalo-hunting Plains tribes. Like the Sioux and Cheyenne, the Arapaho celebrated the Sun Dance and had a number of warrior societies. Though speaking different languages, the Arapaho and Cheyenne were allies during the nineteenth century and intermarriage between the two tribes was common. The Arapaho are noted for their fine beadwork. Today some five thousand Arapaho share Wyoming's Wind River Reservation with the Shoshone tribe.

Arikara

The Arikara, also known as Ree, are a tribe belonging to the northern Caddoan linguistic family. They are closely related to the Pawnee. Their name means "Horn," from their custom of wearing two upright bones on each side of their hair crest. When first encountered by whites, they occupied a number of villages on bluffs above the Missouri River, dwelling in partially subterranean lodges. They were expert farmers, calling corn their "Mother" and worshipping it as "the Giver of Life." In 1837, they were decimated by smallpox, which was introduced by white traders. They now live at the Fort Berthod Reservation in North Dakota, which they share with members of the Mandan and Hidatsa tribes.

Assiniboine

The Assiniboine (also spelled Assiniboin) were a warlike, buffalo-hunting Plains tribe. Though belonging to the Siouan language group, and though the Assiniboine and the Dakota languages are almost identical, the Assiniboine and the Sioux were bitter enemies throughout most of the nineteenth century. Culturally, the Assiniboine are a typical Plains tribe. Today's Assiniboine live on two reservations in Montana—the Fort Belknap Reservation, which they share with the Gros Ventre tribe, and the Fort Peck Reservation, which is also the home for a number of Sioux.

Athapascan

Athapascan refers to a language group, and it represents the most far-flung of the original North American tongues. Athapascan dialects or related languages are spoken by people in the interior of what is now Alaska, on the western coast of Canada, among some tribes in northern California, and by the Navajo and Apache of New Mexico, Arizona, and Utah.

Biloxi

Now practically extinct, the Biloxi were a small tribe living in the southern part of Mississippi. Belonging to the Siouan language group, some descendants of this tribe are said to live near Lecompte, Louisiana.

Blackfoot

The Blackfoot people were really three closely allied Algonquian tribes—the Siksikas, or Blackfoot proper; the Bloods; and the Piegans. Siksikas means Black-footed People, and they may at one time have worn black moccasins. The Bloods probably got their name from the vermilion color of their face paint. *Piegan* means "People with Poor or Badly Dressed Robes."

These tribes drifted down from Canada into what is now Montana, driving the Kootenay and Shoshone before them. They were much feared by early white trappers and fur traders, because they killed all white men who entered their hunting grounds in search of beaver. Though they inhabited the northern edge of the buffalo range, the Blackfoot tribes lived in tipis and hunted bison like other Plains Indians.

The Piegans' main ceremonials were the Sun Dance and the All Comrades Festival held by the warrior societies.

About seven thousand Blackfoot, twenty-one hundred Piegans, and two thousand Bloods now live on the Blackfoot reservation at Browning, Montana, at the southern edge of Glacier National Park, and some have joined the Piegan Agency in Alberta, Canada.

Cherokee

The name *Cherokee* probably comes from *chiluk-ki,* the Choctaw word meaning "Cave People." The Cherokee are one of the so-called Five Civilized Tribes, a term that first occurs in 1876 in reports of the Indian Office; these tribes had their own constitutional governments, modeled on that of the United States, the expenses of which were paid out of their own communal funds. They also farmed after the manner of their white neighbors.

Wealth and fertile land were the Cherokees' undoing. Under the "Indian removal" policy of Andrew Jackson and Martin Van Buren, troops commanded by General Winfield Scott drove the Indians out of their ancestral lands so that white settlers could occupy them. Herded into the so-called Indian Territory west of the Mississippi, one-third of those removed perished on the march, remembered by them as the infamous Trail of Tears.

Most Cherokee now live in Oklahoma, though a small number managed to stay behind. Their population has increased to about seven thousand people, living on about 56,600 acres on the Cherokee Reservation in North Carolina.

Cheyenne

The name *Cheyenne* derives from the French *chien,* "dog," because of their ritual dog eating. The Cheyenne call themselves Tis-Tsis-Tas, the People. They are an Algonquian Plains tribe that came to the prairies from the Great Lakes region some two to three hundred years ago. They lived in tipis and were buffalo hunters, great horsemen, and brave warriors. They were closely allied with the Western Sioux tribes and fought with them at the Little Bighorn against Custer. Forced after the last battles into a malaria-infested part of the Indian Territory, one group under Dull Knife and Little Wolf made a heroic march back to their old hunting grounds, eventually settling on the Lame Deer Reservation in Montana. Another part of the tribe, the southern Cheyenne, remained in Oklahoma.

Comanche

The Comanche, "Lords of the Southern Plains," were famous for their horsemanship. Early visitors described them as the "finest light cavalry in the world." An offshoot of the Shoshone, the Comanche were a nomadic buffalo-hunting tribe, forever on the move. One of their most famous chiefs was Quanah Parker, the founder of the Native American Church, which uses peyote as its holy sacrament. Today they are part of the Kiowa agency in Oklahoma.

Cree

The Cree (abbreviated from Kristeneaux) are a large tribe of Algonquian Indians living mainly on the Canadian Plains. Linguistically and culturally closely related to the Chippewa (Ojibway), they are settled nowadays on various Canadian reserves, mostly in Manitoba. A few of them still remain on the Fort Belknap and Fort Peck Reservations in Montana, intermingled with Assiniboine and Gros Ventre. Among some of the Canadian Cree, trapping is still a way of life.

Creek

One of the so-called Five Civilized Tribes, the Creek formed a powerful confederacy within the larger Muskogean family. Once occupying the greater part of Alabama and Georgia, they were fierce fighters, defending their territory from encroachment by whites. They were defeated in the great Creek War of 1813–1814, by General Andrew Jackson. Most of them were forcibly removed to Indian Territory in Oklahoma.

Crow

The Crow, or Absaroke ("Bird People"), are a Siouan tribe, formerly a part of the Hidatsa. Originally living along the Missouri River, they moved to the eastern shelf of the Rocky Mountains. A typical buffalo-hunting Plains tribe, they were continually at war with the Lakota (Western Sioux) and the Cheyenne. During the Indian Wars of the 1870s, they sided with the whites, serving as scouts for the U.S. Army.

Great Lakes Tribes

Such tribes as the Ojibway, Menomini, Winnebago, and Potawatomi are sometimes refered to as Great Lakes People.

Gros Ventre

The Gros Ventre (from the French for "Big Bellies") are a Plains tribe, originally from the vicinity of the Missouri River. The name *Gros Ventre* was bestowed on two different tribes—the Atsina, an offshoot of the Arapaho, and the Hidatsa, or Minitaree. Being culturally typical Plains Indians, they lived in earth lodges rather than in tipis like the Sioux or Cheyenne. Today most Gros Ventre live on the Fort Belknap Reservation in Montana, which they share with the Assiniboine.

Haida

The Haida (*Xa'ida*—"the People") live on Queen Charlotte Island off the coast of British Columbia. The first European to visit them was Juan Pérez, who arrived in 1774 in the Spanish corvette *Santiago,* followed in 1786 by the famous French explorer La Pérouse. Contact with Europeans, as in most cases for Indians, was catastrophic for the Haida, bringing them impoverishment, smallpox epidemics, and venereal diseases.

The Haida were great hunters of whales and sea otters. Canoes were to them, as one visitor remarked, what horses were to the Plains Indians. Their sometimes very large vessels were hollowed out of single huge cedar trunks. The Haida are best known as totem-pole carvers and as the builders of large, decorated wooden houses. Their gifted artists are still turning out splendid masks and other carved objects.

Hoh

The Hoh are a small offshoot of the Qtileute tribe, a fishing people from the Pacific Coast living in Washington.

Hopi

The Hopi (from *Hopitu*—the "Peaceful Ones") are the westernmost Pueblo Indians, living in six villages within their reservation in Arizona. Members of the Spanish Coronado expedition reached the Hopi Pueblos in 1540. One of their villages, Oraibi, is thought to be the oldest permanently occupied site in the United States, possibly founded as long as one thousand years ago. Peaceful, settled farmers, the Hopi were known as Moquis or Mokis during the nineteenth century. The Hopi are known for their beautiful traditional ceramics and jewelry. They belong to the Shoshonean language family and are the only Pueblos who perform the famous Snake Dance. The well-known Hopi Kachina dolls are made to familiarize children with the supernatural spirits called Kachinas, represented by masked dancers during solemn tribal ceremonies. The Hopi reservation is an enclave within the larger Navajo reservation.

Kalispel

The Kalispel, or Pend d'Oreille ("Ear-Drop"), Indians are a Salishan tribe, originally living near the lake of the same name in Montana. They were Plateau Indians, hunters and fishermen, roaming over parts of Idaho, eastern Oregon, and eastern Washington. They now occupy the Kalispel Reservation in Washington.

Karok

The Karok (from *karuk*—"upstream") called themselves Arra-Arra, meaning "Men" or "Humans." A tribe of salmon fishers, they lived along the Klamath River between the more numerous Yurok below and the Shasta above them. Due to the absence of redwood in their own area, they made no canoes but bought them from the Yurok. Their culture closely resembled that of their Hupa and Yurok neighbors.

Klamath

Together with the Modoc, the Klamath are part of the Lutuamian language family. Calling themselves the People of the Lakes, they lived in north-central Oregon, at peace with the whites. They did not join their brother tribe in the great Modoc War of 1872–1873. They had a reputation for being excellent bowmen, able to send their arrows through, and beyond, the body of a horse or buffalo.

Kutenai

The Kutenai, or Kootenai, are a small Plateau tribe, settled on their own reservation in Idaho. A nomadic hunting and fishing tribe, they acquired horses in the early 1700s and became breeders of the famous Appaloosas. The Kutenai were also fine basket makers.

Menomini

The Menomini, or Menominee, the "Wild Rice People," are a tribe of Wisconsin Indians belonging to the Algonquian language family. They are a forest and lakes tribe that lived by hunting, fishing, and harvesting wild rice. They used birch-bark canoes for their journeys. They also used birch bark for their handicrafts. Their wigwams of saplings and birch bark were easily moved and put up.

Métis

The Métis, who are part French and part Indian, live in Canada. Their name comes from the French *métis*, "mixed." The Ojibway called them *wissakodewinini*, "burned trees" or "half-burned wood man," alluding to their part-light, part-dark complexions. Some Métis have adopted Indian customs and speak a patois made up of Indian, French, and English words. Some consider themselves white Canadians; others proudly call themselves Métis and stress their Indian ancestry. Their tales show marked European influences.

Micmac

Micmac comes from *migmak*, or *nigmak*, meaning "allies." The Micmac are a large Algonquian tribe of Nova Scotia, Cape Breton Island, Prince Edward Island, and New Brunswick. They were first visited by Cabot in 1497; in fact, the three Indians he took back to England were probably Micmacs. The Micmacs were expert canoeists and fishermen. Fierce and warlike, they sided with the French during the French and Indian Wars.

Miwok

The Miwok, whose name means "Man," were a central California tribe of Penutian stock, living between what is now the modern city of Fresno and the Sierras. They ate nuts, acorns, even grasshoppers; fished; and hunted deer and rabbit. They lived in conical houses made of poles, and their women used communal, many-holed grinding stones to make meal from seeds, nuts, and acorns. Their mystery ceremony was the *kuksu* dance, in which the participants wore feathered headdresses. The Miwok had a rich mythology and, before the gold rush, were a large tribe occupying a hundred villages. They are now practically extinct.

Navajo

The Navajo are an Athapascan tribe that drifted down from northwestern Canada into the Southwest around 1300. They call themselves Dineh, the People, as do their linguistic cousins in Canada and Alaska, from whom they are separated by some fifteen hundred miles. Fierce, skin-clad, nomadic raiders, they terrorized the sedentary corn-planting tribes of the Southwest. The Pueblos called them *apachu,* meaning "enemy-strangers." This led to the mixed Tewa and Spanish "Apaches de Nabahu," which ultimately became "Navajo."

The Navajos adopted many cultural practices from their Pueblo neighbors, such as masked dances *(yebichai),* basketry, and pottery. They became fine silversmiths, learning the craft from the Spaniards, just as they learned weaving from the Pueblos. During the mid-nineteenth century they began making jewelry and weaving rugs; their simple chiefs' blankets have evolved into the well-known Navajo rugs of today.

With a population of over one hundred thirty thousand, the Navajo are the largest tribe in the United States. Their reservation extends over two hundred miles of New Mexico and Arizona, from the Gallup area all the way to the Grand Canyon, and contains such natural wonders as Monument Valley and Canyon de Chelly, as well as large coal and oil deposits. The Navajo are a comparatively wealthy nation; they farm and raise large herds of sheep, as well as some cattle. The women still wear their traditional costume—velveteen blouses, colorful ankle-length skirts, and silver and turquoise necklaces. Their traditional home is the hogan, a low, dome-shaped structure of mud-covered logs with a smoke hole at the top.

Nez Percé

The Nez Percé (French for "pierced nose") got this name from their custom of wearing a piece of dentalium shell through their septum. They belonged to the seminomadic Plateau culture, roaming over the dry, high country of Idaho, eastern Oregon, and eastern Washington. They were known for their trading acumen, their bravery and generosity, their skill in breeding the famous

Appaloosa horses, and the fine basketry of their women. They were consistently friendly to the whites. A large tribe of the Shahaptian language family, they lived in large communal houses containing several families. Unjustly driven from their beloved Wallowa Valley, they fought fiercely and skillfully during the Nez Percé War of 1877 under their great leader Chief Joseph, who won the admiration even of his enemies by his courage and humanity in conducting this war. Today some fifteen hundred members of the tribe live on the 88,000-acre Nez Percé Reservation with headquarters at Lapwai, Idaho.

Omaha

The Omaha are a Siouan tribe, now living on their own reservation in Nebraska. Culturally they are about midway between the corn-planting Mandans and the buffalo-hunting Sioux. Their name means "Those Going Against the Wind." They lived in earth lodges similar to those of the Mandans. In the first half of the nineteenth century, their numbers were greatly reduced by smallpox, introduced by white traders and trappers.

Osage

The Osage, or Wazhazhe, are Plains Indians of the Siouan language group. Their original villages were situated in Kansas, Missouri, and Illinois. According to their legends, they originated in the sky and descended through four layers of sky until they alighted on seven rocks of different colors near a red oak tree. Later the people received four kinds of corn and four kinds of pumpkin seeds, which fell from the left hind legs of four buffalo.

The tribe was divided into *gentes,* which monopolized certain tasks, such as making moccasins, pipes, war standards, or arrowheads. One *gente* furnished heralds (camp criers) to the tribe.

The Osage were eventually removed to Indian Territory in Oklahoma, where they now live.

Paiute

The Paiute ("true Ute" or "Water Ute") are a Shoshonean tribe of hunters and gatherers. As they lived in a land where food was hard to come by (the so-called Great Western Desert), most of their life was spent in a fight for survival. They hunted small game, such as jackrabbits, and gathered piñon nuts and other seeds, which they ground into meal to make bread. Wowoka, the famous shaman who introduced the Ghost Dance of 1889–1890, was a Paiute.

Forever on the move in quest for food, the Paiute used to live in brush shelters called "wickiups." Today, the Paiute live on the Pyramid Lake and Walker River Reservations in Nevada.

Passamaquoddy

The Passamaquoddy—a small tribe belonging to the Abnaki confederation and to the Algonquian language group—were able hunters, trappers, and fishermen, and accomplished at bead and quill work. They used wampum as their medium of exchange and were famous for their canoeing skills. They now live on two reservations in Maine, and are the easternmost tribe of the United States.

Penobscot

The name Penobscot means "Rockland" or "It Flows on the Rocks," alluding to a waterfall near their village of Old Town, Maine, a few miles above Bangor. The Penobscot are a once-powerful New England tribe of Algonquian stock. They belong to the Abnaki confederation, which included such tribes as the Malecite and Passamaquoddy. They made canoes, fishnets, shell wampum, carved pipes, and intricate beading and quillwork. They had a reputation for peacefulness and hospitality.

Some five hundred Penobscot now live on a reservation comprising 4,500 acres at Indian Island, Old Town, Maine.

Pueblo

"Pueblo" (Spanish for "a village" or "a people") is a general name for farming tribes living in settled villages of stone and adobe throughout New Mexico and Arizona. While the Pueblos shared many cultural traits and lifestyles, they belonged to different language groups such as Tewa or Keresan. For centuries they have subsisted on corn and squash, and are famous for their artistic work in basketry, pottery, weaving, and jewelry making. They came into contact with whites before any other tribes. The Coronado expedition arrived at its first Pueblo village at Zuni in 1540. The Great Pueblo Revolt, during which the Indians drove the Spaniards all the way back to the Rio Grande, occurred in 1680. (The Spaniards reconquered the Pueblos twelve years later.) These people are known to have inhabited some of the oldest villages in the United States; at least two of them—Old Oraibi, a Hopi village, and Sky City at Acoma—have a living history of habitation for a thousand years.

Quileute

The Quileute are a typical Pacific Northwest tribe making their living from the bounty of the ocean. They are salmon fishers, hunt seals, and are daring whalers. They live on the Quileute Reservation in Washington.

Salish

The Salish, sometimes known as Flatheads, were a powerful tribe of the Salishan language family. They lived mainly by hunting. They were called Flatheads not because they artificially deformed their heads, as some of their more northern neighbors did, but because they left their hair in a natural shape, flattened on top. They live on the Flathead Reservation, which they share with the Kutenai, near Flathead Lake, Montana.

San Ildefonso

San Ildefonso is a Tewa-speaking pueblo, eighteen miles northweat of Santa Fe, New Mexico, on the banks of the Rio Grande. San Ildefonso is culturally a typical northern pueblo of settled farmers who inhabited this village for seven hundred years. San Ildefonso is famous for its black-on-black pottery, the best-known artists having been Maria and her son, Popovi Da. San Ildefonso played a prominent part in a general uprising against Spanish colonial rule during the Great Pueblo Revolt of 1680.

San Juan

San Juan is a Tewa-speaking pueblo twenty-five miles north of Santa Fe, New Mexico. In 1598, the Spaniards, under Don Juan de Onate, founded their first capital on New Mexico near this village, originally called Oke. The capital was moved to Santa Fe in 1610. The harsh Spanish rule, which enslaved the native population, led to the Great Pueblo Revolt of 1680. Its leader was Pope, a San Juan Indian.

Santee

Santee (Isanyati, Isanta-mde, "Those Who Live at Knife Lake") is the name of a group of eastern Sioux tribes, speaking Dakota, such as the Mdewakantons and the Wahpekutes. They lived in Minnesota, but after the so-called Great Sioux

Uprising of 1862, they were driven out of Minnesota to Nebraska and South Dakota. Today there is a Santee Reservation at Flandreau, South Dakota.

Shasta

The Shasta were a group of small tribes in northern California near the Klamath River and in the Mount Shasta Valley. They were sedentary and lived in small villages of half-sunken plank houses. Their main food was fish, particularly salmon, which they netted, trapped, and speared. They preserved their fish for winter by drying and smoking it. Acorns, seeds, and roots augmented their diet; hunting played a comparatively small role, and their main weapon was the bow. The intrusion of gold miners and prospectors in 1855–1860 spelled the Shasta's doom, and they have now virtually vanished.

Shoshone

The Shoshone, or Shoshoni, sometimes called the "Snake People," are a Plains people who, like the Sioux and Cheyenne, lived in tipis, hunted the buffalo, and celebrated the Sun Dance. They maintained friendly relations with the whites. Sacajawea, the young woman who guided and assisted Lewis and Clark, was a Shoshone. Today the Shoshone share the Wind River Reservation in Wyoming with their ancient enemies, the Arapaho.

Sioux

The term "Sioux" comes from an Ojibway word meaning "snakes" or "enemies." The tribe is divided into three branches: the Lakota, the Dakota, and the Nakota. The language is the same for all three, except that the Lakota pronounce an "L" where Dakotas and Nakotas pronounce a "D" or an "N." For all practical purposes, we are here concerned only with the Lakota, or Tetonwan, the seven western subtribes living now on reservations in South and North Dakota.

Originally, the Sioux lived in the Great Lakes region, but when their Ojibway enemies obtained guns from French traders, they pushed the Sioux westward, across the Missouri River. Once the Sioux acquired horses they became the proverbial Red Knights of the Prairie, the finest light cavalry in the world. The center of the Sioux's existence was the buffalo, which they hunted on horseback. Buffalo gave them everything they needed for life: meat; skins for robes and tipis; bones for knife handles and needles; horns to be carved into spoons and other implements; and sinew twist for string, thread, and bow strings.

Early in the white westward expansion, the Sioux were friendly toward the settlers, but were eventually forced to fight for their hunting grounds against the onslaught of gold seekers, buffalo skinners, and a "river" of settlers. They proved themselves to be formidable fighters. At the battle of Little Big Horn, the united Lakota tribes and their Cheyenne allies wiped out Custer's Seventh Cavalry. The slaughter of the buffalo by white hunters and the relentless pressure by the army finally forced the proud tribes into reservations. Some of the most famous names in Indian history were Lakota, Sitting Bull and Red Cloud among them.

Taos

Taos is the northernmost pueblo in New Mexico, fifty-eight miles north of Santa Fe. The people of Taos, together with those of the nearby pueblo of Picuris, speak Tigua, a language that is part of the larger Tanoan linguistic family. Taos is divided into two large, ancient communal house complexes— Hlauuma, or "North Town," and Hlankwima, or "South Town." Discovered by the Spaniards in 1540, Taos played a prominent part in the Great Pueblo Revolt of 1680. It was at Taos that Pope, its leader, organized the uprising. In 1847, egged on by Mexicans, the people of Taos rose again—this time against their new masters, the Americans. During this uprising the American governor Charles Bent was killed. The revolt was mercilessly crushed and the leaders hanged. Today the picturesque pueblo is a much-photographed tourist attraction.

Tewa

Tewa is the language spoken by several pueblos in New Mexico—San Ildefonso, San Juan, Santa Clara, Nambe, and Resuque, and by Hano in Arizona. The people of Hano, fleeing from the Spaniards after the Pueblo Revolt of 1680, sought shelter among the Hopi villages.

Tlingit

The Tlingit, the northernmost of the great Northwest Coast tribes, lived in numerous villages from Prince William Sound down to the Alaska Panhandle. Like the Haida, Tsimshian, and Kwakiutl, they occupied large, rectangular, decorated and painted wooden houses; fished in big dugout canoes; held potlatches upon the death and burial of important persons; and made war to capture slaves as well as the booty necessary for giveaways during the potlatch.

The sea provided nearly their entire diet. The Tlingit were also great sculptors and carvers of totem poles, masks, ceremonial rattles, bowls, and painted boxes. Their women wove the famous Chilkat blankets and also fine, multicolored baskets. Their dress was highly decorative, often covered with the images of eagles and other animals, the outlines formed of round pieces of pearl shells or buttons acquired from whites. Women wore ornaments in their lower lips, so-called labrets.

The Tlingit were harshly treated and exploited by Russian fur traders. Today some 250 Tlingit live at Craig on Prince of Wales Island in Alaska.

Tsimshian

The Tsimshian, or "People of the Skeena River," are a typical Pacific Northwest Coast tribe, culturally related to the Haida and Kwakiutl and, like them, artistic carvers and weavers of Chilkat blankets. Their main food was salmon, halibut, cod, and shellfish, and they also hunted whales. Their original home was on the Skeena River in British Columbia. In 1884 a Church of England clergyman persuaded them to move to Alaska. About a thousand Tsimshian now occupy the Annette Island reserve of 86,500 acres in southeastern Alaska and take an active political and economic role in the state.

Ute

The Ute, who belong to the Uto-Aztecan language family, are a Shoshonean tribe of western Colorado and eastern Utah. They shared many cultural traits with the more northern Plains tribes; they performed the Sun Dance and lived in tipis. They acquired horses in 1740 and ranged from southern Wyoming down to Taos. The Ute were generally friendly to the whites; their best-known chief, Ouray, made a treaty of peace and friendship with the government. He was a welcome guest, as well as host, among white silver miners.

The Ute now raise cattle for a living. Some seven hundred Ute live on a reservation of 300,000 acres at Ignacio, Colorado. The northern Weminuche Ute consist of eighteen hundred people on 560,000 acres on the Ute Mountain Reservation in Colorado. Still another twelve hundred Ute live on the million-acre Uintah and Ouray Reservation at Fort Duchesne, Utah.

Winnebago

The Winnebago (from Winipig—"People Near the Dirty Water"), a Midwestern woodlands tribe, belong to the Siouan family. Among their deities and supernaturals, to whom they made offerings, are Earth Maker, Disease Giver, Sun, Moon, Morning Star, Night Spirit, Thunderbird, Turtle, and the Great Rabbit. The tribe is divided into two so-called phratries, the upper or air people, and the lower or earth people.

During the War of Independence and the War of 1812, the Winnebago sided with the British. Between 1829 and 1866, whites forced the Winnebago to give up their land and go to new homes no less than seven times. Some Winnebago joined Black Hawk in his war of 1832. They were removed to the Blue Earth River in Minnesota but were driven from there by white settlers, who were afraid of Indians after the great Sioux uprising. Today some eight hundred Winnebago live on their own reservation in Thurston County, Nebraska.

Wichita

The Wichita formed a federation of nine tribes, closely related to the Pawnee. An agricultural people, they were first encountered in 1541 by Coronado and his Spaniards, vainly searching for the fabled golden city of Gran Quivira. Instead of the golden city, Coronado encountered the Wichita and their large grass lodges, looking like haystacks, in what is now Kansas. Together with the Wichita, the Spaniards also came across the first buffalo ever seen by white men.

Yakima

The Yakima occupy the high mountain country of eastern Washington and live on one of the biggest reservations in the Northwest. It is a large and thriving community with a very viable and intact culture.

Yokuts

The Yokuts were a California tribe of the Mariposa language family, living mainly in the San Joaquin Valley. They lived in communal houses and had earthen sweat lodges. There are only a few of this once numerous tribe left today.

Yurok

The Yurok are a tribe of northwestern California, living along the Klamath River. With their redwood canoes they also ventured out on the ocean. They had their own reservation on the Klamath River. When it was abolished by the government, the tribe became self-sufficient.

Zuni

The Zuni were the first Pueblo encountered by the Spanish. Fray Marcos de Niza saw the Zuni village from afar. The light adobe walls glistened like gold in the evening sun, and he reported back to the Spanish viceroy in Mexico City that he had found the fabled Seven Cities of Cibola, whose streets were paved with gold. As a result Don Francisco de Coronado, with a large party of heavily armed adventurers, appeared in 1540 at Hawikuh and on July 7 of that year stormed and plundered the pueblo. At the time of their reconquest by the Spaniards in 1692, twelve years after the Pueblo Revolt, the Zuni fled to one of their strongholds on top of a high, inaccessible mesa. Eventually they built one single village on the site of their ancient pueblo of Halona, and have dwelled there ever since.

Today about five thousand Zuni live on their 40,000-acre reservation some thirty miles south of Gallup, New Mexico.

SOURCES

Introduction

Quotes from Ekkehart Malotki and Michael Lomatuway'ma, *Stories of Maasaw, a Hopi God*, American Tribal Religions 10 (Lincoln and London: University of Nebraska Press), 1987.

Part One: Coyote Creates the World—and a Few Other Things

The Beginning of the World (Yokuts)
From Frederic Ward Putnam, *American Archeology and Ethnology* 4 (Berkeley: University of California Press), 1906–1907.
Sun and Moon in a Box (Zuni)
Retold from various nineteenth-century sources.
Coyote Steals the Sun (Miwok)
Retold from various late-nineteenth- and early-twentieth-century sources.
The Origin of the Moon and the Sun (Kalispel)
From Ella Clark, *Indian Legends of the Northern Rockies* (Norman: University of Oklahoma Press), 1966.
How People Were Made (Miwok)
Retold from various late-nineteenth- and early-twentieth-century sources.
Coyote Steals the Summer (Crow)
Retold from many variations.
Coyote and Eagle Visit the Land of the Dead (Yakima)
From Ella Clark, *Indian Legends of the Pacific Northwest* (Berkeley and Los Angeles: University of California Press), 1953.
Coyote Steals Fire (Klamath)
Retold from early-nineteenth-century sources.

Coyote Kills Terrible Monster (Salish)
    Retold from a combination of early sources.
The Seven Devils Mountains (Nez Percé)
    Retold from Clark, *Indian Legends of the Pacific Northwest*. And from an
    account by Caleb Whitman, a Nez Percé, told to Alfonso Ortiz on the
    Umatilla Reservation, August 1950.

Part Two: Up to No Good

Coyote Taunts the Grizzly Bear (Kutenai)
    Retold from Franz Boas, *Kutenai Tales*, Bureau of American Ethnology
    Bulletin 59 (Washington, DC: Smithsonian Institute), 1918.
How Locust Tricked Coyote (Zuni)
    Retold from earlier sources.
Coyote-Giving (Paiute)
    Retold from a combination of early sources.
Putting a Saddle on Coyote's Back (Northern Pueblo)
    From the notes of Alfonso Ortiz.
A Satisfying Meal (Hopi)
    From the notes of Alfonso Ortiz.
A Strong Heart (Arikara)
    From George A. Dorsey, *Traditions of the Arikara* (Washington, DC:
    Carnegie Institute), 1904.
Better Luck Next Time (Hopi)
    From the notes of Alfonso Ortiz.
Long Ears Outsmarts Coyote (Pueblo)
    From the notes of Alfonso Ortiz.
Old Man Coyote and the Buffalo (Crow)
    From S. C. Simms, *Traditions of the Crows*, Field Columbian Museum Publi-
    cation 85, Vol. 2, No. 6 (Chicago: Field Columbian Museum), 1903.
Coyote and Bobcat Have Their Faces Done (Ute)
    Retold from various early sources.
The Adventures of a Meatball (Comanche)
    From Elliot Canonge, *Comanche Texts* (Arlington, TX: Summer Institute of
    Linguistics), 1958.
Coyote Gets Stuck (Shasta)
    Retold from Roland Dixon, "Shasta Myths," *Journal of American Folklore* 23,
    1910, and other sources.
Anything but Piñon Pitch! (Navajo)
    From William Morgan, *Coyote Tales* (Phoenix: Bureau of Indian Affairs,
    Phoenix Indian School Print Shop), 1954.

Fat, Grease, and Berries (Crow)
    From Simms, *Traditions of the Crows.*
Don't Be Too Curious (Lakota)
    John Fire Lame Deer, from tape recordings by Richard Erdoes, 1969–1975.

Part Three: Coyote's Amorous Adventures

Coyote's Amorous Adventures (Shasta)
    Livingston Farrand, "Shasta & Athabascan Myths from Oregon," *Journal of American Folklore* 28, 1915.
Two Rascals and Their Wives (Pueblo)
    This is one of many versions of a commonly told tale.
Coyote Sleeps with His Own Daughters (Southern Ute)
    Retold from a combination of half a dozen versions, collected between 1900 and 1932.
Old Man Coyote Meets Coyote Woman (Blackfoot)
    Retold from various sources.
Coyote and Fox Dress Up (Nez Percé)
    Retold from various sources, including Herbert Spinden, *Nez Percé Tales*, Memoirs of the American Folk-Lore Society, Vol. 6 (New York: G. E. Stechert), 1917.
Coyote and the Girls (Karok and Yurok)
    Retold from Austen D. Warburton and Joseph F. Endert, *Indian Lore of the North California Coast* (Santa Clara, CA: Pacific Pueblo Press), 1966.
Coyote Keeps His Dead Wife's Genitals (Lipan Apache)
    Retold from *Myths and Legends of the Lipan Apache Indians*, Memoirs of the American Folklore Society, Vol. 36 (New York: G. E. Stechert), 1940.
The Toothed Vagina (Yurok)
    Jean Sapir, "Yurok Tales," *Journal of American Folklore* 41, 1928.
Something Fishy Going On (Athapascan)
    Retold from the nineteenth-century stories gathered by Livingston Farrand and others in *Journal of American Folklore* 28, 1915.
Where Do Babies Come From? (Karuk)
    From John P. Harrington, "Karuk Indian Myths," Bureau of American Ethnology Bulletin 107 (Washington, DC: Smithsonian Institute), 1932.
Winyan-shan Upside Down (Sioux)
    George Eagle Elk, from tape recording by Richard Erdoes, Rosebud Sioux Reservation, South Dakota, 1975.

Part Four: The Trouble with Rose Hips

Coyote, Skunk, and the Beavers (Wichita)
George A. Dorsey, *Mythology of Wichita*, Field Columbian Museum (Washington, DC: Carnegie Institute), 1904.
Monster Skunk Farting Everyone to Death (Cree)
Retold from various nineteenth-century sources.
Coyote Sells a Burro That Defecates Money (Lipan Apache)
Melville Jacobs, *Santiam Kalapuya Myth Texts* (Seattle: University of Washington Press), 1945.
Coyote the Credulous (Taos)
Elsie Clews Parson, *Taos Tales*, Memoirs of the American Folk-Lore Society 34 (New York: J. J. Augustin), 1940.
The Trouble with Rose Hips (Lipan Apache)
Myths and Legend of the Lipan Apache.

Part Five: Iktomi the Spider-Man

Seven Toes (Assiniboine)
From Robert H. Lowie, *The Assiniboine*, American Museum of Natural History Anthropological Papers 4, Part I (New York: American Museum of Natural History), November 1909.
Tricking the Trickster (Sioux)
From George Eagle Elk tape.
Iktomi and the Man-Eating Monster (Lakota)
From Lame Deer tapes.
Iktomi, Flint Boy, and the Grizzly (Lakota)
From Lame Deer tapes.
Iktomi and the Buffalo Calf (Assiniboine)
Robert H. Lowie, *The Assiniboine*.
Ikto's Grandchild Defeats Siyoko (Rosebud Sioux)
Told to the authors by Jenny Leaning Cloud, White River, South Dakota, 1968.
The Cheater Cheated (Lakota)
From Lame Deer tapes, 1971–1972.
The Spider Cries "Wolf" (Rosebud Sioux)
From Lame Deer tapes.
Tit for Tat (Omaha)
Told to the authors after a ceremonial gathering at Crow Dog's place, Rosebud, South Dakota, 1969.

Iktomi Takes Back a Gift (Rosebud Sioux)
> From tape recordings by Richard Erdoes at Rosebud Sioux Reservation, South Dakota.

Iktomi and the Wild Ducks (Minneconjou Sioux)
> Lame Deer tapes, 1969.

Iktomi Trying to Outrace Beaver (Santee)
> Ida Lame Deer, interview with Richard Erdoes, Rosebud Sioux Reservation, South Dakota, 1968.

Too Smart For His Own Good (Sioux)
> Jake Herman, from tape recordings by Richard Erdoes, Parmelee Rodeo, 1964.

Part Six: Spider-Man in Love

Oh, It's You! (Lakota)
> Lame Deer tapes.

Too Many Women (Lakota)
> Bill Schweigman, from tape recordings by the authors, 1969.

Forbidden Fruit (Lakota and Rosebud Sioux)
> Lame Deer tapes, 1970.

The Spiders Give Birth to the People (Arikara)
> Retold from George A. Dorsey, *Traditions of the Arikara* (Washington, DC: Carnegie Institute), 1904.

The Winkte Way (Omaha)
> Told to the authors at Rosebud Sioux Reservation, South Dakota, 1971.

Part Seven: The Veeho Cycle

He Has Been Saying Bad Things About You (Northern Cheyenne)
> Strange Owl, interview by the authors, Birney, Montana, summer 1972.

The Possible Bag (Northern Cheyenne)
> Strange Owl.

Hair Loss (Northern Cheyenne)
> Strange Owl.

Brother, Sharpen My Leg! (Cheyenne)
> From *Journal of the American Folklore* 13, 1900.

Veeho Has His Back Scraped (Northern Cheyenne)
> Strange Owl.

He Sure Was a Good Shot (Cheyenne)
   Richard Erdoes, notes taken at Birney and Busby, Montana, 1971–1972.
The Only Man Around (Northern Cheyenne)
   Strange Owl.

Part Eight: The Nixant and Sitconski Cycles

When the People Were Wild (Gros Ventre)
   From A. L. Kroeber, *Gros Ventre Myths and Tales*, American Museum of
   Natural History Anthropological Papers 8, Part III (New York: American
   Museum of Natural History), 1907.
The Talking Penis (Gros Ventre)
   Kroeber, *Gros Ventre Myths and Tales*.
Hairy Legs (Gros Ventre)
   Kroeber, *Gros Ventre Myths and Tales*.
Sitconski and the Buffalo Skull (Assiniboine)
   Lowie, *The Assiniboine*.
She Refused to Have Him (Assiniboine)
   Lowie, *The Assiniboine*.
Ni'hancan and Whirlwind Woman (Arapaho)
   From George A. Dorsey, *Tradition of the Arapaho*, Field Columbian Museum
   Publications in Anthropology, Publication 81, Vol. 5 (Chicago: Field
   Columbian Museum), 1903.
Ni'hancan and the Race for Wives (Arapaho)
   G. Dorsey, *Tradition of the Arapaho*.

Part Nine: Magical Master Rabbit

Little Rabbit Fights the Sun (Ute)
   Retold and abbreviated after J. W. Powell, *Sketch of the Mythology of the
   North American Indians*, Bureau of American Ethnology Annual Report 1
   (Washington DC: Smithsonian Institute), 1879.
The Long Black Stranger (Omaha)
   Retold from various early sources.
Why the Possum's Tail Is Bare (Cherokee)
   From James Mooney, *Myths of the Cherokee*, Bureau of American Ethnology
   Annual Report 19 (Washington, DC: Smithsonian Institute), 1897–1898.
Rabbit Escapes from the Box (Creek)
   From John R. Swanton, *Myths and Tales of the Southeastern Indians*, Bureau
   of American Ethnology Bulletin 88 (Washington, DC: Smithsonian Insti-
   tute), 1929.

Rabbit and Possum on the Prowl (Cherokee)
   Mooney, *Myths of the Cherokee.*
Tar Baby (Biloxi)
   From J. Owen Dorsey, "Two Biloxi Tales," *Journal of American Folklore* 5, 1892.
Don't Believe What People Tell You (San Ildefonso and San Juan)
   From notes of Alfonso Ortiz.

Part Ten: Nanabozho and Whiskey Jack

Nanabozho and the Fish Chief (Great Lakes Tribes)
   Retold from various nineteenth-century sources.
Why We Have to Work So Hard Making Maple Sugar (Menomini)
   Abbreviated and retold from Walter James Hoffman, *The Menomini Indians*, Bureau of American Ethnology Annual Report 14, Part I (Washington, DC: Smithsonian Institute), 1896.
Who Is Looking Me in the Face? (Menomini)
   Retold from Hoffman, *The Menomini Indians.*
Why Women Have Their Moon-Time (Menomini)
   Retold from Hoffman, *The Menomini Indians.*
Whiskey Jack Wants to Fly (Cree and Métis)
   Oohosis-Desjarlais, from tape recordings by the authors, 1971–1972. See also *Journal of American Folklore* 42, 1929.
Wesakaychak, the Windigo, and the Ermine (Cree and Métis)
   Oohosis-Desjarlais tape, 1972.

Part Eleven: Old Man Napi Chooses a Wife

Choosing Mates (Blackfoot)
   From James Willard Schultz, *Blackfoot Tales of Glacier National Park, Montana* (Cambridge, MA: Riverside Press), 1916; and from George Bird Grinnell, *Pawnee, Blackfoot and Cheyenne* (New York: Charles Scribner), 1913.
Napi Races Coyote for a Meal (Blackfoot)
   From Percy Bullchild, *The Sun Came Down: The History of the World as My Elders Told It* (San Francisco: Harper & Row), 1985.
Magic Leggings (Blackfoot)
   Retold from various nineteenth-century sources.

Part Twelve: Glooskap the Great

How the Lord of Men and Beasts Strove with the Mighty Wasis and Was Shamefully Defeated (Penobscot)

> From Charles Godfrey Leland, *Algonquin Legends of New England; or, Myths and Folklore of the Micmac, Passamaquoddy, and Penoboscot Tribes* (Boston: Houghton Mifflin), 1884.

Glooskap Turns Men into Rattlesnakes (Passamaquoddy)

> Maynard Stanley, interview with the authors, New York, 1974.

Kuloskap and the Ice-Giants (Passamaquoddy)

> From John Dineley Prince, *Passamaquoddy Texts*, American Ethnological Society Publications 10 (New York: G. E. Stechert), 1921.

Questions, Questions (Passamaquoddy)

> From nineteenth century-sources and from Stanley notes.

A New Way to Travel (Micmac)

> Retold from various 1880s sources.

Glooskap Grants Four Wishes (Micmac)

> Retold from various nineteenth-century sources.

A Puff of His Pipe (Micmac)

> Anna Mae Aquash, interviewed by the authors, New York, 1974.

Part Thirteen: Skeleton Man

While the Gods Snored (Hopi)

> Retold from various early sources, including Alexander M. Stephen, "Hopi Tales," *Journal of American Folklore* 42, 1929.

How Masaaw Slept with a Beautiful Maiden (Hopi)

> From Ekkehart Malotki and Michael Lomatuway'ma, *Stories of Maasaw, a Hopi God*, American Tribal Religions 10 (Lincoln and London: University of Nebraska Press), 1987.

Scared to Death (Hopi)

> Malotki and Lomatuway'ma, *Stories of Maasaw, a Hopi God*.

Part Fourteen: Raven Lights the World

Hungry for Clams (Hoh and Quileute)

> From the notes of Alfonso Ortiz.

Give It Back! Give It Back! (Haida)

> From the notes of Alfonso Ortiz.

Raven Steals the Moon (Haida)

> From the notes of Alfonso Ortiz.

Yehl, the Lazy One (Haida)
   Retold from various sources.
Raven and His Slave (Tsimshian)
   Retold from Franz Boas, *Tsimshian Mythology*, Bureau of American Eth-
   nology Annual Report 31 (Washington, DC: Smithsonian Institute), 1916.
A Lousy Fisherman (Haida)
   Abbreviated and retold from various early sources.
Raven Lights the World (Tlingit)
   From late-nineteenth- and early-twentieth-century sources.

INDEX OF TALES

FOR THE BEST IN PAPERBACKS, LOOK FOR THE

In every corner of the world, on every subject under the sun, Penguin represents quality and variety—the very best in publishing today.

For complete information about books available from Penguin—including Penguin Classics, Penguin Compass, and Puffins—and how to order them, write to us at the appropriate address below. Please note that for copyright reasons the selection of books varies from country to country.

In the United States: Please write to *Penguin Group (USA), P.O. Box 12289 Dept. B, Newark, New Jersey 07101-5289* or call 1-800-788-6262.

In the United Kingdom: Please write to *Dept. EP, Penguin Books Ltd, Bath Road, Harmondsworth, West Drayton, Middlesex UB7 0DA.*

In Canada: Please write to *Penguin Books Canada Ltd, 90 Eglinton Avenue East, Suite 700, Toronto, Ontario M4P 2Y3.*

In Australia: Please write to *Penguin Books Australia Ltd, P.O. Box 257, Ringwood, Victoria 3134.*

In New Zealand: Please write to *Penguin Books (NZ) Ltd, Private Bag 102902, North Shore Mail Centre, Auckland 10.*

In India: Please write to *Penguin Books India Pvt Ltd, 11 Panchsheel Shopping Centre, Panchsheel Park, New Delhi 110 017.*

In the Netherlands: Please write to *Penguin Books Netherlands bv, Postbus 3507, NL-1001 AH Amsterdam.*

In Germany: Please write to *Penguin Books Deutschland GmbH, Metzlerstrasse 26, 60594 Frankfurt am Main.*

In Spain: Please write to *Penguin Books S. A., Bravo Murillo 19, 1° B, 28015 Madrid.*

In Italy: Please write to *Penguin Italia s.r.l., Via Benedetto Croce 2, 20094 Corsico, Milano.*

In France: Please write to *Penguin France, Le Carré Wilson, 62 rue Benjamin Baillaud, 31500 Toulouse.*

In Japan: Please write to *Penguin Books Japan Ltd, Kaneko Building, 2-3-25 Koraku, Bunkyo-Ku, Tokyo 112.*

In South Africa: Please write to *Penguin Books South Africa (Pty) Ltd, Private Bag X14, Parkview, 2122 Johannesburg.*